How To Find And Work With

The Good

Financial

Advisor

So You Both Make Money!

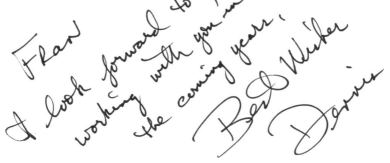

Dennis L. Morin, MBA, CFP®

Foreword by Peter Montoya; Author of The Brand Called You

First published by Dog Ear Publishing
4010 W. 86th Street, Ste H
Indianapolis, IN 46268
www.dogearpublishing.net

ISBN: 978-159858-626-8

This book is printed on acid-free paper.

Printed in the United States of America

Table of Contents

Foreword

3 Reasons Why I Have a Financial Advisor...
...and You Should Too

Retirement is a Big, Complex Issue

Health Care, Increasing Lifespan, and an overwhelming selection of financial products are making retirement too complex for the average person.

Retirement health care costs are increasing at a rate faster than inflation, and at a 4% rate of increase, your costs will double in 18 years. The good news is that the higher quality of health care you receive will increase your active and productive years in retirement.

If you retire at 65, you may spend 30 years in retirement...and your money will have to last. You may live a third of your life in retirement, and you want to maintain your lifestyle, independence and dignity throughout those years.

The proliferation of new (and many times better) products is overwhelming to the average person. Even financial advisors are finding the need to specialize due to the complexity of variable annuities, life insurance, long term care insurance, and new investment products such as exchange traded funds.

In the end, there is no substitute for experience. You may only work on your financial plan, but professionals have worked on hundreds of cases building experience and knowledge.

Comprehensiveness

A good financial advisor will not only look at your ability to accumulate wealth, but more importantly how to protect your principal, distribute income as required, and potentially distribute the balance to your heirs. Good financial advisors integrate investment management with tax planning and estate planning, creating a comprehensive plan. Unfortunately, most people have "silo-ed" their professionals (CPA, Attorney and Estate Planner) and may have conflicting strategies or massive holes due to lack of a comprehensive approach. A good financial advisor knows how to work with all professionals to create a complete and integrated plan.

Full Time Protector in an Ever-Changing Financial Landscape

Life in the United States is busy. Family, work, vacation and hobbies can consume all your time…and then some. Most people want to enjoy their lives and not spend their nights and weekends worrying about what they don't know about their finances. Your financial advisor's job is to understand the ever-changing and complicated financial landscape, and make sure that your plan still meets your objectives. Tax laws change constantly. New Federal laws affecting estate planning change every year. The Federal tax code has about four times as many words as the bible. Accompanying the law are a staggering two-and-a-half million pages of regulations.

Life is meant to live and enjoy. A good financial advisor will help you to do both.

Peter Montoya
Peter Montoya Inc.
The Financial Services Marketing Firm
150 El Camino Real, Ste. 200
Tustin, CA 92780

Author of "The Brand Called You"

Introduction

"We have met the enemy and it is us."

Many books have been written about investing and financial planning, but nearly all of them are targeted toward the would-be expert or avid do-it-yourselfer. The majority of those publications are based on the premise that the typical financial planning/investment management client is an unsophisticated and uninformed sheep going to the slaughter, so it is therefore preferable to do it yourself.

Very little has been written for those who cannot, or choose not, to manage their own finances. This book is aimed at helping clients, or prospective clients, to find a Good Financial Advisor, and efficiently use his or her services. It is also designed to provide a financial planning guide for those who wish to achieve financial independence.

The New Profession

The financial planning profession is relatively new compared to other service professions such as law, accounting or medicine. Despite more recent prominence, the financial advisor remains a relatively unknown, and oftentimes misunderstood, professional. This can partially be attributed to a lack of published material about who they are and the true nature of their job. This book will help to fill that information gap.

It is unfortunately not uncommon to see articles in books and well-known publications warning investors about greedy, incompetent and unethical financial advisors. Equally disturbing are true stories about the few greedy, incompetent and unethical financial advisors who break the law, and cost their clients money in the process. In my experience, there are few financial advisors in this category, and the average client is more able to spot them than generally perceived. With the information in this book you should be capable of weeding out the few mediocre or unethical advisors from the many good financial advisors waiting to serve you.

Competence is the Real Issue

A critical and more important issue is the level of competence of the financial advisor. This is such a new profession that it has yet to define itself, either internally or in the eyes of the public. We all know what to expect from our attorney, doctor or accountant, but we are generally unsure of what to expect from a financial advisor. There are no published standards to follow or specific educational requirements, nor is there a common designation to tell you when a person is a true financial advisor. Unfortunately there are too many designations (more than 100!) that do not tell you what the person is capable of doing, but are primarily designed to help the advisor acquire clients. In addition, people in the business can call themselves by titles that are misleading at best. This must change if the financial advisor is to take his proper place with the other service professionals.

Public Perception

A serious perception problem for financial advisors comes from the comparison of their profession to the other service professions. To many it appears that they do little or no work. Your accountant or CPA prepares your taxes and presents you with a thick stack of paper for signature. You sign it, return it to the IRS, and your taxes are done for another year. Your attorney prepares a package of documents that contains a will, power of attorney and other relevant papers, you sign them, and your estate plan is completed. A doctor examines you, performs tests on you and pronounces you healthy for another year.

By contrast, your financial advisor talks to you for an hour or two, asks you to sign a few sheets of paper, and accepts your check. When he does a financial plan, he talks to you and gathers data for an hour or so, and then produces a computer-generated document that is barely understandable. He invests your money, sets up a protection plan, and reviews the results with you periodically. He encourages you to defer gratification for the next 20 years, before you know if the end result is satisfactory. Are you having fun yet?

Misperceptions

A common misperception is that a financial advisor will make you rich through brilliant stock selection or by his knowledge of some secret investments. Sorry, but that is not the case. There are few secrets you can't find out by diligent study, and no one is that brilliant a stock picker (with apologies to the great stock pickers of the world). Look elsewhere for instant riches. I cover the financial advisor's role in detail in Chapter 3E.

Another common misperception is that the financial advisor always profits, even if the client loses money. A book from 1940 that asked where the customer's yachts are promulgated this myth, despite much evidence to the contrary. I added that line to the cover of this book because only when each of you make money can a relationship last, and then you both can prosper.

It's Hard to Keep Score

No matter what your interim results are, someone will always tell you that you could have done better (although at what risk?) Your protection plan will be viewed as having little value unless you die or become disabled. Your estate plan means little until you die, with the exception of peace of mind and gifting programs. Tangible results come after many years, and they can come erratically, depending on how you are invested. This delayed reward effect is difficult to overcome, in spite of having a longer and deeper relationship with your financial advisor than you do with any other professional.

Whatever the final result, someone will always be able to say they could have done it better, since there is no way to contradict them. And, financial advisors are certain to make mistakes on occasion, just like other professionals. You will seldom see any of the effort that justifies the financial advisor's fee.

Help Was Scarce before Now

As part of my job as a financial advisor, I have read numerous books about personal finance. Most of them contained only a few pages about how to find a financial advisor, and almost nothing about how to work with one. Most of those pages were focused on how to identify a bad advisor, instead of how to find a good advisor. The former advice is almost useless, while the latter is vital to those who are seriously seeking professional assistance from a Good Financial Advisor.

Some books, and even websites that purported to be dedicated to helping you to find a financial advisor, were actually lead generation methods for advisors to find new clients (advisors had to pay to be listed on the website). Don't be surprised, but if you find one of these, please ignore it or don't read it. Most of their content was extremely cynical in nature, and came off as a rehash of every problem the financial services industry has experienced since the 1929 stock market crash. Some pretended to reveal the secrets of the financial advisory profession. (There are few secrets, only facts that are not widely known. I attempt to correct that problem in this book.)

The Bias of Do-It-Yourself Books

Every personal finance book written for the do-it-yourself crowd seemed to have a built-in bias against financial advisors, including finding a good one. They ranted on about how advisors actually collect commissions, have conflicts of interest, and make a living off your assets. They warned about advisors who were incompetent or lacked proper credentials or education. They even claimed that some advisors lacked character and integrity. I was shocked, shocked, to find out that financial advisors suffered from all the human frailties that afflict every profession. Obviously, helping you to actually find a financial advisor was not their purpose, since those clients who use a financial advisor have little use for a do-it-yourself book.

My personal experience as a financial advisor was in direct contradiction to most of what I read. The vast majority of financial advisors I knew were hard-working and ethical, and truly tried to help their clients. I felt it was time to stop living in the past, and take a positive approach to the subject that would benefit people who want to find and work with a financial advisor, but lack the ability or knowledge to do it on their own. It was for those reasons that I decided to write a book for the millions of people who might benefit from the services of a financial advisor.

The Relationship - A More Important Issue

After you found a financial advisor (a difficult task with so little guidance), there was little to tell you how to work with them over time to achieve any kind of financial goal. This was the reason you wanted to find an advisor in the first place, but for the next ten to thirty years you were on your own. The largest and most critical aspect of working with a financial advisor was left almost completely unaddressed. It seemed to be all or nothing, where you could either do it all yourself, or turn the whole job over to a financial advisor and hope for the best. Working with the financial advisor, a period that can encompass many years, is by far the most important part of the process, and deserves more than a few pages thrown into a book on some aspect of personal finance. The financial advisor/client relationship is essentially a long-term partnership and should be treated with the importance it deserves.

I also noticed in the course of my business that many of the problems experienced by clients were self-inflicted. Whether through fear, ignorance or laziness, some clients looked for the quick, painless, solution to their particular concerns. There are no quick, painless solutions to complex financial issues. By accepting a seemingly easy way out, those clients left themselves at the mercy of the advisor looking for the easy way to earn his fee. The end result was usually less than satisfying to either party. My colleagues and I frequently observe that a client will spend more time planning their annual vacation then their retirement. Your retirement is more important, so treat it accordingly.

Millions of Potential Users

With that in mind, this book is written for the two groups of people that may really benefit from the services of a financial advisor. With more than 40,000,000 families estimated to have investment or financial planning needs, there is no shortage of clients who need a financial advisor's services.

First, for the millions of people who already have a financial advisor and want to improve their ability to communicate with him, as well as enhance their working relationship, this book will give you the information you need to take that relationship to the next level.

Second, for the millions more who do not have a financial advisor and would like to find one, this book will guide you along the way to finding the right person for you and making the relationship work successfully over many years.

Finally, I try to take some of the mystery out of this profession, to enable you to better evaluate and work with a financial advisor to achieve your financial goals. I provide some knowledge in the areas of financial planning important for you to understand in order to effectively communicate with your financial advisor. This probably comes under the "A little knowledge is a dangerous thing" category, but some subjects are necessary for you to have a little knowledge of if you are to get the most out of your relationship with your financial advisor. If you want to know more about the various subjects I touch upon in this book, I urge you to expand your knowledge by reading quality books by experts in that particular field. Trendy self-help books are like cotton candy; tasty but not very filling.

Self-Help Books

Most self-help books should carry a warning label similar to over-the-counter drugs. They are not for everybody, and they can have harmful side effects when used improperly. You should probably avoid simplistic self-help books with titles like these made-up examples. Finding a good one in this batch is like finding a diamond in a road apple:

- The Only Book On (*You Name It*) You Will Ever Need
- The 147 Greatest Stocks You Must Own Today
- Financial Planning Made Easy In 93 Easy Steps
- The Complete Guide to (*You Name It*)
- You Don't Have To work To Get Rich
- Understanding Life Insurance in 5 Minutes A Day
- 43 Ways To Invest In Variable Annuities
- Secrets Never Before Revealed About (*You Name It*)
- Retire Rich at 30 In Three Easy Lessons
- Low Cost Estate Planning - Without An Attorney
- Flipping Real Estate For Fun And Profit
- Everything You'll Ever Need To Know In Your Lifetime About Personal Finance

There are numerous books like these, written by people who claim to have many years of experience and expertise. Yet they expect you to understand how to handle your life's savings and plan for your financial future after reading their book for a few hours. Then they publish an updated version of their book a year later with "The latest information that you can't do without." It's a great way for them to sell books, but a poor way for you to manage your finances.

Staying Current Is Hard Work

Staying current on the latest information is a full-time job for me as a Certified Financial Planner (CFP®). It requires about ten to fifteen hours of reading a week, and 25 to 30 days each year spent at seminars run by experts in a particular field. I have the advantage of more than 20 years experience investing other people's money, and I work on five to fifteen client portfolios each week. I also have the resources of my broker/dealer, sophisticated and costly software, educational support from wholesalers, and the Financial Planning Association to keep me knowledgeable on the latest information in the areas of financial planning, taxes, investments and protection planning. Staying informed over an extended period of time can be overwhelming for the do-it-yourself crowd, and it will gradually wear you down. The problem is not learning enough to get started successfully; it is maintaining a sufficient level of expertise over the years to finish successfully.

Set Your Expectations

After reading this book, you should have a working understanding as to what a financial advisor does, how they became one, and how they run their business. You will also know how to select and successfully work with one, so that you both make money, which is the only way you each of you can be successful in the long run. Expect nothing less.

Only You Can Make It Happen

You should also understand what an advisor can and cannot do for you, as well as what you must do for yourself. Advice is just advice, and only action produces results. It is up to you to produce a plan for your future, because without a plan your future is unnecessarily uncertain. With a plan, financial independence can become a reality. Financial independence is that point when you work because you want to, not because you have to.

I am convinced that many of the problems people encounter when working with a financial advisor are of their own making. Through a lack of understanding as to the role of both the advisor and the client, they fail to take full advantage of the advisor's services. They become disappointed and eventually terminate the relationship to seek a new advisor, when the process starts all over again. This is a lot of hard work and you lose time developing the relationship of trust between you and the advisor necessary for long-term success.

The Good Financial Advisor

Finally, with some effort on your part, you will be able to select what I will refer to in the remainder of this book as the Good Financial Advisor: That is the capable advisor who has experience, character, integrity, and competence. Note that I did not refer to the Great Financial Advisor or the Perfect Financial Advisor (if one exists). There are certainly a few great financial advisors around, but it may be hard to find one unless you have millions to invest. Never let the great or perfect be the enemy of the good.

The Good Financial Advisor will keep you from making the Big Mistake. The Big Mistake is an error so great, that it permanently alters your financial plan, and your future. It is like taking a bullet. You sometimes survive, you sometimes don't, and sometimes you are never the same.

Wealthy People Use Them

The majority of already wealthy people use the services of a financial advisor, and most of those who wish to be wealthy probably should. Those who do use a financial advisor are typically intelligent people in their own right, who could, if they chose, manage their own finances. They have instead decided to do other things with their time (See Chapters 4A & 11), and let their financial advisor handle that aspect of their life, with their role being that of an overseer.

The Playing Field Is Now Level

Armed with this book, you should be able to obtain quality service and results from your Good Financial Advisor. Confronted with someone who has read this book, the Good Financial Advisor will know that expectations have been raised, and will raise his own bar for performance. The playing field will be level, and both sides will be seeking the same results. In the long term, this could mean a difference of hundreds of thousands of dollars more in your retirement plan, or make the difference in whether you can retire at all.

The Choice Is Yours

Whether you elect to do it yourself, or seek the services of the Good Financial Advisor, I wish you success. If you choose the latter, may your relationship with the Good Financial Advisor be long and mutually prosperous. Both paths can lead to financial independence, although I believe a guide can make for a safer and more comfortable journey.

After reading this book you will not be uninformed,

and

you definitely will not be one of the sheep.

Chapter 1 – Overview

"If we fail to plan, we plan to fail".

This book is not intended to educate you to become the next great investor, or help you to become an expert in some area of financial planning. It is not designed to replace all of the important and helpful books that are meant to assist you in improving your understanding of financial planning. Instead, it tries to put in plain language what you need to know to <u>find</u> and <u>effectively use</u> the services of a financial advisor; the latter being critical to your financial success.

The Two Big Issues

There are two main issues regarding financial advisors.

The first step is finding one. If you know where to look, and how to separate the good from the rest, this step is fairly easy to accomplish. Financial advisors do not hide from people, since they are usually looking for you. Many advisors solicit clients regularly through seminars, advertising, and mailings. Most advisors will accept new clients as long as they fit their practice. This hurdle is easy to overcome if you try.

A note of caution here is to beware the "Hunter". That is the advisor who appears only to be interested in making you a client, after which you will be handled by some other person at his firm. These advisors enjoy the thrill of the hunt, but care little for service and long-term relationships.

The second step is learning how to work with a financial advisor, once you have found the one whose services you want to engage. This is far more important to you than finding the advisor, since it involves many years in a close working relationship that eventually determines your financial future. Until now, this second step has been widely overlooked and treated as an after-thought by those giving advice in the personal finance area. That is now going to change.

What This Book Is About

This book addresses both of these concerns to allow you to take control of your financial future, manage your investments in your own best interest, and minimize your risk of financial loss. Ultimately, the goal is to help you enjoy a better life and achieve financial independence.

It discusses the important areas necessary to allow those interested in financial planning to make an intelligent assessment regarding what general direction to take. With the information provided and questions posed in this book, you can go to the appropriate financial professional or institution armed with enough facts to avoid selecting the wrong products or services, or paying too much. In short, it will help you to make good decisions about your financial future, as I expand upon in Chapter 3B. And, it should keep you from making the Big Mistake.

This book will give you an understanding of what financial planning means, and how to use the services of a financial advisor to meet your own financial goals. You will get to know how a financial advisor works with people and the economics of their business. You will understand why and how they get paid, and when and why you should or should not use their services. When you decide to use the services of a financial advisor, this book will help you get the most out of your relationship.

You Have a Role Too

And equally important, I believe you will have a sound understanding of what you need to do in order to meet your own financial planning goals. It takes a lot of effort on your part for the financial advisor to do a good job. You must communicate regularly, stick to a plan in difficult times, and sacrifice today for the promise of a better tomorrow. While this may seem like a daunting task, you can do it if you have the desire, a few helpful tools and bits of information, and the services of the Good Financial Advisor.

Information is Not Knowledge or Wisdom

Information is relatively easy to come by in this world of unlimited access to data. Knowledge is only gained by doing something well over time, and many people have little spare time in this busy, overscheduled world.

Wisdom is said to be the combination of knowledge and experience. Hopefully, the reader of this book will gather some wisdom from the knowledge and experience of others that will serve them well as they attempt to reach financial independence in today's complicated and confusing world of financial planning. You will read more about this in Chapter 3M.

I have added a number of corny, trite and familiar sayings to this book to try to reinforce the obvious, and put in a touch of humor. Forgive me, for I am a financial advisor, not a writer, and I lacked the wisdom to do anything else. One of the stories I told in my seminars and adult education classes is about recognizing help when it is right in front of us, and the tale of this old couple sums it up well.

And old farmer and his wife lived in a low-lying area when rain started coming down heavily, making their road impassible. The forecast was for continued rain and severe flooding, and one of the townsfolk came by in his four wheel drive pickup truck and offered to take the farmer and his wife to higher ground.

"No thank you "said the farmer, "the Lord will provide for us."

A few hours later the water had reached the farmer's front porch, and the local sheriff came by in a small boat and offered to take the farmer and his wife to safety.

The farmer again refused saying, "Thank you Sheriff, but the Lord will provide for us."

By the end of the day, the water had flooded the first floor of the house, and the farmer and his wife had gone upstairs to stay safe.

A helicopter came by, and through a bullhorn the pilot shouted, "Let me take you to safety, before the water covers your house and you drown."

The farmer shouted back from the upstairs window, "Go help others, the Lord will take care of us."

As the water level went higher, the farmer and his wife climbed out on the roof and prayed for the rain to let up. Soon after, the floodwater washed them off their roof and they were both lost.

Standing in front of the pearly gates, the farmer and his wife were shocked to find themselves in front of their maker. In a pleading voice the farmer cried out, "Why did you not save us Lord? We have been faithful all of our lives."

In a booming voice the answer came back.

"I sent you a truck, a boat and a helicopter and you refused help from all three. What more could I have done? "

There is a serious need for the retiring wave of baby boomers to get control of their financial future. Most will be unable to do it successfully without help. This book will provide that assistance to many, by giving them the confidence and ability to seek out the Good Financial Advisor.

I believe that everyone deserves and should be able to enjoy financial independence, and the Good Financial Advisor is the best hope for many to achieve that goal in their lifetime. Poverty is an avoidable condition for most people.

My hope is that this book provides the assistance you need to make your financial future as bright as it can be, and keeps you safe from life's storms.

Help has now arrived.

Chapter 2 – Financial Planning

"We don't know what we don't know. And what we do know that isn't so can be dangerous."

The old concept of financial planning meant you should talk to your stockbroker or insurance agent. In the past thirty years, many things have changed. Defined benefit plans have been replaced by defined contribution plans, and the risk of paying for retirement has shifted from the employer to the retiree. Investment options have increased significantly, and the products we have available to us are so complex as to defy analysis. Add to that a dramatic increase in life expectancy, and it is obvious that the simple methods of yesterday will no longer work in the complex future in which we plan to live.

Financial Planning

What are we talking about when we use these foreboding words? It is more than simple investing, and not just buying an insurance policy or an annuity. Financial planning is a complex process that encompasses wealth accumulation and distribution, protection planning, investing, tax planning, retirement planning and estate planning. This is the essence of what working with the Good Financial Advisor is all about.

Comprehensive financial planning means developing a complete forecast of expenses, income, and savings into the future, factoring in inflation and investment returns, allowing for taxes and foreseeable circumstances, protecting what is at risk, and assisting in the orderly transfer of your estate to those you choose. If a financial advisor tries to give you something significantly less, view it skeptically. Some financial plans are simply spreadsheet projections of little value in guiding your future, and some free internet plans are worse.

However, just because a plan is thick and complex, it is not necessarily better than a simple plan. Large and complicated financial plans that you cannot easily understand are sometimes worse than no plan at all, because they will confuse rather than enlighten. And some plans are designed to be complex in order to hide their true agenda, which is to promote the sale of products, sometimes at higher than necessary levels.

The Future Is Uncertain

As silly as that opening quote might sound, think about it, and it will eventually make sense. No one knows the future with any degree of certainty. Projections of inflation are relatively meaningless more than a few years ahead, as evidenced by the last 20 years. Look at the impact that the inflation rate assumption has on most financial plans and you begin to see the problem.

Even our government, with many skilled people and sophisticated computers, projected both budget surpluses and deficits as far as the eye could see within a few years of each other just a few years ago. And what we do "know" that is not true can be really dangerous because it leads us to make bad decisions.

So the next time someone tries to tell you what is going to happen 37 years into the future, explain to him, or her, what you know that they don't know. In my opinion, financial advisors who do a financial plan for a couple who are in their thirties, and then proceed to tell them exactly what they will need for assets and income when they are in their eighties, need a reality check.

Financial Plans Set a Direction

In practical terms, do not try to "foresee" the future farther ahead than is meaningful. Financial plans, while necessarily imprecise, can help you set a direction. But they need to be reviewed often and adjusted as needed, to reflect what you know today that you did not know yesterday.

A good financial plan is like a map of the United States that you can use when heading out on vacation. If you want to get to California from Connecticut, it will get you on a major route headed west, instead of north or south. But it won't tell you which secondary roads to take, where to stop for food or rest, how fast to travel, what the weather or traffic conditions will be along the way, how much the trip will cost, or how long it will take to arrive at your destination. It is just a lot better than no plan at all.

To parody a famous movie line, "A plan's got to know its limitations." Make sure you understand the limitations of any financial plan that someone prepares for you, or that you prepare for yourself. Also, do not confuse a financial plan with investment management. A financial plan may almost always include managing investments, while investment management may not necessarily be done in the context of a financial plan.

Financial Planning Software

If you are interested, there is financial planning software you can purchase that will allow you to create your own financial plan. For those with the initiative and time, these can be used to your advantage. Just be aware of their limitations, since they all have some. Even the most sophisticated software is only as good as the data you provide to it.

Many financial services firms offer software on their website that will do some basic financial planning for you. Use it carefully, since it is general in nature and may not apply to your specific situation. Any internet-based software should be carefully scrutinized before you use it to guide your future.

Free financial plans offered by various firms or on websites should probably be avoided altogether. The few that I have seen are inaccurate to a fault, and are only designed to get you to engage the firm and invest your money with them. By varying the assumptions, a financial plan can reach any desired conclusion, and lead to a totally erroneous course of action.

The Plan's The Thing

Bear in mind this one inarguable fact. If you do not have a plan, you have little chance of achieving your goals. In fact, you probably do not even have goals if you have no plan, and without goals, your future lacks direction and purpose. If you wish to reach financial independence, a financial plan is an absolute necessity. It can be simple or it can be complex, as long as it is yours.

Whichever path you choose, it must be comprehensive if it is to have a good chance to succeed. You cannot leave out the parts that you do not like or seem too difficult and still call it a plan. This is far too important a task to skimp on the fundamentals here.

A Comprehensive Financial Plan Works

The surest way to prepare a comprehensive financial plan that will give you proper direction is to have it done by the Good Financial Advisor. Of all the tasks that a person should leave to a professional, this is more important than any other in the financial services area. It is the basis of everything else we do to achieve financial independence. It need not be complex, but it must be right.

Plan to get a plan,

sooner, rather than later.

Chapter 2A – Setting Lifetime Goals

"You must have dreams, or sadly, you will never have a dream come true."

Without goals we can drift aimlessly, deluding ourselves that we are making progress. We have little risk of missing what we do not lay out as a goal, and never experience the satisfaction of reaching what we sought. My son had a tee shirt that said it pretty well, with a picture of a basketball and the saying: *"You miss 100% of the shots you never take"*.

50 Lifetime Goals

I often ask clients to write down the 50 things they wish to accomplish in their lifetime, and it is interesting to see the results. The sheer act of trying to discover 50 things that you wish to accomplish before you die is educational in itself. Think outside the box and don't be limited by past experiences. You will find that you and your spouse or partner will have similar interests that you were not aware of before you tried. Go ahead and get a pen and paper and take a stab at it. The entertainment value alone is worth the effort.

Will you always find 50 things to write down? Probably not, but just trying will open up your mind to things that you did not previously consider or were even aware existed. When my wife and I tried this we came up with about 15 items, and discovered that we both wanted to visit Ireland. In June of 2006 we made that dream a reality. In Chapter 4A on Retirement Planning I stress that you must retire to something if retirement is to be at all meaningful and satisfying. Here is where you can uncover some of your lifelong desires. Now you are starting to have some fun.

Questions to Ask Yourself

Some specific questions to prompt you to look at your life and what kind of legacy you want to leave might be these. Try writing down the answers to maximize the impact.

- What is your unrealized passion? Can you do it if you really try?

- Do you have a talent that you have not used but would like to?

- Who do you want to spend more time with?

- How would you be living if money were no object (because you had all the money you wanted)?

- If you found out you had only 5 to 9 years to live, what would you change in those years relative to how you plan to live them now?

- If you found out you only had 5 to 9 weeks to live, what would be your biggest regret?

- If you found out you only had one more day to live, what would you say to the people you love and your closest friends?

- What is one thing you have wanted to do, either for yourself or for others that you have not yet accomplished?

- Where is one place that you want to go that you have not yet been?

- What do you want to be doing 5 or 10 years from today?

- What do you want your legacy to be? (In Chapter 5 there are a few added words on legacies as part of estate planning.)

- When you reach financial independence, where will you be living? With whom?

- Have you made a real difference in someone's life? Do you want to?

These questions will get you started, but you will surely find others. Take your time; dreams should be made with care.

Financial Goals Are a Necessity

Goals are an absolute necessity, or you will be doomed to tilting at windmills forever, and you will never know when you do reach your desired destination.

Specific, quantifiable, financial goals are equally necessary, or you will forever be doomed to chasing investment performance (a losing strategy), and you may never realize true financial independence. For example, when setting a goal for an investment portfolio, select a dollar value at a point in the future instead of just a target rate of return. I expand on this in chapter 6A in The Investment Policy Statement.

Do not fall into the performance trap, where all you do is look at the last quarterly returns to gauge how well you are doing. It is similar to looking at the guard posts on the side of the highway to see how well your trip is progressing. You see a lot of motion, but you have no idea where you are or where you are heading.

The "I Am Rich" Problem

One problem with wealth accumulation is what I call the "I am rich" problem. When a person saves $5,000 a year from age 18 to age 40 they can accumulate a large nest egg. At a 9% return this will become more than $400,000. Looking around at friends who did not save as well and have much smaller nest eggs, they see themselves as rich. They then change their lifestyle to reflect that perception, and by doing so lose their ability to continue to save in the same manner. This is another reason that you need a financial plan, so that you understand you are not rich, just on the road to a comfortable retirement.

Goals – The Basis for a Financial Plan

The Good Financial Advisor will ask many of these questions as part of developing your financial plan. If he doesn't, ask them of yourself. Without them a financial plan may have little substance and provide minimal help in achieving your financial goals. With them you can start with the first item on your list of things to accomplish.

Now go ahead and take that shot, and see which dream will come true.

If you miss, shoot again.

Chapter 2B – Net Worth: The Big Picture

"We sometimes miss the forest for the trees."

When evaluating your financial situation, if you focus only on your invested assets you may be missing the bigger and more meaningful picture. In the market crash of 2000 to 2002 there was a large transfer of wealth from stocks to real estate. Those who saw and understood this were less concerned about the drop in the market than those who merely looked at their declining investment accounts. They watched their house value rise as their investment accounts decreased and tracked their net worth, which in many instances rose. They were also less likely to make bad decisions by moving assets out of the market for an extended period.

Net Worth Statement

To more accurately track your financial position, calculate your net worth (total assets minus total liabilities) and update it annually, or whenever there is a major change in your status. Your net worth is a more accurate and helpful tool to determine the soundness of your financial position than merely looking at your invested assets. Since your house may be one of your largest assets, it could be a source of retirement income later in life through the utilization of a reverse mortgage, which is discussed in Chapter 4H. If you need help in preparing an accurate net worth statement, your Good Financial Advisor can assist you.

Debt Management

Just as an increase in debt can reduce your net worth, a reduction in debt is an addition to net worth, so careful debt management is essential to your financial health. You should know how much you owe, what it is costing you, and when it will be paid off at all times. It is absolutely necessary to discipline your spending so that the total amount of debt you owe does not become unmanageable. The Spending Plan described in Chapter 2D is vital to your success.

If your debt load does become too much to handle, you can be faced with a damaged credit rating for many years, or a personal bankruptcy. In the present, debt service (the interest and principal we must repay) robs us of the flexibility to do other things with our life. When payments become a problem, it will seriously and adversely impact your quality of life for years afterward.

A financial advisor is not a debt counselor, but they should recognize overspending or credit abuse in a minute. When you do not have the ability to invest anything over the course of a year there is a problem. Few people consciously decide not to save anything because other spending takes priority. They almost always spend with abandon until they have nothing left to save, and then make excuses to justify why the spending was absolutely necessary. If you hide your debt situation from your financial advisor, you know you have a problem. One of the most important things the Good Financial Advisor can ask you in the initial interview is how you feel about debt. Don't take it personally. It is important to determining an appropriate financial plan.

Creating Wealth

Creating wealth in the form of tangible net worth can be reduced to this over-simplified process:

- Spend less than you earn.

- Save the difference regularly and diligently.

- Invest what you save prudently.

When you spend more than you earn, the process is broken right from the start and you will never make headway towards financial independence. Therefore, watch your spending and debt load before you get in trouble.

You Must Invest

Remember that you cannot <u>save</u> your way to wealth in retirement without adversely impacting your lifestyle before retirement. The numbers don't work unless you plan to live in an efficiency apartment, and go out only to restock the peanut butter and tuna fish in your cupboard. The detrimental impact of taxes and inflation makes it necessary for you to achieve a return in excess of normal savings rates. You must <u>invest</u> if you wish to accumulate wealth.

Save.

Invest.

Watch your net worth grow.

Chapter 2C – Starting A Financial Plan

"I'm going to stop procrastinating, starting tomorrow."

Here's a news flash. If you don't start your financial plan, you will never have one. If you never have a plan, you will never know where you are going. If you don't know where you are going, you won't know when you get there, and the journey will be filled with anxiety and doubt.

Procrastination

Many of us are too apprehensive about the possible final result to get started. We tell ourselves that we will get started right after: Summer vacation, the start of school, Thanksgiving, Christmas, tax season, Spring cleaning, school gets out, the fourth of July, and oops!, it's Summer vacation again. We are afraid a financial advisor will tell us that we are so bad off that we will have to work until we drop. Yet with a plan we have a greater chance of retiring with financial independence than without one.

It takes substantial effort to create a plan, and it may involve finding the courage to change your lifestyle when you implement it. However, the end result will be a sense of financial security that far outweighs the sacrifices needed to reach your financial goals.

Financial Plan Components

There are three essential parts to a financial plan if you want a high probability of success in reaching your goals.

The first is a Spending Plan that shows what you <u>must</u> spend (your fixed expenses) and what you <u>want to</u> spend (your discretionary expenses). Everyone has to have a Spending Plan or you will almost inevitably spend more than you should on things that you shouldn't. Spending is fun. Saving is not. You are only human.

The second part is a Savings Plan that shows how much you plan to save and where you will invest it. This determines how much you will have to spend when your income from working stops and you must live on the income from your pensions, social security, and that generated by your invested assets.

The third part is a Protection Plan to make sure that the first two parts go as planned. Do not neglect this third part because you feel it is unimportant. Without adequate protection, your income and assets can disappear in a heartbeat, or when your heartbeat stops. The funding for your Protection Plan should be part of the fixed expenses in your Spending Plan.

Time is important to all three parts of your plan. Procrastination can undo the best of plans by removing the magic of compounding from your investment time horizon.

Remember that time is relentless:

- When you have enough, it is a great friend.

- When you have too little, it is your worst enemy.

- Use your time well, and do not let it pass without purpose.

Make time your friend.

Start your plan today.

Chapter 2D – Spending and Savings Plans

"Waste not, want not. Waste a lot, got not."

Developing your Spending Plan and Savings Plan is a difficult job, since they each compete for your money. Typically you will go back and forth between them until you reach a happy compromise between living too frugally and having a lifestyle that leaves nothing for the future. Seek a balance that gives you both a good life today and when you retire.

The Spending Plan – Not a Budget

Before you can effectively do anything else you must develop a Spending Plan that provides for the lifestyle you choose to live, and leaves enough left over to accomplish your financial goals. A Spending Plan is not a budget. It is a comprehensive and thoughtful plan on how you will spend your income, both today and in the years ahead. Your decisions on how expensive a house to live in, how costly a car to drive, and similar lifestyle choices, will define to a large extent your ability to accumulate wealth for retirement, or any other purpose. Deferred gratification is not just something we teach our children, it is what we must learn if we are to plan for the future.

The Spending Plan – Two Major Parts

Your Spending Plan consists of two major parts, both of which are important for your financial plan to work.

The first is what you <u>must</u> spend, such as the fixed expenses related to your choice of house price and size, car price and size, school tuition if you elected to send your child to private school, and similar expenses that are difficult to change in the short run. Debt service is a fixed expense, and usually constitutes the largest portion of this part of your plan. Protection planning and its associated expenses are part of the <u>must</u> spend portion of your plan.

The second is what you <u>want or like</u> to spend, or discretionary expenses that are relatively easy to adjust on a day-to-day basis. These are typically dining out, vacation selection, entertainment, clothing purchases, household maintenance, and miscellaneous daily purchases. These are not completely discretionary, but you can alter them if you make serious lifestyles changes.

If your income minus your Spending Plan leaves a negative balance, you cannot have a Savings Plan, and you will have to either change your lifestyle, or prepare for an inevitable financial train wreck that could end in bankruptcy. I feel this is the most important and critical step in the financial planning process. It is usually taken for granted because it lacks cachet and sophistication, and your financial advisor might prefer to impress you with his expertise in other areas. Don't let this happen. Until you actually put pen to paper and focus on your Spending Plan, the end product of any financial plan you develop could be the result of chance or good luck. A larger than expected bonus, or unanticipated overtime, might lead you into spending habits today that are unsustainable in future years.

If your Spending Plan shows that you will use every dollar you earn to sustain your current lifestyle, then you will be unable to accumulate wealth (other than perhaps some equity in your home) and your future options will be limited. Your retirement will not look so good either.

Only when your Spending Plan allows for sufficient savings to meet your wealth accumulation goals will your future be filled with good and abundant choices. There are many books available that help you to spend wisely, and they are in the personal finance section of your bookstore. Use them to find the myriad of small ways to save money that will add up to some significant savings, without sacrificing a quality lifestyle.

Credit Reports

To help monitor your spending, you can and should check your credit reports. These are what creditors look at when they try to decide if you are a good risk, and you can now get one free every 12 months. Make sure they are accurate, or you could be denied credit or pay higher rates on loans. If you find an error, notify the appropriate party immediately to get it corrected. If you see maxed out credit cards, it's a sign that you may be overspending. You will find your credit reports with three companies: Experian (1-888-397-3742), Transunion (1-800-888-4213) and Equifax (1-800-685-1111). In general, you want to keep your balances low relative to your available credit, and minimize the number of applications you take out. Pay to find out your FICO score, which is the number used to determine what rate you get on a loan. You can check this out on www.myfico.com. Check www.annualcreditreport.com for more information, or call 1-877-322-8228. Just don't take it for granted.

The Savings Plan

Assuming you have a workable Spending Plan, what do you do with what remains after you have spent all that you must and want to? (If nothing remains, go back to the Spending Plan because you do not have a viable plan. Start over and repeat as necessary.) Structure a systematic Savings Plan that will cover all of your savings needs so that one day you may reach financial independence.

The first step, before anything else, is to establish cash reserves in an amount equal to at least four months expenses. This is vital in order to avoid the unforeseen forced liquidation of long-term investments in a financial crisis. Once your cash reserves are in place, you can proceed to your Savings Plan.

In order of importance you should fund your Savings Plan before your Spending Plan. This is the old concept of paying yourself first and it works. A hypothetical basic Savings Plan might look something like this:

- Participate in your employer plan at work to get the company match (it's free money) and defer taxes.

- Contribute to your Roth IRA (if eligible) to avoid future taxes.

- Develop a non-qualified investment portfolio to a level of $50,000 within the next seven years by allocating 50% of salary increases to this goal.

- Contribute to a 529 college savings plan for your children at the rate of $300 per month.

- Save for a vacation in Hawaii in two years at a rate of $150 per month

- Save up a $10,000 down payment for your next car in two years using annual bonus money.

- Save for a second home in 15 years at the rate of $250 per month.

You should fund these goals in order of their priority. If that second home is not within your reach, pass on it until your income permits you to include it in your Savings Plan. Don't sacrifice other goals in an attempt to have it all.

If your Savings Plan gets beyond your ability to fund, revisit your Spending Plan until they both fit within your income.

If you decide not to fund a Savings Plan because you do not want to change your current lifestyle, you have little need for the Good Financial Advisor. Learn to be frugal, because eventually you will be forced to live in that manner.

Save Early – Let the Magic of Compounding Work

For high school or college graduates, a complicated spending and saving plan is not necessary on day one. Start by saving about 10% to 15% of your gross earnings, and you are well on your way. The Good Financial Advisor will direct you to a quality investment vehicle to start your plan, and guide you each year until you are ready to develop a comprehensive financial plan. Read Chapter 8 on protection planning, so you don't forget to get sufficient coverage. You need to do this while you are young, and insurance is inexpensive, as well as available.

The Good Financial advisor will help you put together, and assign amounts to each portion of, your Savings Plan. The rest is up to you. Systematic savings with defined goals produces results better than any other method you can use. Don't try to "put in a slug at the end of the year". When the end of the year arrives, the money is usually gone. Postponing the start date ((as I stated in chapter 2C) not only doesn't work, but you lose valuable compounding time for your money to grow. Remember it is a Spending and Savings <u>Plan</u>, not a Spending and Savings <u>attempt</u>. Anytime you do not pay yourself by funding your Savings Plan, you have sacrificed a piece of your future.

Arrive at retirement ready to spend.

Not spent.

Chapter 2E – Common Advice Pitfalls

"Either find out where the land mines are, or find someone who does."

When starting your financial plan, you have to be careful as to where you get your advice. A big part of winning the financial planning battle consists of avoiding the minefields that people typically step into when attempting to do financial planning on their own. Some advisors also refer to this as avoiding the Big Mistake, though some of these errors can be smaller and correctable. Some of the common errors are: Saving too little, investing too aggressively, investing too conservatively, failing to protect what you have, not having an estate plan, failing to set a goal, and failing to diversify what you invest. There are many others of greater or lesser degree, and you do not want to discover them on your own.

You must find out where the mines are, or find someone that knows where they are, and can lead you around them. Even the most severe critics of financial advisors usually concede that helping you to avoid Big Mistakes is an important service that they can provide. An example of a Big Mistake is this: Someone invests all of his assets too conservatively when younger (not taking sufficient risk), and misses his wealth accumulation goal. Later on in life when he discovers that he will not have enough to retire in a few years, he takes on too much risk to try to make up lost ground, and loses more principal than he can recover in his remaining working years. Retirement is now postponed for a time or reduced in quality. Big Mistake. (In Chapter 6C on Return <u>of</u> Investment I write more about loss of principal).

Seek Quality Advice

To minimize your chances of hitting a mine, seek the advice of those who can and want to help you. When you are seeking advice, you must carefully evaluate the information you receive no matter what the source. Even advice from a professional can be biased, inappropriate for your circumstances, or just plain wrong. Yes, financial advisors can make mistakes, as my own experience shows. But hopefully they are small, infrequent, and can be corrected without permanent damage.

Media Information and Advice

Clients have often brought to my attention things they have seen on TV or read in a magazine, usually to ask for my opinion as to its accuracy. Typically it is free investment advice, such as what stock to buy, or some new system that guarantees successful results if followed. After pointing out the foolishness or fallacy in the advice (although once every few years someone does come up with a piece of advice that is worthwhile), I tell them how to properly evaluate the quality of this type of information.

Ask the Right Questions

Ask yourself this question: What is the goal or purpose of the person giving the advice?

Is it to help you personally? Certainly not, since they know nothing specific about you, your background, your goals, financial position or risk tolerance.

Is it to educate you? No, because there is insufficient context for the information. You have no frame of reference to evaluate the meaning of the information (See chapter 3M).

The media actually encourages the retail investor to move in and out of investments by playing on the emotions of greed and fear. A financial advisor is protection against this type of whipsaw action.

How can you take seriously the "Stock of the Day" or "Mutual Fund of the Week" when you are investing for the next decade? Keep in mind that if you buy and hold for a lengthy period of time, a lot fewer commissions are generated. Unfortunately, a large portion of the securities industry still depends on a steady volume of buying and selling for their income. They are biased towards having you turn over your investments on a frequent basis.

A Simple Goal

The goal of the media is simple and straightforward: they are trying to sell magazines, or newspapers, or to get you to watch their TV show, listen to their radio show or buy their book. (Some books actually try to provide helpful and useful information, and I hope you are reading one of them right now.)

They don't understand you and really do not care what results you get from using their information. It is not because they are bad people, or that they are giving bad advice, it's just that they don't know you. They have no relationship with you and never will.

Contrast this with the Good Financial Advisor, who depends on your success, and continued patronage, if his business is to prosper. Advice that costs nothing is usually worth every penny, and you should be extremely wary of advice from people who are not licensed professionals in that field. Family members who fancy themselves experts in investing are an example of those who you should avoid. The relationship is too close, and will eventually lead to a bad ending when the inevitable problem occurs. How do you fire your brother?

Advice from the Unqualified

For reasons I don't understand, educated professionals seem to like to give advice outside of their area of expertise. I often find attorneys giving advice on insurance, and accountants giving advice on investments. I tell my clients that I do not give advice on taxes or legal issues because as a Certified Financial Planner (CFP®), I am prohibited from doing so by the ethics of my profession. They should judge other professions using that same standard. When given advice by a professional outside of his field, always get a second opinion from one within the field.

Worse yet is advice from friends and acquaintances. The hot tip on a stock or mutual fund is every bit as dangerous as gambling, and somewhat similar as I view it. Equally egregious is the person who pretends to have knowledge on a subject like insurance, and proceeds to give bad advice along with actual examples (usually exaggerated or partly made-up) from their own experience.

Seek Advice from the Qualified

Avoid these common pitfalls by never taking advice from someone who is not truly qualified to give it, and always get a second opinion on complex issues, unless you are certain beyond any doubt as to the accuracy of the advice you receive. You may in fact find that your Good Financial Advisor will get that second opinion himself, just to make sure that his advice is accurate. The last thing he wants to do is lose your trust because he inadvertently gave a piece of inaccurate advice.

If you are up front about your concerns, the Good Financial Advisor will respect your wish to get a second opinion on a difficult subject, since it will usually confirm the quality of his advice. Two heads can be better than one if both have wisdom to offer.

Watch Out For Scams and Schemes

Since much of our behavior is guided by either fear or greed, compounded by ignorance, it is easy to fall victim to scams and schemes promoted by unethical crooks with a fancy title. Due to the scarcity of educational material or programs to alert people to these scams, people fall victim to a host of Ponzi-style schemes and bad "investments". You don't have to be a victim if you take a few precautions.

If It Looks Too Good To Be True - It Isn't.

The financial services industry is highly regulated and extremely competitive. No one has any secret ways to earn returns that are significantly higher than anyone else. Never fall for an idea that promises more than seems reasonable, or you will likely wind up losing your money. Always take the time to evaluate a proposed investment and get a second opinion when warranted. You should not depend on the government to watch out for you.

Regulators Can Only Do So Much

No matter how hard the Securities Exchange Commission (SEC) or the other regulatory agencies try, they must walk a fine line between warning people to the extent of scaring them out of investing at all, and allowing an entire industry to run unsupervised. The financial services industry provides important advice and services to a vast segment of the population. We need effective programs to educate people to use it correctly, instead of patchwork public service announcements that usually come after the fact. Until those are readily available, this book will assist you in your everyday interactions with those in this industry who are genuinely trying to help you on the path to financial independence.

Experience is a tough teacher.

You get the test first and the lessons later.

Chapter 2F – Seminars and Workshops

"If you keep doing the same things, you will keep getting the same results. Believing otherwise is one definition of insanity."

Advice obtained at public talks also needs to be put in perspective. There seems to be an unending number of seminars, workshops, free informational dinners, adult education classes, lunchtime speeches and the like, available today. They are given on almost every financial planning topic imaginable, sometimes with catchy titles like, "Avoid the Ten Terrible Mistakes Every Retiree Makes With Their Money" or "Avoid Paying Taxes Forever".

These talks can be helpful and informative, but please do not delude yourself that they are a substitute for specific advice from the Good Financial Advisor. In a few cases, the information you receive is not just wrong, but intended to get you to take a certain action that may not be in your best interest. In rare cases the speaker is a charlatan, who has no motive other than to get his hands on your assets. If you sense this, eat your meal and leave early!

Skepticism is Warranted

Listen with a skeptical ear whenever you attend one of these events. If you do not know the speaker, listen more skeptically. If you do not know the speaker's credentials, ask yourself how much confidence you should place in what you hear. The speaker may be the Good Financial Advisor that you have not yet met, but you will not know that unless you take the time to schedule a follow-up meeting with him and determine that for yourself. I write more about how to do that in chapter 3B.

If you are asked to sign up for a free consultation on the spot, this is a warning flag that you should heed. The Good Financial Advisor will wait for you to think about what you heard, and call them for an appointment if you feel it desirable. The initial consultation is almost always at no charge, and you should never be pressured into making a quick decision. That is a sure sign of someone you want to avoid.

Common Characteristics

As someone who has given many of these talks (hopefully the helpful and informative ones), I can assure you that they all have some common threads:

- They are not intended to give specific advice. That would be inappropriate, since the speaker knows little about the audience and therefore does not know what advice is suitable for any particular member of it.
- They are not intended to educate the audience sufficiently to make judgments on their own. Years of training and experience cannot be conveyed in an hour or two of general talk and discussion.
- In most cases they are intended to solicit new clients, although some of my speeches were done as a favor for a group, or to help me to sharpen my own knowledge of a certain subject. Being introduced to a financial advisor in this manner is perfectly acceptable, providing that it is followed by a consultation so that you can properly evaluate the person.
- Some talks are done by professionals for exposure in the community. This is a perfectly good way to assess a prospective advisor, by listening to him expound publicly on a particular subject. Just be sure to properly follow up with a private consultation as described in Chapter 3B.

Please understand the real purpose and limitations of any public talk before you try to take action based on what you heard about a specific subject. Would you attend a talk on how to remove pre-cancerous lesions in the privacy of your own home? Some things are just not amenable to doing it yourself no matter how much you learn.

If you have a financial advisor and attend a seminar given by someone else, tell your financial advisor before you ask him questions about what the speaker said. It will save you both from wasting time on a review of someone else's material. If you didn't attend just for the free dinner, your advisor will likely want to know why you are asking him about the subject first.

Proceed With Caution

Before taking action based on a seminar, always evaluate the professional who gave it, and get a second opinion whenever you need a better understanding of the subject. There is no need to hurry in this instance. The Good Financial Advisor will not ask you do anything without careful and thoughtful consideration.

Never confuse a gifted speaker

with a Good Financial Advisor.

Chapter 2G – Health and Life Expectancy

"If I'd known I was going to live this long, I'd have taken better care of myself."

Your financial plan will be highly dependent on the assumptions you use for life expectancy. The good news is we are going to live longer than we ever imagined, provided of course that we take care of ourselves, both physically and mentally. It reminds me of this old joke, which since I turned 60, has not seemed as funny.

Two old timers in their 70's were sitting on a park bench talking, when a much older friend of theirs walked by in a feeble and stooped manner. The first old timer said to the other, "Who on earth would want to live to be as old as Jake Richards. Why he just turned 93, and he can hardly get around anymore." Without turning his head the second old timer answered, "Anyone who is 92 would be my guess."

Longevity - The Next Big Thing

The bad news is we are not prepared for longevity. When you contemplate retirement, do you really think of being in retirement for 20 to 30 years? I doubt it. People used to plan for a retirement of 5 to 10 years when their life expectancies were in the late 60's to early 70's. People must now plan for longer and healthier years after their primary working career is done. A second career may become commonplace in the next decade for just those reasons, or people will have to rethink their planned retirement age.

Not only must you plan to live a long time, but you will likely be healthy and active for many years beyond what your parents were, and your retirement plan should take that into account. I go into this in detail in Chapter 4B when discussing a phased spending model. In my opinion, Longevity Risk is the "next big thing" in retirement planning. I discuss the myriad of other risks we face in Chapter 6B.

Lifestyle Choices

While we are on the subject of health and life expectancy, smoking, which was the primary cause of death for both of my parents, is definitely a hindrance to developing a retirement plan. If you smoke a pack a day from age 18 to age 66, the opportunity cost (Chapter 6D) will be about $1,500,000 over your lifetime, to feed that habit. The offsetting news is that your lifetime will most likely be shorter. You have found a sure way to address Longevity Risk.

The same goes for excessive drinking, drug use, or obesity. As I wrote this book, my best friend of over 40 years was faced with a significantly shorter life expectancy due to diabetes and the related problems that accompany it, so I speak from first hand experience. Financial health alone is empty and meaningless. Maybe my next book will be "Eat, Drink and Smoke Your way to A Secure, Early and Short Retirement".

Physical Health Is Vital

Without physical health, your financial health may become moot, so plan to live well in every way. A preponderance of studies indicates that the more active we are both physically and mentally, the longer we will remain healthy in every respect. I have several stories in my files about people actively working in their chosen careers beyond age 70 and into their 90's. These stories all seem to indicate that the socialization aspect of working, as well as the sense of purpose you get from contributing to a job, makes it worthwhile. A secondary benefit is that people who work tend to be physically healthier and mentally sharper than those who sit in front of a TV all day.

Factor all of this into your planning when you consider what you will retire to (Chapter 4A), when you should elect to begin taking Social Security, and when you decide to stop working altogether. The Good Financial Advisor will take into account your health and life expectancy when helping you to establish your financial plan, since it affects many assumptions, especially the age at which you begin taking Social Security as discussed in Chapter 4I. When did you get your last physical checkup? When will you get your next one?

Live long, stay healthy, and prosper.

Chapter 2H – Doing It Yourself

"Physician, heal thyself, and you will have a fool for a patient."

The basic premise of this book is that most people would be better off working with a Good Financial Advisor than trying to do-it-themselves. Not very much is written about the pitfalls and pluses of doing it yourself, so I thought it appropriate to include a few of the obvious and maybe not so obvious problems that do-it-yourselfers face, compared to the advantages of paying a professional to do the work for you.

The Advantages of Doing It Yourself

- You pay no fees or commissions to anyone, whether you make or lose money

- No one nags you to act, so you can procrastinate for indefinite periods.

- You are completely in charge of your portfolio 24/7, during vacations, when you are ill, in good market times and bad.

- You get 100% bragging rights if you are successful, and you can brag to everyone, if you get it right.

- You can boast to your spouse or partner about how great an investor you are, if you make money.

- Emotions will guide many of your investment decisions. You will constantly hope that you don't make the Big Mistake.

The Disadvantages of Doing It Yourself

- You pay no fees or commissions to anyone, so you get to do all of the work yourself whether you make or lose money. Fatigue will be your constant companion.

- No one nags you to act, so you will likely procrastinate on every major decision to your detriment.

- You will worry about your portfolio 24/7, during vacations, when you are ill, and especially in declining market periods. Stress will be with you always.

- You must take 100% of the blame <u>when</u> you are wrong, and you will avoid telling anyone how badly you did <u>when</u> you make the Big Mistake.

- Your spouse or partner will know you ruined your retirement plans because you invested badly, since you have no one else to blame.

- Emotions will guide many of your investment decisions. Historically, you will be wrong more times than you are right and come to doubt your every decision.

Prioritize Your Life

After netting out the advantages and disadvantages, it comes down to this tradeoff. You can do a lot of work, save the fees and commissions that an advisor would charge, and hope to get the same (or better) result. But, you must do at least as good a job as a professional financial advisor, or you have done a lot of work for many years for nothing. Since we only have a finite amount of time in a day, it comes down to setting priorities on what we will do, and what we will have others do for us. There are practical limits on how much we can do ourselves.

I am amazed that today we develop our own pictures, scan ourselves through a register, pump our own gas and assemble our own furniture, but there are no serious consequences when we make a mistake in these areas. I believe (backed by my experience) that most people would be better off allowing a professional to guide them in the area of financial planning, and expending their energy on tasks where the cost of mistakes is small and the impact is only short-term.

What do the "Experts" do?

I have never seen the public figures who advocate doing it yourself come forward with their own investment and financial planning results, so we can see how they have done <u>without</u> a financial advisor. If their results were good, I am confident that we would know about it. If their results were poor, they couldn't reveal that without destroying their credibility. I am therefore suspicious that some of them get poor results and tell no one, or they might actually use a financial advisor, and keep that fact hidden from the rest of us.

Do They Have A Plan?

It would be interesting to see 1,000 financial advisors and 1,000 do-it-yourself advocates (who handle all of their own finances) face off for a 1, 3, and 5-year period. I wish someone would survey these advocates to see how many do handle all of their own finances, and how many have a written financial plan. If they have no financial plan they have no business telling others to do their own financial planning. If they do have a plan, is it consistent with the advice they give to others? If more than 50% use a financial advisor, the question has been answered.

Look at the Dalbar study in Chapter 6G to see how poorly self-directed investors have done in the past, and how investor behavior affects you in Chapter 6L. The record of individual investors acting without professional advice is so weak that it begs the question as to why anyone would want to assume all of the responsibility for their own portfolio.

Some Can - Some Can't

Seriously consider the pros and cons of using an advisor before taking on the burden of handling all of your financial affairs yourself. I have seen too many Big Mistakes made by people in the last decade to believe that the <u>average</u> person can achieve the same results on a consistent long-term basis as the Good Financial Advisor. It is not only stressful work, but it demands a great deal of time to do it right. The Good Financial Advisor can rationalize spending twenty hours a week on investments because it benefits all of his clients. For the individual it is difficult to justify spending that amount of time on a single account, even when it is your own.

There is no doubt that some people are capable of handling their own finances and doing an excellent job. I am equally confident that most people cannot do it themselves, and there is compelling evidence that this is true. Optimism and over-confidence are discussed in Chapter 6L, and few are exempt from this category. Given all of the obstacles facing them, it is my opinion that there are only a few people who have both the time and ability to manage their own financial affairs and do a good job of it. If you are one of them, please give this book to a friend who might benefit from reading it.

Do-It Yourself Books

If you wish to learn more about financial planning and its related subjects, prepare for years of studying. You can also go to a website such as www.swlearning.com and add to your knowledge. You will not learn much that is helpful, or useful, by reading the usual do-it-yourself monthly magazines. The personal finance section of the local bookstore is better, but only if you are selective and avoid the self-help books mentioned in the Introduction.

Perusing the personal finance section of the major bookstores, I notice that there are now books on every topic imaginable. However, their advice is usually the same. First, the author brags about being an expert, with years of training and experience. Then they tell you that you will learn all you ever need to know about a particular product, or subject, by reading their book. Finally, they warn you to be careful when taking action based on what you learned (They blame the warnings on the lawyers). Read the disclosures and you might be surprised.

Dangerous or Useless?

This type of advice borders on useless, and nearly dangerous, when applied to complicated financial services and products. Look closely at the titles to see just how ridiculous some books are before you buy them. Then think about this common sense test: If learning how to manage your finances could be accomplished by simply reading a book, why would major institutions, corporations, college endowment plans and billionaires pay large fees to financial advisors year after year? They are sophisticated, and have the resources to hire anyone they choose, yet they still use financial advisors. The answer is that financial advisors minimize risk and get results.

Clients Know Better

Common sense tells you that clients would desert financial advisors in droves if they did not produce satisfactory results for the fees they charge. If problems were as pervasive as the media leads you to believe, clients would be filing complaints in overwhelming numbers. If financial advisors were as bad as portrayed by the do-it-yourself experts, clients would not seek out another advisor after experiencing a problem with their current advisor. Cynicism is far too prevalent in some of the pundits, but it is based on the past thirty years, not the drastically different past five years. It also ignores the vast changes that will govern the next twenty years. Economic conditions, investment products, inflation, insurance products and financial analysis have all seen huge improvements in how they work for the typical investor. They cannot be ignored.

When you see books ostensibly written for idiots, dummies and fools, it tells you something about the mindset of the author. Look elsewhere for knowledge and understanding. They are only trying to sell books. If you wish to learn, choose the serious books written by experts in a field. They are not as much fun, but they won't waste your time on simplistic explanations of complicated subjects.

Results Are What Count

I cannot resist relating one example of how some do-it-yourselfers may have fared in the last major market downturn from 2000 to 2002. If you heeded the advice of many media talking heads, and just bought an S & P 500 Index fund in January 1998, when the market was rising steadily, you would have made about 39% on your investment by the end of 2004. If instead, you bought a balanced asset allocation mutual fund, and paid a 4.75% sales charge (plus higher ongoing expenses), you would have made about 57% on your investment, at significantly less risk. If, like many investors without a financial advisor to help them stay the course, you sold in panic or desperation at the end of 2002, and went to a 5% Certificate of Deposit for safety, you made about 7% on your investment. The investor who used a financial advisor, paid sales charges, and paid higher expenses had an 18% higher return than the index fund investor, and a 50% higher return than the investor who cut and ran.

Those who tell you to simply buy and hold an equity index fund, instead of investing in a balanced portfolio, have been discredited often, and yet they still keep advocating this approach. Now you have been warned. Low expenses are good, but net results at low risk are what counts. Focus on risk and results, not costs. If active portfolio management did not work, sophisticated institutions would have abandoned it long ago.

Results are Relative

Remember that old story of the two hikers who spotted a bear following them on the trail. One hiker stopped and removed his sneakers from his backpack and started to put them on. The other hiker looked at him and said, "You don't think you can just outrun that bear do you?" The first hiker looked at him and said, "I don't have to outrun that bear, I only have to outrun you."

In the same way, if you decide to use a financial advisor, they do not have to outperform the market or some equally irrelevant benchmark unrelated to your goals. They only have to outperform you. Put another way, if the total cost of using a financial advisor is 1.00%, you have to perform within 1.00% of what a professional would have done over the long haul, or you have done all that work for very little reward.

The Good Financial Advisor does not have to beat the market.

He does not have to beat a benchmark.

He only has to beat you.

Chapter 3 – Financial Advisors

"The Holy Grail, Atlantis and the Good Financial Advisor."

Finances have become much more complex than they were twenty or thirty years ago. And our government can't seem to resist the urge to change tax laws and retirement plan rules on an almost annual basis. For these reasons along with other changes, and because financial planning and investing are so important, many people elect to use the services of a financial advisor rather than managing these aspects of their lives themselves.

Where can you find a great person, pure of heart, clear of mind, sharp of wit, laden with knowledge and experience, energetic and capable, overflowing with ethics and integrity, this side of heaven? You probably can't, anymore than you can find Atlantis or the Holy Grail, but you can find the Good Financial Advisor if you know where and how to look.

A financial advisor is a professional who provides advice and may sell products and services in conjunction with that advice. The most common person in this general category is the stockbroker, who now usually goes by another title. Insurance agents also hold themselves out as financial advisors if they have a securities license. There is no required training for a financial advisor nor is there a designation that all financial advisors must have, so it is up to you to determine if someone is acceptable as a financial advisor.

Financial advisors usually work for a firm called a broker-dealer (in a few cases they may own their own broker-dealer). If their broker-dealer is a Registered Investment Advisor they will be Investment Advisor Representatives and be able to charge fees instead of commissions. In some cases a financial advisor may operate solely as a Registered Investment Advisor and not work under a broker-dealer, and I will cover these in a later paragraph. To understand your financial advisor you should be familiar with the type of firm under which they operate.

Broker-dealers

Broker-dealers come in two types: <u>proprietary</u> broker-dealers who make some of the products they sell, hence, they are a dealer of those products, and <u>non-proprietary</u> broker-dealers who make no products, and simply broker products made by others. When dealing with a financial advisor you should know his broker-dealer so you can determine whether or not you are buying proprietary products. Proprietary products may contain different incentives and commissions for the advisor, and you should know this when recommendations are made for their purchase. In many cases these products cannot be transferred to another broker-dealer (if you ever need to change advisors in the future), and must be liquidated, with possible tax consequences. In a few cases the proprietary products are not as good as other competing non-proprietary products.

There is a growing preference for non-proprietary broker-dealers on the part of clients in order to eliminate any bias towards the sale of proprietary products. Chapter 3C discusses this in more detail. Given the choice, with all other things being equal, you should always prefer the non-proprietary broker-dealer to eliminate any concerns regarding product bias.

Financial Planner or Not?

Financial planners or registered investment advisors operate under a different set of guidelines than brokers. Financial planners act as a fiduciary and must make decisions based on the "best interests of the client" with full and fair disclosure. A broker only need make investment recommendations that are "suitable" for the client with minimal disclosure. There is a significant difference between the two, and there is an ongoing dispute today about how each should be regulated. You should know under which guidelines your advisor works and whether they are acting as a fiduciary. You should always prefer a fiduciary over one who is not. A stockbroker is almost always not a fiduciary. One key question to ask your prospective advisor is: Are they a financial planner or investment advisor? Brokers cannot call themselves a financial planner or investment advisor, so they will use titles such as financial consultant, investment counselor, or financial advisor to describe themselves.

For this book I chose to use the generic term financial advisor to describe the person you should work with because I feel they are an advisor, not a planner, in most of what they do. As a Certified Financial Planner (CFP®) myself, I feel that you should always prefer a CFP® to any other designation. The financial services industry is having a vigorous public debate over what designation is the best one, and as of now, the CFP® is winning. There are other designations that you can rely on to tell you about the capabilities of an advisor, and I will go over credentials in Chapter 3B.

Registered Investment Advisors

Some financial advisors are Registered Investment Advisors (RIAs), and some are not. If you do not wish to pay commissions or asset-based fees, you must work with someone who is an RIA and can provide advice for a fee. RIAs do not have to have securities licenses to provide advice on a fee-only basis, but if they do not have licenses they cannot collect commissions. Most Good Financial Advisors are RIAs or represent a broker-dealer who is an RIA, in which case they are Investment Advisor Representatives. Even though there are Good Financial Advisors who are not RIAs, I would always select an RIA over someone who is not able to provide fee-based advice.

Check Your Expectations

But who said finding the Good Financial Advisor would be easy? It isn't, and the more effort you put into the financial advisor selection process, the more likely you are to be successful in the long term. Before you decide to ask someone to help you with your financial planning, take time to review these three things:

1) Determine why you want an advisor.

- Are you too busy to do it yourself?
- Are you unable to do it yourself?
- Are you afraid of making the Big Mistake?
- Do you feel a professional will do a better job?
- Do you just want a second opinion?
- Are you looking for continuity after you are gone?

2) Think about what you will expect from a financial advisor, and what they will expect from you.

- Are your expectations realistic?
- Are you ready to enter into a close relationship?
- Are you ready to keep up your side of the relationship?

Are you prepared to develop a close, long-term relationship with your financial advisor, perhaps more so than with your doctor, accountant or attorney? You may come to share your most private thoughts with your financial advisor, even those of a non-financial nature such as health issues. I have had clients confide an impending divorce in me more than a year before it was to occur, so that they could restructure their finances in an appropriate manner. Those confidences I did not even share with my staff, except to the extent necessary to do their work. This is why confidentiality is so important, as discussed in chapter 3G.

Getting Started Is Tough

Going to a financial advisor has sometimes been likened to going to a dentist. (My apologies to my dentist, who has always made my trip to his office pleasant). You tell the advisor what you want. The advisor tells you what you should do, and you make promises that you have little hope of keeping. At the next meeting, which you have postponed for as long as possible, you admit that you have not done the things you said you would do, and promise to do them again. At some point, you realize that if you had followed the advisors' advice, you would be in great shape financially with a good retirement ahead of you, but you would have had to defer some gratification today to get there. No wonder getting started is tough.

Once you have determined that you definitely want a financial advisor, make sure you really need one, and for the right reasons, as discussed in the next chapter.

Expect the best from the Good Financial Advisor.

Chapter 3A – Do You Need An Advisor?

"A little knowledge is a dangerous thing, but a lot of ignorance can be worse."

There are two main groups of people who need a financial advisor: Those who are able to manage their finances, but won't, and those who are unable to manage their finances. You probably fit into one of these two groups if you are considering using a financial advisor to handle your finances.

Evaluating your need for a financial advisor is important so that you don't engage the services of one for the wrong reasons. Do not engage a financial advisor to make you rich by finding the next Microsoft stock. It won't work. Be certain as to why you want to work with a financial advisor before deciding to become a client. See if you fit any of the following categories.

Who needs a financial advisor?

You <u>might</u> need a financial advisor if:

- You think the S & P 500 is a new NASCAR race.

- Your idea of diversification is to open another CD at a different bank.

- You think asset allocation means figuring out how much money you spend at the casino vs. the local Wal-Mart.

- You think protection planning means keeping a loaded gun in the house.

- You think the stock market is where they pen the hogs at the auction.

- You think a bond is what you post to get out of jail.

- You think tax deferral means filing your income tax return late.

- Your idea of estate planning is deciding where to plant the garden in your yard.

- Your motto is "Live for today and to hell with tomorrow."

However, you might <u>really</u> need a financial advisor if:

- You are more than 1 year into your first job and you do not participate in the company 401(k) plan because it is too much hassle, even with a company match. You don't really believe they're giving you free money anyway.

- You are over thirty and have not started to plan or save for retirement because you have plenty of time left. You are not even sure how to get started.

- You have two children in school and have not figured out how you will pay for their college education. In fact you have not started saving for college because you are not sure of the best way to do so.

- You are within 20 years of retirement and figure you will have to work until you drop dead. Therefore you don't want to bother with a retirement plan.

- Your estate plan consists of a will you drafted when your first child was born. The other two children have not been included yet. Living wills, durable powers of attorney and health care powers of attorney are just too complicated to deal with until you are really old.

- You are afraid to invest in the stock market because of the crash of 2000 to 2002. Besides it's already gone back up so you are sure you missed it.

- You are afraid to invest in the stock market because you read about the stock market crash of 1929 and you are sure it will happen again to you.

- You don't have a Roth IRA because you don't know what a Roth IRA is. In fact, you don't even have a regular IRA.

- You just got married.

- You are getting a divorce.

- You like paying taxes, because you figure you have no choice in the matter

- You hate paying taxes, but you figure you have no choice in the matter.

- You don't seem to have enough money to live in retirement, but you are afraid to spend any of your principal because you don't want it to run out.

- Your financial plan consists of never overdrawing your checkbook.

- You are caring for your parents.

- You think an annuity is an updated version of an old ity.

- You get your 401(k) plan advice from a friend at work.

- You have a child with special needs.

- You depend on free advice from a relative who works for a bank.

- You have all the life insurance you need at work, and no one really needs life insurance when they are young anyway.

- You have read several books on personal finance and you plan to save a fortune by doing it all yourself.

- You don't need disability insurance because you aren't planning to get disabled, and besides, you're pretty sure you have some of that at work too.

- The receptionist at work assured you that you are doing the right thing because the big boss has no additional insurance of any kind either.

- You really do live for today without regard for tomorrow.

This is not an all-inclusive list, but if you can answer any of these questions with a yes, you might benefit from a visit to a financial advisor to see just how far off the track you are.

Financial Embarrassment

One reason (there are many) that people do not seek out a financial advisor is what I term financial embarrassment. They fear being ashamed that they have little or no assets, especially if it is due to a past mistake on their part. This is particularly evident with the friends or relatives of advisors who need help but can't bring themselves to bare their financial souls to someone who knows them.

If you fit this description here is an answer. Go to the advisor who you know and tell him that you want to speak to an advisor, but you are uncomfortable at this point with sharing your financial situation with someone you know. Ask for a colleague with whom you can have an initial meeting to determine your financial position. The advisor will refer you to an associate he trusts to handle your concerns and keep them strictly confidential.

The most important thing to look at is not just whether you really need a financial advisor, but also, can you benefit from the assistance of a financial advisor. Like other professionals, a good financial advisor can save you far more than the cost of their services. If nothing else, they can prevent you from making the Big Mistake. Once you have determined that you do need and want a financial advisor, then the hard work begins.

The services of a financial advisor are not a free lunch,

just a good meal

that you don't have to prepare yourself.

Chapter 3B – Selecting an Advisor

"Character and integrity are how we act when no one is watching us."

One of the primary reasons that people do not have a financial advisor is that finding one can be a very difficult task. It is similar to finding a doctor and dentist when you move to a new town, and everyone can relate to how much fun that is.

Some of the apprehension is due to the mischaracterization of the profession in the media, who have a fondness for stories of financial misconduct in every area of the financial services industry. It is very unlikely that you will find a bad financial advisor, any more than you will find a bad dentist or doctor. However, you do want to find someone who is trained and experienced, and will have the judgment to help you achieve your goals, and avoid making bad decisions. This story makes the point.

> *A woman was talking with a financial advisor about becoming a client, and she asked the advisor what was the secret to his success.*
> *"Simple" said the advisor, "and it can all be summed up in just two words. Good Decisions."*
> *"How do you make Good Decisions?" asked the prospective client.*
> *"Simple ", said the advisor, "and it can all be summed up with just one word. Experience."*
> *"But how do you get Experience?" asked the prospective client*
> *"Simple" said the advisor, "and it can all be summed up in just two words. Bad Decisions."*

Although this humorous tale has been told in many ways, the lesson is the same. You don't want someone making bad decisions on your behalf, and you don't want someone gaining experience at your expense. Therefore you have some work to do to find your Good Financial Advisor.

The Selection Process

Selecting the right financial advisor may be the most important step you take on the road to financial independence, so be prepared to invest some time and effort in doing so. You do not want to have to change advisors later or quickly because you were lax in the selection phase. There are four basic steps to the process:

1) Finding advisors from whom to make your initial selection.

2) Narrowing the field to those meeting your criteria. (Which means you must have criteria.)

3) Interviewing advisors to ensure they are right for you in terms of chemistry and trust.

4) Selecting the Good Financial Advisor and beginning to work with him.

Before you envision a two year marathon process where you find 18 potential advisors, narrow the field to the best four, conduct two interviews with each advisor, hold a final runoff with the two finishers and then meet with the finalist for a two hour interrogation to conclude the process, I would advise you to take a deep breath and relax.

Most experienced and successful advisors will not put themselves through a process that treats them in the same fashion that you would an advisor new in the business. (Nor will they enjoy being treated like a used car salesman.)

Speaking personally, I am willing to invest up to ninety minutes in the initial interview with a serious potential client. My experience shows that I can tell a potential client everything they should know about me in less than thirty minutes. I can find out everything I need to know about them in less than thirty minutes. That leaves thirty minutes for socialization and in-depth questions.

There is no hard and fast rule here, but common sense tells you that only so much time will be useful and productive. If you are well prepared, which you will be if you follow the guidelines I spell out in this book, ninety minutes is more than sufficient time for an initial interview.

The actual process can be simple or complicated, depending on your particular circumstances. In the easiest scenario, you may have known a financial advisor for years and can simply contact her and ask for a meeting.

You may know a friend or relative who has used the same advisor for many years and will refer you to her.

There may be a firm in your town that has been established for years and has a great reputation that you can stop in and see.

Whatever your first step, do not get bogged down at the initial stage of the process. There are many ways to select the Good Financial Advisor.

Chemistry and Trust Is Critical

There are many characteristics of a good relationship, but trust is the single most important aspect of the client/advisor relationship. You must trust your advisor, and your advisor must trust you. There has to be certain chemistry for the relationship to work well. No one can define this; you must follow your gut instincts here. Without the right chemistry, you will be unable to develop a sufficient level of trust to make the relationship work over the long-term. If you do not sense that there is a good chemistry between you and the prospective financial advisor at the conclusion of your first meeting, look elsewhere.

Do the Basic Checks

It is important that you learn about someone with whom you plan to do business for a long time. There are some basic checks you can make to ensure you have found someone who has no background problems.

1)   Check on their credentials with your state banking commission and insurance department.
2)   Contact FINRA at 1-800-289-9999 and see if they have any marks on their record.
3)   Check with your local Chamber of Commerce for complaints against them.
4)   Check out their form ADV on the government's website to see if they have anything in their background regarding disciplinary actions.

Websites Can Be Helpful

These are some of the websites that you can use in your search:

www.finra.org is the National Financial Industry Regulatory Authority website (Formerly NASD). It is a great source of information.

www.fpanet.org lists financial planners in your area, but it is by no means complete. (I am not on it.)

www.feeonly.org lists planners who charge fees instead of commissions for those who want a fee-only planner.

www.cfp.net lists advisors who are Certified Financial Planners.

www.garrettplanningnetwork.com lists advisors who charge by the hour. (Most advisors can and will charge by the hour when it is appropriate.)

www.nasaa.org provides links to state regulators.

www.sec.gov/investor/brokers.htm lets you check the record of an advisor with securities regulators.

www.napfa.com lists members of the National Association of Personal Financial Advisors who are fee-only planners.

Let's jump right into the first step in the process, finding people from which to start making the selection.

Step One - Finding Financial Advisors

Just how do you find someone who is competent, trustworthy and compatible with you? And who will not be making bad decisions on your behalf as they learn their trade. It is not easy, but these are some general guidelines to improve your chances of finding the person right for you.

- Ask your friends or family for a referral or introduction to someone they know and have worked with for a substantial period of time. In my opinion, this is still the best way to select a financial advisor.

- Talk to someone you know who is a financial advisor.

- Attend a seminar or adult education class on a subject that relates to your needs in financial planning. Remember to carefully "interview" the speaker before committing to work with someone you meet in this way. (See Chapter 2F)

- Ask the Chamber of Commerce for a list of affiliated financial advisors in your area. Check them out before you contact them.

- Look in your local phonebook. Most established firms will be listed there. You can screen many firms with a single phone call.

- Use the internet and check out the websites of advisors in your area.

Use Caution Using the Internet

As I mentioned in the Introduction, there are some websites that purport to help you find an advisor, but they are actually sites where a few advisors pay to be listed and do not represent a cross-section of advisors available in your area. There are also websites sponsored by investment firms to lead you to their advisors. These have no pretense of objectivity and are not worried about what kind of advisor you find, as long as it is one of theirs. Some of these advisors may be the Good Financial Advisor, but it will be up to you to find the right one to interview. Never pay to find an advisor on the internet; that is a sure sign that something is not right.

Once you have found some advisors (you will find many in my experience), it is time to apply a few criteria to narrow the field to those who might qualify as the Good Financial Advisor.

Step Two - Narrowing the Field

Regardless of how you found them, choose a person with adequate experience as a financial advisor, or in a closely related field. In my opinion this is at least ten years, or less if they have trained under an experienced advisor. This may appear to eliminate all but the most experienced advisors, but that need not be the case. A new advisor can work with an experienced advisor or firm and still get the job done.

What is not desirable is the independent new advisor working alone and learning (making bad decisions) at your expense. Doctors work as interns, and attorneys sit in the second chair, before they work alone. It is an equally wise path for a financial advisor to follow.

Experience is Mandatory

Financial advisors should have extensive training and demonstrable expertise in the area in which they work. Do not be afraid to ask what their background and experience is before selecting a person to handle your financial affairs. Many financial advisors come from a previous career due to a bias against young and inexperienced advisors, and you should ask what their prior work experience is, since it most likely will affect how they perform their current job.

Choose an advisor that has sufficient experience in the field to serve your needs. Do not select a new advisor to the field, unless they work for a firm under the guidance of someone who is experienced. You should not allow an inexperienced financial advisor to train on your accounts. If they are new to the field, they should join with another experienced advisor until they are capable of working on their own. Three to five years of experience under an experienced advisor should be the minimum for someone working on their own, depending on their background.

Choose someone who has relevant prior work experience. Someone who has worked with people before may have an advantage over a person who worked alone. A teacher might be more suited than a research chemist.

A College Education Is a Must

Choose an advisor that has a college educational background that is appropriate to the financial services field. A former electrical engineer may not have the educational experience needed to serve you as well as one with an economics background or a business degree. Someone without a college education may not have the depth of training to become skilled at the technical aspects of being a financial advisor. I would not consider someone without a college degree, since I believe that a college background provides a valuable and relevant learning experience. A college degree is now a requirement for the Certified Financial Planner (CFP®) designation.

Passion is Wonderful

Look for someone who is passionate about their work. It is a wonderful attribute to have in a financial advisor. Because this profession is one of stressful periods and constant rejection, passion is a great attribute to have to overcome these obstacles. The passionate advisor believes that financial independence is one step short of heaven, and is worth whatever the cost to achieve. She eats, sleeps and breathes this stuff. You will recognize passion in the initial interview.

The Right Credentials Are Important

Choose an advisor that has credentials that are relevant to financial planning. A Certified Financial Planner or CFP® is, in my opinion, the best example of this, and indicates someone who has taken courses in Investments, Taxes, Estate Planning, Financial Planning, Insurance, and Retirement Planning. It is a difficult designation to acquire, requiring three years of experience, two to three years of study followed by a two-day ten hour comprehensive exam, and starting in 2006 a bachelor's degree. It is probably more indicative of someone who is a true financial planner than any other designation today. There are about 55,000 financial advisors with a CFP designation today, and about 17,000 have graduate degrees or higher.

Some other designations that are common are CLU or Chartered Life Underwriter and ChFC or Chartered Financial Consultant. Both of these are common with insurance agents. The CFA or Chartered Financial Analyst is a highly respected designation that is more prevalent with money managers. There are a number of others, and you simply need to understand what they are and if they are relevant to what you need in an advisor.

If someone has no designations at all, you might want to consider whether they would work hard for you if they do not have the motivation to work for an advanced designation. If someone has too many designations it might be a sign that they spend more time gathering letters than using them, for purposes other than serving you.

Worthless Designations Proliferate

There are now more than 100 designations that one can earn through various courses, workshops and other types of training. Some have value to you as a financial planning client but most do not. They are designed to portray the holder as one with some unique capability that is in fact only cosmetic and used to sell his services. You can check out designations at www.finra.org to see which have significance to your needs and which are intentionally misleading.

Be skeptical of the numerous designations that require little study to obtain, since they have minimal value to you. Especially suspect are designations that target seniors. They are sometimes no more than marketing gimmicks using words like "Chartered", "Consultant", "Senior", "Retirement", "Planning", "Advisor", "Specialist" and "Certified" to infer a degree of expertise that does not exist.

Ask the prospective advisor these two questions: 1) How much training did it take to obtain the designation he has and 2) What value does it have to you as a client? Listen carefully and be guided by the answers. If it took only one or two days to obtain through a weekend workshop (or a few hours in a hotel conference room), or its focus was to teach the advisor how to market to a specific age group, the designation is worthless to you as a client.

One state is now conducting an investigation into misleading credentials and other states are sure to follow. Use common sense and caution when considering a financial advisor's credentials. The Good Financial Advisor will take great pride in explaining his credentials and how they might benefit you.

Too Close to Criticize

Be careful when doing business with an advisor who is too close to you. When something goes wrong, as it inevitably will, given sufficient time, you may find yourself unable to criticize the advisor's actions or advice, and demand a change. This especially applies to turning your assets over to a friend's daughter or son who just got into the business to "help them get started". It may be nearly impossible to "fire" someone who is close to you, leading to bad feelings on both sides, and losses for you.

I have made it a practice to avoid doing business with close neighbors or relatives for just those reasons. I have made exceptions to this rule for some friends, but only for those who I felt truly wanted or needed my help, and where turning them away would have created hard feelings. In these circumstances, there is a lot of pressure on an advisor to avoid making a mistake that could impact the relationship.

Advisor Continuity

When selecting an advisor, consider what will happen when the advisor is no longer in business, either through retirement, disability or death. Continuity of coverage is an important consideration and I talk more about it in Chapter 3E. Ask the prospective advisor what their business continuity plan is. If they have none, you must decide if that is important to you, and if it is, look elsewhere. If the prospective advisor is older and nearing retirement, does he have a younger partner who will phase into the business to ensure a seamless relationship with you and his firm? Are you comfortable with the partner? Can the firm handle your needs in the future? Ask now to avoid problems later.

Character & Integrity Count

Lastly, select an advisor who appears to have character and integrity. They cannot be bought, and are difficult, if not impossible, to fake. The old definition of character is how we conduct ourselves when no one else can see us, and that is precisely one of the qualities you want in your financial advisor.

An advisor who appears to be too slick, or talks too fast, may just be a slick, fast-talking advisor and should be avoided. Look for substance, and stay away from those who insinuate that they can show you how to completely avoid taxes, or have a foolproof system that provides above average investment results. Look for a financial advisor who speaks well about his profession (even his competitors) and his clients. In financial planning and investing, as in the rest of life, anything that seems too good to be true almost certainly is.

Once a prospective advisor has made it through the process of narrowing the field, it is time to meet for an initial interview. Sometimes these meetings will occur at the same time. You may speak with an advisor on the phone or simply set an appointment because they were referred by a close friend. However it happens, the initial interview will take place, in which you will personally size up the advisor and he will do the same.

<u>Step Three - Interviewing Potential Advisors</u>

The purpose of the interview is for you to evaluate the acceptability of the advisor, and for the advisor to assess your potential fit in his practice. It is not meant to evaluate you, although the advisor will do so to some extent in order to determine what your suitability requirements are regarding an investment portfolio. This is information required to be obtained by FINRA to be sure the advisor knows his customer if you become a client, and you should not be concerned when the advisor asks questions regarding your income, assets, goals, financial situation, job, residence, debt, and investing background. Like everything else you discuss it will be kept confidential, and it is important for the advisor to know so that he will be able to recommend the right investments for your situation.

Most advisors will avoid wasting time trying to impress you with their knowledge, instead of asking you about your financial position and goals. You should keep in mind that it is an interview, not an interrogation. Some experienced advisors may resent a lot of insulting questions based on a lack of preparation, or questions that are obviously not appropriate. Do your homework before the interview and this should not happen.

In the initial interviewing process there are some things that the Good Financial Advisor will probably not agree to do. Some of these will provide no meaningful information to judge the quality of the advisor (how much do you have in your own retirement plan?) and others are simply inappropriate (too personal or unrelated to his job). Still others are too time intensive to be practical (can you describe a portfolio for a retired couple with a cash flow problem?). Pick your questions carefully to avoid ruling out a Good Financial Advisor because of an overdone interviewing process. Again, try to keep in mind how you would select a doctor, accountant, or attorney.

Serious professionals will not submit to an overbroad interrogation disguised as a fact-finding interview. Nor will they agree to three meetings of two hours each as an interview. Few will spend the time to put a lot of answers in writing because it is so cumbersome relative to a face-to-face discussion. Don't ask an advisor to complete a 50 question questionnaire (test?) before you meet with them. That is overkill until you have met the advisor and determined that the chemistry is right. After that it is probably not needed.

The interview is almost always at no charge and should last about 45 minutes to an hour. Prepare well for the interview to maximize its value. Write down your questions so you don't forget the important ones. A careful reading of this book should arm you with all of the questions you need to ask. If the advisor gets defensive, or refuses to answer a reasonable number of legitimate questions, you should seek help elsewhere. I have included a sample Advisor Selection Questionnaire in the Appendix. Use it as a guide for your own needs.

Here Comes Trust Again

Be ready to share enough financial information about yourself to allow an advisor to determine if you will be a good fit in his practice. Even though you are not a client, the information you share must be kept confidential by the advisor. The failure or unwillingness to provide basic financial information will almost certainly prevent the Good Financial Advisor from taking you on as a client. It shows a lack of trust that he can even keep your information confidential. He will feel that trying to develop a relationship of trust in the future might prove fruitless. Let the advisors you are talking to know that you are interviewing other advisors (if you are), so that they will understand what you are doing. It is simple courtesy and it will cause them to sharpen their presentation of themselves to you. Let the ones you do not select know why and avoid any hard feelings. The Good Financial Advisor knows he will not be the right person for every client.

References Are Good - But Easy To Find

Asking for references is acceptable, but any financial advisor with clients who have been with him for a few years can find a few who will say great things about him. Do not put a lot of weight on references unless the advisor reacts badly when you ask that question. Remember that confidentiality prevents the advisor from freely using testimonials from his existing clients, and only a few very close clients will agree to provide a reference.

Good - Not Necessarily Perfect

Finally, do not let the search for the perfect financial advisor prevent you from selecting the Good Financial Advisor. Just as in any profession, few advisors will be the best at everything you ask them to do. In time, if you have selected a person compatible with you, an advisor will give you the confidence and knowledge you need to make good decisions on your own behalf, as well as for the advisor to do the same.

Making Your Selection

Don't let the complexity of selecting the Good Financial Advisor overwhelm you. Most competent and experienced advisors would meet your criteria if they followed these Four Simple Rules, told to me by a wise veteran advisor early in my career (with my interpretation):

- Say please – The advisor asks for your business, after providing you with sufficient information to decide if you should take a specific course of action

- Say thank you – The advisor appreciates your business and works to keep it.

- Show up on time – the advisor provides what you need on a timely basis.

- Keep your word – The advisor does what he said he was going to do.

Those are words for the Good Financial Advisor to live by, and you should look for these characteristics in the advisor you select.

Get All Your Facts Before You Decide

Before making a final decision you need to understand the firm your prospective advisor works for to make sure it meets your needs. By the end of Chapter 3P all of the other areas required to make an informed decision will be covered. Don't make your decision until you have covered all aspects of the financial advisor's business.

Tell the advisor you select as soon as you decide. It is acceptable to do so at the initial interview if you have made up your mind at that point, and my experience shows that to be fairly normal. If you want time to decide, tell the advisor when you will decide, a time that should not exceed a week unless you have other interviews to conduct.

Congratulations!

The first leg of your journey is nearly complete.

Soon will come the heavy lifting.

Chapter 3C – Advisor vs. Broker-Dealer

"Never judge a book by its cover."

When selecting an advisor, it is important to know something about their broker-dealer. This is the company that oversees the activities of the advisor, called compliance in the trade, and handles his securities transactions. A typical business card says: Smith & Jones Financial Services, LLC. Elsewhere it states "securities provided by XYZ". Smith & Jones Financial Services, LLC is the business name and structure under which your advisor operates, and XYZ is the broker-dealer.

National vs. Regional

It can be reassuring to go to a well-known broker-dealer with a national reputation, but recognize that they sometimes require large account sizes ($250,000 to $500,000) before they will accept you as a client and provide a person to serve as your personal advisor. They will typically provide a full range of products and services, although some of those may be proprietary.

It can be equally comforting to work with a smaller regional broker-dealer that will treat you as an important client and give you more personalized service. These will usually be independent broker-dealers with no proprietary products.

Both should be protected by the Securities Investor Protection Corporation (SIPC) to provide protection to you against the insolvency of the firm.

Both have their strengths and weaknesses, and I don't think either should be omitted (the advisor ruled out) in the initial phases of your selection process. Today, people seem to prefer the smaller regional firms, because the larger firms have not provided the high levels of service clients want, and continue to promote proprietary products over non-proprietary products.

Proprietary vs. Independent Broker-dealers

Regarding types of broker-dealers, as stated in Chapter 3, you should understand the difference between a proprietary firm and an independent firm.

The proprietary firm manufactures some of its products. They may make mutual funds, annuities, insurance or other products and have a bias towards selling those products vs. similar products made elsewhere. They make more profit on their own products than on products made by others. Advisors who work for the firm may be pressured to sell proprietary products or be given special financial incentives to sell them. This is not in your best interest. Only if the product is equal to or better than other available products is the sale of a proprietary product warranted, and even then it is unlikely that you can easily move a proprietary product if you change broker-dealers. You may have to liquidate it and suffer any tax or cost consequences that occur.

The independent or non-proprietary firm makes no products at all. They allow their advisors to choose from a fairly unlimited universe of products, from all of the major manufacturers of financial products. Non-proprietary products are usually transferable to another broker-dealer when necessary. The independents show no bias towards any one manufacturer and provide no incentives for an advisor to favor one over the other.

Current trends favor the independent broker-dealer because of the elimination of bias, and the perception that they can provide objective advice in the best interest of the client. Make your own evaluation of the broker-dealer before deciding to select an advisor. A little web searching or discussion with other clients should help you to decide which type of firm is the best fit for your needs. There are Good Financial Advisors at all broker-dealers, so your decision should be based on what is in your long-run best interest.

Manufacturers

Manufacturers of products (also called investment companies or wholesalers) are allowed to provide financial support directly to an advisor for specific purposes, such as client dinners or educational seminars, but these are limited in the level of dollar support that one advisor can receive. The Good Financial Advisor is not going to be swayed by a small amount of support from the wholesaler of a product, since it primarily benefits his clients. What is important is the quality of the manufacturer and the support they give their products.

As evidenced by recent mutual funds scandals, good firms have a reputation to protect and they want to ensure that clients are satisfied with their products. Avoid firms without a good track record of reasonable costs and steady, solid performance over many years. It's a risk you need not take.

Employee vs. Independent Contractor

Some advisors are employees of their firm and work for a salary. The firm pays all of their expenses, and the advisor is compensated with wages that are not directly tied to the level of business they produce. Some employees receive wages and bonuses that are tied to the revenue they produce. Employees usually must produce some minimum level of revenue to remain at their firm.

Other advisors are independent contractors and pay some or all of their own expenses. They receive no wages, only a share of the revenues they produce. Their revenue production is up to them, but at lower levels of production they will likely receive a lower share of those revenues from their broker-dealer.

The Good Financial Advisor can be either an employee or an independent contractor, although being an independent contractor removes almost any issue of bias towards products manufactured or promoted by their broker-dealer.

Advisors who provide advice on a fee-only basis do not have to work for a broker dealer and do not need a securities license. They are Registered Investment Advisors or RIAs, and only need a license to give advice. You should ask a potential advisor what licenses he has. A Series 7 license allows him to sell securities while a Series 6 license is limited to mutual funds. A Series 66 allows him to give advice only, and he cannot receive commissions. A series 65 is a state securities license required of all advisors that sell securities or variable annuities.

Advisor vs. Broker-dealer

There can be a difference between small boutique firms and large national firms in how they treat clients and handle problems. However, if you have a problem with the broker-dealer that your advisor works under, don't fire the advisor in hopes of solving the problem. Remember that this is a relationship built on trust, and you will then have to begin building a new relationship with another financial advisor all over again. In addition, when you tell your next (new) advisor what happened (he should ask), it will be apparent to him that you showed no loyalty to your previous advisor, leaving him for problems not of his making. This can make it hard to establish a strong working relationship going forward. I have a rule that I will not accept a new client who is simply deserting their previous advisor without a good reason, because I would always feel that they might repeat their actions down the road with me.

Conversely, if you have a problem with an advisor, but you like the broker-dealer, ask the broker-dealer to replace him with someone else that can better serve your needs. Advisors understand that sometimes the chemistry just is not right and a change is in the best interest of both parties. The broker-dealer also understands that it sometimes takes two tries to get the chemistry right.

If you change advisors too frequently, you will be seen as the problem, making it difficult for you to find a new advisor who will accept you as a client. Change advisors carefully and infrequently, or it could adversely impact you in the long term.

Following Your Advisor to a New Broker-dealer

If your advisor changes broker-dealers voluntarily, for good reasons which are explained to you, then you have a decision to make. You can follow him to the new broker-dealer and transfer your accounts where possible without incurring charges, or you can remain at the old firm and ask for a new advisor.

If you have a good relationship with your advisor and he has served you well, think it over before letting him go. You may have to leave some proprietary investments or insurance products at the old broker-dealer, but it would be unwise to simply discard a long-term relationship because it is easier to stay put.

It is common for people to have two advisors in situations where their financial advisor moved to a new broker-dealer and some products, such as insurance or annuities, had to remain at the old broker-dealer.

Transferring your accounts to the new broker-dealer is easily done using standard transfer forms. The costs of transferring to the new broker-dealer, if any, are many times borne by the advisor where he can legally reimburse you for transfer costs. There can be termination fees and surrender charges to move your accounts and you should watch this carefully to make sure they are not excessive or unwarranted. You may also incur capital gains taxes when you liquidate a position at a profit. Check this before you sell to avoid any unwanted surprises. However, don't be afraid to take profits when you have them.

Remember that the relationship of trust is developed with the financial advisor, not the broker-dealer under which he works. Act with this and your own interests in mind.

Think of the old New England adage about friendships.

Be slow to make them, and slow to break them.

Chapter 3D – Evolution of a Practice

"There is nothing so exacting as the test of time."

Before you decide to do business with a financial advisor, it is helpful to understand where his practice stands, relative to how long he has been in business.

The following sequence is not exact, but it does give you an idea as to how a financial planning practice might evolve, so you can decide if it is a good fit for you.

Practice Inception

At inception, a financial advisory practice usually looks like this:

- No Clients
- No Client Service to Perform
- Few Incoming Phone Calls
- No Referrals from existing clients
- Total focus on Client Acquisition – Any kind and any size
- Level of competence - depends on prior experience
- No staff (if independent)
- Experience – Minimal except for prior job related experience

Established and Growing

After four to five years it typically looks like this:

- Some clients – Perhaps 100 to 150
- Some client service, but not too much, 3 to 6 appointments per week
- Some incoming calls each day
- A few referrals from existing clients
- Trying to acquire clients with a higher net worth
- Struggling to manage the practice

- Experience – Good, since it comes quickly if you survive the first few years
- Higher level of competence
- Part time staff if cash flow permits

Mature and Stable

After ten plus years a mature practice might look like this:

- A substantial client base – 200 plus clients
- Extensive service on a daily basis, 5 to 10 appointments per week
- Telephone rings all day long
- Usually has a full time staff person or two
- Depends solely on referrals for new clients
- Selective as to new clients accepted
- Experience – High. They have knowledge of many areas.
- High level of competence
- Financially stable

The Group Practice

There are a few very large practices that fall outside the scope of this discussion. They generally work with a select group of clients with exceptionally high levels of investable assets. They are usually group or team practices and may look different, but have the characteristics of a mature and stable practice. They may be set up as a simple cost-sharing group, where several advisors share the costs of operating the business in order to hold overall costs down. Others may share some or all of the revenues of the firm. This is the way of the future in my opinion, since it provides a higher level of service for the clients of the practice. Just as solo attorneys and accountants found it necessary to form groups to allow them to specialize, hold down overhead and improve their level of service, the Good Financial Advisor will follow for all of the same reasons. All things being equal, you should receive better service in a group practice.

Know Where You Fit In

Understanding where your financial advisor stands regarding the evolution of their practice is important in order for you to know how and where you fit into the practice. If you have few assets and are looking for minimal service, you are not likely to be a good fit in a mature practice unless they are expanding to accommodate new partners. On the other hand, if you have substantial assets and need a high level of service, a new practice may not be able to provide what you need. It is okay to ask your advisor how many clients he has and how much he has in assets under management. You want to know how you fit into the advisors' practice. If you are too small (in terms of assets you can invest), you may not get the service you wish. If you are too large, the advisor may not be able to provide the level of service you require.

Larger practices, with more than one advisor, may provide better service than that offered by a sole practitioner. They also offer continuity if your advisor should retire, leave the area, leave the business or die. Don't necessarily rule out a sole practitioner, because there are many good ones that have been in business a long time, and provide excellent service to their clients. Just be aware of their limitations, and what it would mean to you if they were no longer around.

Discuss your expectations when you meet your potential new advisor to determine if there is a good fit between your needs and his firm. You may wish to grow with a smaller firm or a newer practice, if you don't want to be a small fish in the big pond of a large practice.

The Presumption of Success

You can usually assume that an advisor is successful if he has been in business for at least five years, and has a substantial client base. Historically, more than 8 out of 10 people who set out to be financial advisors drop out of the career in their first 5 years. It is a difficult profession in which to succeed, and is not for everyone. Even though a smooth talking advisor might fool some of his clients for a while, it is not possible to fool all of his clients forever, because results speak for themselves. Even the least capable advisors will have a moderate level of competency in order to get their licenses. In addition, a financial advisor must really enjoy dealing with people at a personal level on a daily basis. You either like people or you don't, and it is not something you can fake.

In the interests of full disclosure, in the year 2006 I had about 250 active clients, managed more than $40,000,000 in assets, and genuinely liked my work and my clients. I often tell my clients that it is a rare profession where you get paid well to talk to nice people whose company you enjoy. (Of course I omit all of the hours of hard work that precedes those conversations.) And the feeling you get when you help people is absolutely wonderful. Now I constantly strive to become the Good Financial Advisor.

It is better to be a big fish in a little pond,

than lunch for a larger fish.

Chapter 3E – A Financial Advisor's Role

"Some people see things as they are and ask why? I see things as they could be and ask why not?"

Contrary to what most people think, the Good Financial Advisor does not sell products, he sells advice. Products are only a means of implementing that advice.

Some financial advisors, when asked what they do, answer, "I sell mutual funds and annuities." Others may say, "I manage assets." The advisor who sees the big picture might say, "I create financial independence for my clients." One of the most important roles of an advisor is to sell themselves to you. This is a prerequisite to developing the relationship founded on trust that is necessary for you and the advisor to successfully work together for many years. These three workmen illustrate the point:

> *Three men were working laying stone in a wall. When asked what they were doing, the first man said, "I'm making $18 per hour." The second man said, "I'm building a wall." The third man looked upward and with a sweeping flourish of his hands said, "I'm creating a church."*

Who do you want working for you? Seek out the advisor who sees the big picture, but maintain an understanding of what they can and cannot do.

What Advisors Cannot Control

When you finally decide to use the services of the Good Financial Advisor, it is helpful to understand what financial advisors cannot control:

- They cannot control the rise or the fall of the stock market

- They cannot control government fiscal or monetary policy

- They cannot control world events or the global economy

- They cannot control the general level of interest rates

- They cannot control the tax laws of this country or your state

- They cannot determine your life expectancy or even predict it with any degree of accuracy

- They cannot control the short or long-term rate of inflation

And in addition,

- They cannot control your general health

- They cannot control the level of your income, or it's continued availability

- They cannot control your expenses, either foreseen or unforeseen

In fact, these last three items are solely under your control. That is why he is only an advisor. And that is why your role in achieving financial independence is critical. Loss of control is a concern for many prospective clients that you should address right up front by telling your advisor what control you expect to give up, and what control you wish to maintain.

What Advisors Can Do For You

Many people will benefit from the services of a financial advisor, because what the Good Financial Advisor can do is pretty important:

1) They can help you to formulate a financial plan which will actually work to achieve your goals. This is no mean accomplishment when you consider that most people have no plan at all. It is worth repeating. Most people have absolutely no financial plan at all, and simply accept whatever happens when they reach the age when they can or must retire.

A number of others have an unrealistic plan that says they will invest with great risk and abandon and hope to find the next great stock that will make them rich. They will usually lose money, and then abandon a sensible investment plan for the security of a bank CD. They will likely retire in poor financial health.

Still others have a simplistic plan that will not accomplish much of anything except to give them a false sense of security. These are the folks who are saving about 1% of their take-home pay and want to retire at age 55 with a large income and live more comfortably than when they worked. They of course usually have inadequate protection in addition to inadequate savings, and will in some cases experience complete financial meltdown due to death or disability.

2) They can help you maintain adequate protection against unforeseen adverse financial events. The majority of home foreclosures result from the death or disability of the primary wage earner in the family. Yet, many people who need it carry little if any disability income protection, and some carry no life insurance beyond what they have at work.

3) They can help you manage the risks associated with your investments in a way appropriate to your goals, risk tolerance and risk capacity. Risk management is at the heart of wealth accumulation. When you get to Chapter 6B, you will see that risk is the single biggest factor you have to contend with when making investment decisions.

4) They can help you to avoid inappropriate investments that could lead to large financial losses (the Big Mistake). Much of successful wealth accumulation results from loss avoidance, not great investment selection. Read up on Modern Portfolio Theory to see why picking the next great stock or mutual fund is rarely the reason for one's financial success. You must preserve your principal if you are to successfully accumulate wealth, as I expand on in Chapter 6C.

5) They can provide advice on almost every area of your financial life that will allow you to make good decisions on your own behalf. A financial advisor can tie together every aspect of your financial situation so that the decisions you make are informed and correct.

6) They help you take the emotion out of investing. Investment decisions based on emotion can be hazardous to your financial health. Behavioral studies indicate that emotions rarely improve an investment decision. People fall in love with a stock, or refuse to sell when they should, out of pure emotion. You have to avoid the buy high and sell low mentality that is pervasive among individual investors. I discuss this in chapter 6L on behavior.

7) They can provide Continuity of Coverage. When the person responsible for managing the family finances is no longer able to perform that function, what person will step in and keep things running smoothly? In my opinion, this is one of the most important and most often overlooked services that a financial advisor can provide. Without a backup, the remaining spouse or partner is left to chance, and

must find someone they trust to carry out their financial plan. This would be a daunting task at best, but when done under the typical stressful circumstances surrounding the loss of someone you loved, it can be overwhelming.

If you are the person solely responsible for your family's finances, think about how you want things to continue when you cannot run things any longer. Share the responsibility with your spouse or partner, or retain the services of a financial advisor to simply work with you on a regular basis, so that they can fill in for you when that day inevitably comes. (See Chapter 3N - Continuity of Coverage.)

8)   They can validate the decisions you have already made, whether by yourself, or with the aid of another financial advisor. An unbiased second opinion (provided on a fee-only basis if appropriate) could be very helpful in confirming that you are on the right track to achieve your financial goals.

9)   They can relieve you of the time and work required to manage your finances, so you can live a higher quality of life. They can uncover your concerns, alleviate your fears, and help you to pursue your dreams. It does take effort, and some stress, to watch over an investment portfolio, and those who engage the services of the Good Financial Advisor experience less of both.

With these services, it is little wonder that the majority of wealthy people use a financial advisor. Financial planning and wealth management is not a hobby, or something to be done on a part-time basis. The Good Financial Advisor can help you attain and maintain good financial health. Remember that their primary role is not to make you rich, since only you can do that through the diligent pursuit of a viable Savings Plan. It is to keep you from ever being poor.

Educating Clients

One thing that a financial advisor cannot (and should not) do is to try and educate a client in all aspects of financial planning. For that reason, this book is written not to educate you to do-it-yourself, but to show you how to effectively use the services of someone who is skilled in these areas. Trying to educate yourself using the do-it-yourself books available today is dangerous, as I mentioned in chapter 2H. If you really want to become knowledgeable and manage your own finances, attend courses taught by professionals. Practice before you take action with your own money. Learn from experience before risking your future. Study long and hard using serious textbooks. Prepare to work hard now and into the future. Good luck, and may the force be with you.

The Future Role of Financial Advisors

For all of the reasons I have discussed, the future role of the financial advisor will become more prominent with the passage of time. When it is widely realized that those who use the services of the Good Financial Advisor have gained a significant advantage over those who did not, nearly everyone will utilize a financial advisor to some extent.

In the future, the Good Financial Advisor will take his or her place among the most respected professions in the world. This will happen in spite of the fact that one of his primary functions is to persuade people to defer gratification, and prepare for a future that may never arrive.

Most of the rest of the world is trying to convince people to spend, spend now, and spend with abandon. In cars, home, leisure and necessities, we are constantly barraged with ads urging us to spend, with no regard for protecting or saving for our future. The Good Financial Advisor stands alone in his objective to see people save, invest, and achieve financial independence.

Acting as either a generalist or specialist they will dispense advice on an unbiased basis. They will be considered as necessary as a family doctor, attorney or accountant. Their credentials will have meaning and their training will be to an even higher standard than it is today. They will always place the client's interests ahead of everything else, and fees will be fair, reasonable, and fully disclosed, regardless of the service being provided. They will earn the respect their profession deserves. This is not some utopian dream, it is the only way the profession can evolve and survive in the long-term. This will be similar to the medical profession's evolution from selling snake oil and chanting incantations, to being our path to a happier, healthier and longer life. Check out my take on the Good Financial Advisor Credo in Chapter 12 to see how I paraphrase the Hippocratic Oath.

It is my hope that this book contributes in some small way

to making this future a reality in my lifetime.

Chapter 3F – Working with an Advisor

"You will care how much they know, when you know how much they care."

The above line describes how most clients feel about their advisor's knowledge of his profession. Perhaps more than any other phrase, it sums up the essence of the advisor-client relationship. If you do not sense that the financial advisor cares for more than just making you a client and gathering your assets, you should seriously consider whether the relationship is worth establishing in the first place.

There are many things you must consider when working with a financial advisor. Depending on circumstances, some are more important than others at a given point in time, but all are necessary to maximize the value of the relationship for both parties. Competence, character, integrity and trust are all necessary, but trust overshadows them all.

Trust Is All-Important

You are entering into a relationship that is primarily one of implicit trust. Due to the all-encompassing nature of your financial life, you will likely find yourself confiding in your financial advisor to a greater degree than your doctor or attorney. An advisor can be likened to a physician in that he examines you, diagnoses your condition, prescribes a treatment, and watches over you as time goes on to see that you stay financially healthy. Some people don't like to go to a doctor because they are afraid of what he might find. In a similar fashion, some people do not like to meet with a financial advisor because they are afraid that their condition might be "incurable". An often-heard phrase is, "What if she tells me I can never retire?" The short answer is that there is seldom anything that cannot be improved upon or fixed, if you are willing to make an effort to do so.

Trust Evolves

Since trust is the essence of the relationship, here is how it might evolve, from your perspective, when it comes to managing money. Starting with your initial meeting and progressing over time, here is how your thought process might go from skepticism to confidence:

- I hope he knows how to manage money.

- He sounds like he knows something about managing money.

- What if we give him some money and he loses it?

- Let's let him manage some of our money and see what happens.

- So far he hasn't made any mistakes or lost our money.

- He seems to be making good decisions.

- It looks like he knows what he's doing.

- He does a pretty good job with our money.

- Let's consolidate our other money with him.

- Don't worry about a thing; our money is in good hands.

Trust Goes Both Ways

The advisor trusts that you will provide him with all of the information needed to help you, and give him your future business if he serves you well. Many times, an advisor will invest a lot of time in you with little or no compensation, in hopes of gaining more of your business over time. Before you renew a CD at your local bank, or purchase a fixed annuity in place of a maturing CD, ask your financial advisor if this is business he would be able to provide. If you have a relationship with a life insurance agent, be sure to tell your financial advisor so he does not interfere with it. If you do not have an insurance agent, consult with your financial advisor before buying insurance over the internet or at the bank. In general, offer your financial advisor an opportunity to serve you before you go elsewhere.

You trust that the advisor will always put your interests above anything else and give you quality advice and timely information. You hope that he will help you to achieve whatever financial goals you have set for yourself. This is serious stuff and any material breach of trust on the part of either you, or the advisor, can be damaging or even fatal to the relationship.

Dos and Don'ts

If you want high quality service from your advisor, there are a few common sense things to avoid, and some things you should do. You should always be candid and open with your financial advisor as to what things bother you and what things you expect out of the relationship. Service is different for each client, and the Good Financial Advisor will tailor the service to your needs where possible.

Things to Do

- Do respect the advisor's time and schedule and be on time for your appointment. Time is a critical element in an advisor's business, and when an appointment is missed it can be costly. (The Good Financial Advisor should respect your time in the same way). Unlike doctors who may have many patients waiting in a given day, a financial advisor may have only one or two appointments in a day and spend hours preparing for them.

- Do prepare for the appointment. If you have a proposal that you should have read, it wastes a lot of time to have to read it from scratch at the advisor's office when he should be going into depth on the finer points of the proposal. In addition, your financial advisor may have spent hours preparing a financial management proposal or a complex portfolio.

- Do return phone calls promptly. (The Good Financial Advisor should also be conscientious about this).

- Do tell your financial advisor when something is not up to expectations so it can be corrected right away.

- Do tell your financial advisor when you like something or he does something exceptionally well, so he makes sure to do it in the future.

Things Not To Do

- Don't tell the advisor or his staff that you are too busy to meet for service. Asking them to call back after a vacation, holiday, in a few months, etc. is the same as telling them you consider your financial health a lower priority than all of these other activities. Your advisor will assume these are less important also, and your service may suffer. Unless you are caring for a sick relative or something equally dire, treat a service meeting as if it were very important, and your advisor will do the same. If you really don't care that much about your finances, your advisor will sense it and is likely to value your service accordingly.

- Don't ignore calls and letters from your advisor. A financial advisor can only invest so much time trying to contact you for either an appointment or a telephone conversation. Eventually you may find your account transferred to another advisor, or to a "house account" with no assigned advisor. When the new advisor contacts your previous advisor to see why your account was transferred, it hurts your case when the answer is that you were unresponsive. In either case your account will get little attention.

- Don't withhold information from your advisor on your finances or spending habits because you are embarrassed or ashamed. He is a professional and needs a complete picture to give you meaningful and appropriate advice. Financial advisors see everything from Chapter 11 filings, drug problems, divorces, and affairs, to million dollar inheritances. One problem that occurs occasionally is having one spouse try to conceal expenditures because they are hiding them from the other spouse. Putting your advisor in the position of discovering these can be awkward at least, or extremely damaging to your relationship at worst.

- Because advisors work in strict confidence, an affair or drug problem will not be divulged, but it will likely mean the advisor may terminate the relationship to avoid future problems. Use caution and discretion in these situations. Occasionally, one spouse will divulge that they intend to divorce the other, creating a conflict of interest for the advisor who represents both clients.

- Don't tell the advisor what you think he wants to hear instead of how you really feel. If you want to spend your money now and live frugally in retirement, that's okay, but your advisor needs to know the truth in order to properly advise you on what to do today.

- Don't stay with an advisor if the chemistry is wrong. This is just something you have to feel, but without a strong relationship, the results will likely be less than fulfilling for both of you. Remember the analogy about the breakfast of bacon and eggs. The chicken is involved, but the pig is committed. Since it is your money that is involved, you are committed. The chemistry must be right for this commitment to last.

·

Don't Get "Dumped"

A complaint expressed by clients is that they were unceremoniously dumped by their advisor for no reason. Many times it is because you ignored his advice. If you don't listen when he provides advice that is not subject to interpretation or your own preferences, you may find yourself transferred to another advisor and wonder why. It may be that the advisor is concerned about his professional reputation down the road.

Say that he recommends a college savings 529 plan for your children, but you decide to leave their money in a bank account. Years later you meet someone who shows you how much more you could have earned in a tax-free 529 plan vs. a bank CD. Will you admit that your advisor recommended a 529 plan and you ignored him? Or will you feel that your advisor did not adequately explain the long-term benefits of a 529 plan? The latter is more likely unless you are magnanimous to a fault, but your relationship may be damaged. If you leave the advisor because of this, he has invested years of time hoping for your future business for nothing.

Perhaps your advisor recommends that you roll over a 401(k) plan so it can be passed on as a stretch IRA to your heirs, but you decide to leave it where it is because it is in a safe stable value fund and forget to name a beneficiary. At your death, the 401(k) plan pays out the balance as a lump-sum taxable distribution to your children instead of a tax-deferred IRA. The attorney handling your estate decides to sue the advisor on behalf of the children for the difference in value between the two outcomes. On a $100,000 IRA that difference could be several hundred thousand dollars. This could cost the advisor financially and his reputation would be seriously harmed.

Whenever you elect a course of action that leaves your advisor open to future criticism, his reputation is at stake, and in the financial services business this is very important. Your advisor also knows that he can expect no referrals to friends or family once you realize the impact of a prior bad decision. It's a lose-lose situation. Advisors who realize what the eventual outcome will be may choose to transfer your account rather than deal with a potentially bad situation later on. When you decline to take advice, be candid with your advisor to avoid problems with your future relationship. There are usually three instances where problems will occur in the normal course of events: The first is where you are getting unmistakably bad advice, in which case you should get a new advisor. The second is where the chemistry and trust are not right, in which case you should get a new advisor. The third is when the advisor fails to make a strong enough or clear enough case for you to take his advice. When this happens, tell him you are not persuaded and allow him to make a better case or alter his recommendation. Do not be passive and say nothing.

Don't "Forget" Your Advisor

Often you will have an opportunity to give your business to others in the normal course of your day. At the bank, they might mention that they have a special on CD's or annuities, or even life insurance. Wherever you are, remember that your financial advisor also provides these services and earns a living from them too. Before you assume that it is too small or maybe they don't have a competitive product, call your advisor and ask them if they would like to compete for the business. Usually they will, and because of your relationship they may provide a better product. If they can't, the Good Financial Advisor will tell you up front.

House Calls and Office Visits

Should you meet your advisor at his office, or should your advisor come to your home? There is a difference that you should understand.

First, if the advisor does not have an office, you need to know why. If it is a lack of commitment to the future of his business, or a lack of success in his practice rendering him unable to afford an office, you should consider looking elsewhere for an advisor (unless given a satisfactory explanation). A few advisors work out of their house, but this is generally limited to those with smaller practices or those phasing out of the business.

Assuming your advisor has an office where he meets clients, the only clients that should expect an advisor to come to their home are those that cannot drive or who cannot easily make the trip to the advisor.

Many times, an advisor will go to your home on the initial meeting to avoid the problem that occurs when you forget to bring important papers to the office, as well as to size up your living arrangements. Clients who have no money, yet live in a large expensive home, sometimes will not tell the advisor. And there are clients with great wealth that live in modest homes, which also tells the advisor something important about them.

Keep in mind that your advisor must be compensated for his time in some form or fashion, and time spent traveling to your home must be paid for in one way or another. It is my strong belief that you will receive more and higher quality service if you go to the office of the advisor. If you use the analogy of the doctor making a house call, it is obvious that you could have been treated in a more comprehensive manner in the doctors' office. The advisor can only carry so much material with him to your home, and may avoid or forget certain products or services, if the material needed to present them is not in his briefcase.

Ask your advisor directly how he prefers to work. I see many of my elderly or geographically distant clients at their home because it is too difficult for them to come to my office. But, I have a large practice and can schedule several clients on a single trip, making it somewhat more efficient for me to be out of the office. All other things being equal, I can do a better job for a client when I have all of the resources of my office and staff at my disposal. You must also be careful not to let your advisor think that you don't value your financial future enough to drive a few miles to see him. I have transferred clients who did not wish to drive a short distance to my office when I felt it was due to lack of sincere interest on their part.

If the advisor comes to your home, it is good manners to offer something non-alcoholic to drink. Depending on the time of day, my voice is in danger of running out of volume without a glass of water to keep it going. Food is a problem, because it is hard to eat and talk. If you are a great cook however, it is okay to offer cookies or pie (my favorites). It is also okay to offer the use of your lavatory, especially if the meeting goes over an hour.

A little item, but don't get upset if your advisor is a little late arriving for a meeting at your home. It is very hard to keep a precise schedule driving from one appointment to another. Whether dealing with traffic or the talkative previous client, it is not easy. I have found that out through years of experience.

Client and Advisor Relationship

Friendship is the logical extension of the close relationship many advisors develop with their clients. This is acceptable, as long as it does not affect the ability of the advisor to give you tough advice, or for you to effectively criticize the advisor's actions. If you become friends with your advisor, watch out for problems developing in this area. Socializing can present problems, if you feel that the advisor is watching your behavior, your spending habits, or violating your personal space. Your advisor may also feel uncomfortable in letting loose in front of you because it might affect your perception of him professionally.

Beyond friendship, the personal relationship between the advisor and you should be strictly professional at all times. If it takes a different direction for any reason, a change in advisors is necessary. The conflict of interest is far too great for both of you. If the advisor becomes too friendly, let him know that you want to keep it strictly professional. If you become too friendly, don't be surprised if your advisor transfers your account before he gets into trouble. A little common sense and courtesy is all it takes to make these parts of the relationship go relatively smooth.

Think about the Golden Rule,

and everything should come out right.

Chapter 3G – Confidentiality is Vital

"If I tell you, I will have to kill you."

That old joke from the military (popularized on the TV show M*A*S*H) is just an exaggeration, but it gets the point across. The current version of it is "If I tell you I will have to <u>bill</u> you."

The issue of what an advisor can say about what happens between he and a client should not be in question. Advisors must keep everything that transpires between them and their clients strictly confidential - period.

The Initial Interview

Even in your initial interview, when selecting an advisor, it is understood between both parties that everything discussed is absolutely confidential. The good Financial Advisor will not hesitate to tell you this, but if you are in doubt just ask. The Good Financial Advisor will also decline any request for information about existing clients unless it is sanitized so that you cannot recognize its source.

When in an advisor's office, if you notice anything that might be something you should not see, point that out to the advisor so he can put it elsewhere. You should also keep whatever you noticed to yourself. Most advisors are very careful about this, but occasionally, on a drop-in visit, something that should be put out of sight is forgotten.

Friends and Family

Advisors should not disclose who their clients are, even to the client's friends or family, and certainly not for purposes of soliciting new clients. "Your cousin is a satisfied client, so why don't we meet" is not acceptable when soliciting a new client unless previously approved by the existing client.

If you disclose your relationship with the advisor to another person, the advisor still should confirm with you that it is acceptable to acknowledge that relationship, and to what extent it can be discussed with that person. This can be a problem at social gatherings, when a client says out loud that he is a client of an advisor who is also present, and many others hear him. Experienced advisors learn to change the subject when this circumstance occurs, to avoid potentially awkward moments.

Under no circumstances is it acceptable for an advisor to discuss the details of a client's account with anyone else, such as an attorney or accountant, unless the client gives specific authorization to do so. This authorization should be renewed for each subsequent occasion.

Staff personnel that work for an advisor or the firm must also observe strict rules regarding confidentiality. They should not discuss either the client or the client's account at any time, or to anyone, outside the requirements of the workplace.

Prospective clients should appreciate an advisor's strict adherence to confidentiality before they become a client, as evidence that they can trust the advisor to keep their information confidential after they become a client.

Clients should also adhere to this confidentiality rule and refrain from discussing details of their account, or workings with their advisor, with others. It is good policy for both parties. Both client and advisor should heed this revised version of an old saying:

See No Information.

Hear No Information.

Speak No Information.

Chapter 3H – How Your Advisor Is Paid

"There are always those advisors who will reduce their price one more dollar, and those clients who will be their willing victims, for they care neither for their future success nor yours."

I want to start by saying that the manner in which an advisor is paid should never affect the advice he gives. I realize that there will be times when it does, but they are few and far between in my experience, and usually relate to the need to get paid for work performed.

Character and integrity do not change with the moment, and the difference in fees between various types of products and payment methods is too small to be meaningful. The only real difference is in the timing of cash flows received by the financial advisor. This fact is overlooked by the cynics who criticize commissions as too high, when in practice, fees may cost more in the long-term. Fees and commissions are seldom sufficiently different to induce a Good Financial Advisor to compromise his reputation and business by giving advice, or selling a product, that is not in the best interests of his client.

That said, you should still understand who is paying your financial advisor. Are his revenues paid by you, the manufacturer of the product, or his broker-dealer? Knowing this, you can determine if there are any conflicts of interest that might affect his recommendations to you.

Do-It-Yourself Book Bias

Contrary to what is often written in various do-it-yourself financially-oriented magazines, financial advisors do not wake up in the morning trying to figure out how to take money from their clients. Successful advisors earn a good living by managing assets and risks, and providing quality advice. However, you would not sell a lot of magazines or books if you took the position that using a financial advisor was better than doing-it-yourself. Shameless self-promotion accompanies many of the books I have found in the personal finance area of major bookstores, (I restrain myself as I write). Be mindful of this as you read them. I wrote this book so you would have a second opinion, and my bias is this, plainly stated and up-front:

> *I believe most people would be better served in the long run by using a financial advisor, rather than attempting to handle their financial planning and investments on their own.*
> *Amen!*

Methods of Compensation

Advisors are compensated in various ways, depending on the structure of their business, and their practice is characterized based on its primary method of generating revenue. The type of practice is not as important as the character and integrity of the advisor who runs it. The main types of practices are:

Commission-Based – Most or all of the advisor's revenue is derived from commissions on products sold. These commissions pay for any advice given to the client prior to the sale, and for follow-on service. Trailing commissions and 12(b)-1 fees are a large part of the revenue stream of a commission-based practice.

Fee-Based – Most of the advisors' revenue is derived from fees instead of up-front commissions, although 12(b)-1 fees may still be significant. The fees are usually a percentage of the amount of assets under management. Commissions are charged only on life insurance or annuities, or accounts too small for fees. Fees may also be charged for services, such as financial planning. These can be hourly or project-based depending on the job.

Fee-Only – All revenues are derived from fees and are not dependent on the level of assets under management. The advisor may not even maintain licenses to sell products and accept a commission. Another firm may handle product imple-mentation, or the fee-only firm may use no load funds inside a wrap account. Insur-ance products are likely handled by another firm via referrals.

Some believe that the fee-only financial advisor can remain totally free of bias regarding products recommended. While this may have some truth to it, one might ask what basis they use for product selection when it excludes all but no-load funds.

One concern I have is that those clients who prefer a fee-only advisor, in the belief that the advice they receive will be unbiased, are then open to paying another fee or commission to the person or manufacturer who provides the actual products. The Good Financial Advisor will typically reduce his fees to reflect any commissions earned as a result of advice given or products purchased.

A second concern is that the client who does not trust anyone other than a fee-only advisor will have difficulty developing the depth of relationship necessary to maintain a long-term working relationship with any advisor. It seems similar to shopping for a doctor who does not dispense drugs to avoid any conflict of interest with the drug company that held the best golf outing (disguised as a learning day).

Lastly, the level of fee set by a fee-only advisor is not usually subject to market discipline, whereas the commissions set by product manufacturers are competitive and known to all. I am convinced that most fees would be lower if clients could readily compare the services provided by fee-only advisors.

Hybrid - Revenues are derived from a mix of fees and commissions based on products and circumstances. This is probably the most common type of practice today, and in my opinion provides the lowest overall cost to you. The good Financial Advisor can select the optimum mix of products and fee structures based on your needs without limitations or restrictions of any kind.

The Debate Continues

The argument over which fee structure is best continues unabated today. I do not believe that the moral high ground belongs to any specific fee structure, and clients should select their advisor based on what they feel is best for their needs. Most advisors run a hybrid practice, and provide quality, unbiased, advice regardless of the source of their revenues. Successful advisors have strong enough revenue streams that the timing of revenue receipt is not a concern.

As the old saying goes, *"You pays your money and you makes your choice."*

How Advisors Receive Their Revenues

Advisors receive sales commissions from the product manufacturer (paid through the broker-dealer) on money you invest or products you purchase from them. These can range from as little as 0.1% on certificates to as much as 8% on a long-term annuity, depending on the product and the size of the investment. Generally, the advisor receives a smaller percentage commission on larger investments.

Depending on the product, you may or may not see these charges on your statement, but they are hidden somewhere. Ask your advisor to show you where they appear. No one works for free, at least not for long. If any advisor tells you that there is no fee or commission on a specific product, it is a fairly reliable sign that you should find someone else (pro bono work excluded).

Client Service Commissions and 12(b)-1 Fees

Client service commissions, or trailing commissions (called 12(b)-1 fees on mutual funds), are paid to the advisor on existing assets under management, and on renewal premiums on insurance products. Again they can range from 0.1% to as much as 5% on insurance premiums, but typically are in the .25% range for invested assets. These are also paid by the manufacturer (through the broker-dealer) to compensate the advisor for the cost of servicing your accounts. You must read a prospectus to find most of these charges, or ask the Good Financial Advisor to point them out to you.

Financial Planning Fees

Some advisors charge fees for financial plans, or advice given where no product is sold. Estate planning, remortgaging your home, or analyzing a portfolio not under the management of the advisor (your 401(k) plan for example), are areas where advisors typically charge a fixed or hourly fee. If you have a substantial account, many advisors may provide some of this type of work without charging additional fees, as a courtesy to a valued client. Because of potential regulatory issues, this is an area that may change drastically in the next year. There is an issue of price discrimination when clients are charged different fees for identical services. In my opinion, it will all be worked out with little impact on either you or the advisor.

Asset-Based Fees

On a managed account (also called a wrap account), an asset-based management fee is paid to the advisor, either monthly or quarterly, instead of commissions. This fee is based on average annual assets under management, and typically ranges from .5% on large multi-million dollar accounts, to as high as 2.0% on small accounts (The fee is negotiable based on your overall account). A fee in excess of 2.0% is difficult to justify, and you should ask how your advisor decided to charge that fee, and is it warranted in light of the anticipated return on the investment. On a conservative portfolio with an anticipated return of 6%, it is hard to support taking 33% of the return off the top for managing the account. You usually pay no other charges or commissions on these types of accounts, except for minimal trading costs that are either passed through, or paid by the advisor, depending on the account.

Discounted Fees Are Suspect

Be wary of an advisor who is quick to cut his normal fee to get you to become a client (unless his fee was too high to begin with, which raises the issue of what his fees will be in the future). Good Financial Advisors, who provide quality advice and a high level of service, will seldom reduce their fees just to acquire a client. To do so would simply add large numbers of clients to their practice, without a commensurate addition of revenue. That would eventually lead to a reduction in service for all of their clients, not to mention more work for the advisor at lower profit margins.

If an advisor seems too anxious for your business, it could be an indication that his practice is not successful, or that he is only interested in gathering assets, not managing them. He might make up for the lower fee later on with a reduced level of service, which could explain his lack of success. Do not rush into anything until you are comfortable with the advisor and his reasons for taking you on as a new client.

Advice Is Not Free

Do not expect an advisor to give you a lot of free advice. Without receiving either a commission or a fee, the advisor will not be in business for long. Serious advisors will seldom give free advice except to their best and most profitable clients, and you should be wary of advisors who say that they will provide a lot of service at no charge. Usually, free advice is worth every penny you pay for it. And, unfortunately, clients do not value free advice with the same importance as advice for which they paid a fee.

Introductions and Referrals

Finally, one of the most important ways an advisor values you as a client, is when you introduce him to another person, whom then becomes a client. Most advisors will accept the children of their good clients, and referrals of friends from good clients, regardless of account size.

An advisor who receives an introduction to a friend or member of your family may express his gratitude with a small gift, and repay you through more attentive service. Simply put, you are a more valuable client if you provide introductions, because these help your advisor grow his practice at little or no cost, through the addition of new, high-quality clients.

The level of service you get will almost certainly reflect your value to the advisor's practice. Each year, an advisor must replace clients who die, move away, or leave, to avoid a reduction in income. Overhead usually goes up each year, so if you can provide an introduction to your advisor, it benefits everyone by keeping costs lower for all clients.

If your revenue to the advisor does not exceed the cost to carry you as a client, then you are not profitable, unless you have some future potential. Either an introduction to a new client, or other business such as a retirement plan rollover or insurance, are the only reasons an advisor would be likely to keep you as a client, unless you are a friend or family of a good client.

In a limited number of cases, an advisor will keep a client for purely altruistic reasons, but out of necessity these will be few and far between. If you are related to another client, you have value to maintain the continuity of the advisor's practice. When a current client dies, the assets generally are passed on to the children or relatives, so the Good Financial Advisor will establish a relationship in anticipation of this happening.

These are some of the economics of running a financial services practice. If you understand them, you increase your chances of developing a strong and mutually beneficial relationship with your advisor. I also hope you understand why a cut-rate advisor may not be desirable. Either you will not get what you need, or they will be gone before you are.

The Bottom Line

An advisor must produce enough annual revenue to support his reasonable expenses, and provide an adequate income, if he is to remain in business. The high drop-out rate in this profession is partially attributable to the failure of newer advisors to charge an adequate amount for their services. Lack of experience and confidence, combined with the fear of losing the business, are the new advisors' enemy.

Each client represents a certain amount of gross revenue, based on their assets under management, and their fee structure. Or, they represent some future revenue to be realized.

Each client must bear a fair share of the overhead and expense of the advisors' practice. Free rides are unacceptable, because they are paid for by other clients.

Remember that you are paying an advisor for their advice based on years of training and experience. Do not begrudge them a good income, any more than you would a successful attorney or doctor. Poor quality lingers for years after the joy of paying a low price is gone. In planning for your financial future you do not get a second try. Once you reach a certain age you must deal with the reality that exists, not what you had hoped it would be. If that reality is what you dreamed it would be, the price you paid to get there was well worth it.

Under the fee and commission arrangements discussed in this chapter, a typical, full-time, successful advisor might generate an annual gross income of $150,000 to $300,000, and take home about 50% to 70% of that after overhead and expenses. Some advisors who choose to work limited hours make less, and some advisors with large practices make substantially more, but those are out of the typical range.

Given the extensive start-up costs, long hours of training, and the high stress levels of the job, this is not as large an income as it might seem. Out of the gross business profit above the independent advisor still has to pay all of social security (not half), Medicare taxes, income taxes, and medical insurance and fund their retirement plan. There is a reason for the very high drop-out rate I previously mentioned.

Some people wonder why an advisor cannot share in the rewards of investing money for a client. If the client earns money, the advisor takes a share of the earnings. If the client loses money the advisor gets nothing. This is not legal, and no advisor would agree to such an arrangement. Hedge funds have this type of fee arrangement and it sounds good until you look at the numbers and realize that it is biased towards the money manager.

The Long-Term Perspective

Just to try to put fees in perspective, look at them in another way. To offset a 5% initial sales charge would take an increase in return of about 0.56% in 10 years, 0.28% in 20 years, or 0.19% in 30 years. If returns are identical, the difference in total assets is about 5.25%. If either of these makes a difference in your ability to retire and live comfortably, your retirement plan is wound a little too tight. Put another way, you might have about 5.25% more assets at the end of 30 years, but you must do at least as well as a Good Financial Advisor, and you will do all the work yourself. Reread Chapter 2H.

I also know one thing from my experience as a financial advisor. No fee will seem unreasonable when your account value is increasing at an acceptable rate. When your account is going down in value, no fee will seem fair. Every advisor has probably heard the words, "I'm not paying you to lose money!" Being a financial advisor in down markets is not a walk in the park.

Successful financial advisors

produce successful clients.

Chapter 3I – Rating Advisor Performance

"Financial advisors live in a world of results, not a world of time and effort."

How can you judge the quality of advice that you receive from your advisor? How do you measure his performance in the various areas that you require his assistance? How do you know he is doing a good job of managing your investments, or just getting lucky? Answering these questions is about as easy as building a bridge to Ireland (See Chapter 8B). My thoughts on this are my own, and sure to be controversial, but here I go for what its worth.

Do You Want To Know?

First, I don't believe most people want a quantitative rating on their advisor, since it might be different than what they feel about him based on trust, character, integrity, and other non-performance related issues. Not every advisor is going to be the best financial planner or investment advisor available, but that may be overshadowed by other factors such as service or likeability. It would be like finding out that your beloved doctor of many years, who has treated you well through various illnesses, graduated at the bottom of his class. Talk about mixed emotions.

Broker-Dealers Know But Don't Want To

Second, the broker-dealer that an advisor works under could rate the advisor's investment results if they chose to, since they have most of the information they need in their possession. If they did, they would then certainly have to publish the results, and which client would want to have the "worst" advisor in the company handling their portfolio? They would also have an obligation to point out apparently weak, or poor performing, portfolios to the client, which would not be conducive to keeping the assets at that broker-dealer. In effect, they would wind up assuming the responsibility, and the liability, for the account instead of the advisor.

In the case of broker-dealers that make proprietary products, an advisor rating that was low, due to the poor performance of their own products, would be embarrassing at the least. I see few incentives for a broker-dealer to rate its advisors, and as of this writing none have done so to my knowledge.

How Do You Measure Performance?

Lastly, there are no defined standards for rating investment advisors. It cannot be based on absolute portfolio performance without adjusting for risk, and this is difficult (if not impossible) to do with any degree of accuracy. A serious concern here is that any performance rating based on absolute levels of performance, could lead to excessive conservatism on the part of the advisor to avoid portfolio losses that would adversely impact their rating. This in turn would lead to lower returns for clients who could accept higher portfolio risk, and that is not a desirable outcome.

You must also know the goal of the portfolio you are rating. A portfolio with a goal of preserving capital under any circumstances will perform in a different manner (lower) than a portfolio with a goal of earning at least 6% through any market.

This is a briar patch Brer Rabbit would have a hard time getting out of, because there is no correct answer. Many believe that a financial advisor should not also be a portfolio manager. They feel that job should be left to other professionals, and the advisor's role should be that of a monitor or quarterback. Practically speaking, this is hard to do in a small practice, so most advisors do have to manage a portfolio. In addition, to be competitive an advisor must have a fair degree of expertise in investment selection and management, whether in mutual funds or individual stocks and bonds, or he will lose business to other advisors because of poor results.

In areas other than investments, it is even more difficult to rate an advisor because of the subjective judgments involved. Who decides when an estate plan needs to be revised? What portion of an account should be in annuities? How much and what type of life insurance should you have? Black and white answers do not exist in most everything the financial advisor does, and therefore a standard rating system is a long way off. Today, we can at best look at extremes and make judgments as to performance. It is left to you the client to make the only meaningful judgment, by transferring to another advisor when current performance is not satisfactory.

In spite of that, in my opinion even the average financial advisor will provide better results than the average client attempting to do it all themselves. Only the truly mediocre (or dishonest) advisor has the potential to do serious harm over the long-term. My experience shows that these advisors are rare, and they are seldom able to attract a large number of clients. Again, this is a reason that you want a successful advisor, with experience, a large client base, and significant assets under management.

The Industry Challenge

It will be a watershed event, when the industry steps up to the challenge of rating advisor performance in a way meaningful to the average client. It is somewhat discouraging that it has not yet happened in other professions, despite efforts by many good people to let some sun shine in on the bad apples. Doctors, teachers, accountants and attorneys might all benefit from a little more light, but it is extremely hard to develop meaningful measurement systems that are fair to all. If a system of rating advisors could be developed, that one change might upgrade the financial advisory profession overnight in the minds of many people.

The Second Opinion Works

One of the best ways available for you to rate your advisor is to seek a second opinion from someone who has no ability or desire to take away the business. Pay a fee for an objective review of your portfolio or financial plan, and see if there are any major flaws in it. Tell the firm doing the analysis that you do not intend to move your portfolio to them, you just want their opinion as to the structure of the portfolio. It will be money well spent.

If the review shows some problems, bring them to the attention of your advisor and ask him if he agrees, and if so, is he willing to correct them. It may just be an oversight, or an honest mistake, and your advisor can easily fix the problem. Or, your advisor may show you that his portfolio design is correct but he failed to properly communicate that to you. Remember that you both have the same goals in mind. And again, you must have goals for the process to have meaning.

Rate your advisor based on the progress

you make towards meeting your financial goals.

Nothing is more important than that.

Chapter 3J – Changing To A New Advisor

"Breaking up is hard to do."

There may come a time when you feel the need to change either your advisor or the broker-dealer for whom he works. Many times the reasons are not of your making. There are a number of instances in which you may wish to simply change your advisor, and you want to do it correctly so it maximizes the benefit to you (or minimizes the problems).

Reasons to Change Advisors

- When you move to a distant location, and your advisor is not licensed to do business there, or chooses not to get a license because it is not financially feasible, it is appropriate to look for a new advisor. You may also prefer a local advisor so you can have regular face to face contact, which is certainly understandable, because it facilitates developing the relationship necessary to establish a high level of trust. In these circumstances, your old advisor may be able to assist you in locating a new advisor and transferring your business to him.

- If you decide that you want services, or a level of service, that your current advisor does not offer, you may have to transfer to another firm with an advisor who can provide what you want. Discuss this with your current advisor before making your move. He may be able to help, or he may be able to work with another firm to provide these services, and avoid making a complete change.

- If your current advisor is not getting the job done, you have every right to change. This is probably not as common as thought, but if the level of service is inadequate, or his performance is poor, don't hesitate to explain to him that you feel your needs would be better served elsewhere.

- When your advisor retires, or sells his practice, you may wish to seek out a new advisor if the transition is badly executed. This is a difficult area for the selling advisor, and he will not expect you to stay unless the purchasing advisor is to your liking.

- If you reach a point when the chemistry is not right, and you cannot maintain the level of trust necessary to make your relationship work, you should change advisors. Only you can decide this issue, and you should explain to your current advisor the reason you decided to leave him. It may help him to avoid losing other clients in the future, and he may assist you in your move.

- If your current advisor tells you to leave, it is time to move on. For whatever reason, even if unjustified in your eyes, when an advisor suggests that you should move to another advisor, don't argue, because he is giving you a message. You will be better served elsewhere.

The Right Way and Wrong Way to Change Advisors

The right way is to tell your current advisor that you wish to move your account and be specific about the reason. A real professional will help you make the transition as easy as possible for both of you. If you have to leave some products behind, he will make sure they are kept in good hands, and may offer to keep them himself if it is agreeable to you.

If there is a chemistry problem that is due to your advisor, then you owe it to the advisor to tell him that you are not confident that the relationship you have will produce the desired results over the long term. As hard as it might be to believe, some advisors can be arrogant, lazy, indifferent, uncaring, incompetent, inattentive, sloppy, unknowledgeable, rude, abrupt, abrasive, and almost dumb (Did I miss anything?). Thanks to the great difficulty in becoming a successful advisor, they are the very few, but you are justified in leaving one if they wind up managing your accounts.

The wrong way is to move your assets without giving your current advisor any notice. You may wish to avoid confrontation or to spare his feelings, but do not expect much help from the old advisor under those circumstances. Keep in mind that your new advisor will likely judge your value and loyalty as a client by the way you treated your old advisor on the way out. If he feels you mistreated the previous advisor, it could affect his willingness to place great trust in his future relationship with you.

I personally will not take on a client who leaves their advisor without good reason, since I believe that this is a client who shows no loyalty, and it would eventually happen again with me. Advisors invest time and effort in developing a new relationship only when they feel the relationship will truly be a lasting one, so be careful in how you terminate your relationship with your existing advisor.

If you have had more than three advisors in the last five years, the problem is more than likely you, and few advisors will be eager to take you on as a client. Expect as much loyalty from your new advisor as you showed to your previous advisor.

Consolidating Assets

In some cases it may make sense to consolidate your assets under one advisor to get lower fees. The Good Financial Advisor will understand this, and will likely suggest that you move all of the assets to her. A better reason to consolidate assets is to ensure that the investment advice you receive reflects your entire financial position.

Some advisors will refuse to take on a client unless they manage all of the client's assets for just that reason. Without knowing a client's entire financial position, an advisor may inadvertently give poor advice.

Consider the client with half of his investments in bank Certificates of Deposit who tells his advisor he is conservative but does not disclose these assets. The advisor then invests the other half of the client's money in a conservative portfolio, resulting in an excessive amount of money in low yielding fixed accounts and inadequate overall growth. Be sure to tell your advisor about your entire financial position to avoid this problem. The Good Financial Advisor will ask about all of your assets in order to ensure that he understands your financial position and gives appropriate advice.

I discuss dual advisors in the next chapter, where you use more than one financial advisor to get a second opinion, or products and services unavailable from your first advisor. The use of more than one advisor may or may not involve splitting assets between them. Split assets only when it gives you a benefit, and avoid splitting assets when it raises your fees with each advisor. Usually you do not have to split assets to engage the services of a second advisor for a readily available second opinion. In Chapter 3N I discuss using an advisor when you manage your own assets.

Change If You Must

People find the need to change advisors for a number of reasons. Some for convenience to find an advisor who is closer to them, some to establish a better relationship, and some due to poor performance or lack of products or services.

One reason that people change advisors is because someone close to them just got into the business and they want to give that person their business to help them get started. This is not a good reason to change advisors and should be avoided if at all possible. You do yourself no favor by entrusting your financial future to a relative or close friend just to be nice. With a dropout rate of over 90% it is unlikely that the person will be in the business in five years, and unless it worked out right for you in that time period, the damage to your relationship could be substantial. If asked to give your business to someone like this, tell them that your investments are not liquid at this time, but you will consider them for your new business in the future.

Most clients, perhaps as many as two out of three, change advisors because they did not feel they were appreciated. Whatever your reason, when the time comes that you feel change is necessary, don't hesitate. Prolonging the change can only harm both you and your advisor.

If your financial advisor does not value your business,

find one who does.

Chapter 3K – Transferring Assets

"From the frying pan into the fire."

Once you have decided to change advisors (or broker-dealers), moving your accounts is not difficult, if you use the proper transfer forms. Normally your accounts can be moved over to your new advisor, or new broker-dealer, in less than a month.

Following Your Advisor or Broker

If you are only following your financial advisor to a new broker-dealer, an event becoming more common with the increase in prominence of the independent broker-dealer, she will assist you in transferring assets in the most cost-effective manner (See Chapter 3C – Page 68).

If you are following a stockbroker to a new firm, check out www.nyse.com for information on what to look for and what questions you should ask.

Changing Broker-dealers

If you are not just changing broker-dealers but are also changing advisors, you should use more care in transferring assets. Ask your new advisor for assistance here.

Many times, you can transfer your accounts in-kind by just moving the actual investments. In the case of highly appreciated assets this is the choice that you will want to make to avoid selling and incurring capital gains. Occasionally, you will have to liquidate (sell) some investments, if the new firm does not handle them, or if they are proprietary products (sold and carried only by their manufacturer). Be sure to review the tax impact of selling assets with your tax advisor before you sell. If the assets are in qualified plans or IRAs there will be no tax liability on the transfer. Use care with non-qualified assets and annuities, especially if you are under 59 1/2 when penalties are assessed for early withdrawal.

Liquidate With Care

Be wary of your new advisor if he wants to just liquidate your old account in its entirety and replace it with all new investments. Complete liquidation of accounts is usually not necessary, except where poor performing proprietary products constituted the bulk of the old account, or where the products were clearly unsuitable for the client due to risk tolerance. In those cases liquidation is the right way to proceed regardless of the tax consequences. Poor future performance will nearly always be more costly than paying taxes on capital gains.

Ask your new advisor for an opinion on your existing account before liquidating it. There may be termination fees involved from the old broker-dealer, or tax consequences on older investments with large capital gains. Annuities may have surrender charges. Insurance programs should never be revised without a thorough review of the pros and cons of changing, replacing, or eliminating a policy. Disability income and long-term care are policies that are almost impossible to replace if they have been in place for a few years. Liquidate only when it is in your best interest.

Be direct with the new advisor as to why you are moving to him and ask which investments or products warrant keeping. It is important to start off the new relationship on the right foot. If you sense that the new advisor is only interested in acquiring your assets, or selling you a new product or service, it would be wise to step back and evaluate whether you should continue the process, or seek out a different advisor.

Remember that many of the decisions you make are irrevocable in the short run, and should not be made quickly, or without careful consideration. In addition, the costs of changing over all of your accounts may be difficult to recover. In some cases, the new advisor may be allowed to offset the termination costs associated with moving your accounts to him. Be sure to ask.

Dual Advisors

It may be advisable to split your assets between two advisors in order to have diversification among products and services, and a readily available second opinion as mentioned in Chapter 31. However, this could work to your disadvantage if the amount with each advisor is too small to afford you their highest level of service. The majority of very high net worth investors (assets greater than $5M) have a second financial advisor.

Don't be afraid to ask each advisor what their opinion is, and work out a fee arrangement with one or both. This will ensure that you get the treatment you want regardless of the size of your account. Having more than one advisor works best on accounts in excess of $2,000,000.

Use Caution

You should be watchful that you do not create the impression with the second advisor that you are not loyal to the first advisor (or vice-versa), or that you are not willing to place your trust in either advisor. If you do, the second advisor will be unlikely to view you as a long-term client, and your service may reflect that concern. He is unlikely to invest time and effort that will only pay off down the road if he feels you are not going to be there. If you create the feeling of mistrust with both advisors you are probably not going to get satisfactory results with either one of them.

Of equal concern is making sure each advisor knows what his role is and that of the other advisor(s). Splitting up your assets between more than one advisor to achieve diversification only works if each advisor is aware of what the other is doing. Otherwise you may find each advisor doing essentially the same thing, with less diversification than if you had allowed a single advisor to handle the entire portfolio. Encourage the advisors to communicate with each other as appropriate to avoid problems.

Transferring assets is an area where angels fear to tread, so proceed with caution. It is your money. The Good Financial Advisor will treat the transfer of your account to him with the importance it deserves.

Do not fear change.

It is the source of much progress.

Chapter 3L – The Advisor's Dilemma

"I have such a poor memory that I have to tell the truth.
Otherwise I might never say the same thing twice."

Those are words for the advisor to live by, especially when he faces the dilemma of fees and commissions vs. what is best for the client. The very nature of the Good Financial Advisor's role has posed this dilemma for as long as the profession has existed.

It is noteworthy that the same concerns do not apply to other businesses. Try to imagine a car dealer disclosing his commissions, margins and expenses as part of the sale of a car, or an attorney describing his profit on a contingency fee case. I add this in to put some needed perspective on the fees vs. commissions argument. It misses the larger point. I believe that fees and commissions are a concern because investors are largely driven by greed when it comes to investing money, and therefore do not take the same precautions as when doing other things with their money. How many people inadvertently buy a Corvette for a family car? Some feel that investing is too important to a person's future relative to other financial matters and thus merits more attention and regulation. You decide, because it is your money.

Reposition/Reinvest/Repeat as Necessary

Once your financial plan is completed, one of the primary roles of a financial advisor is to structure your invested assets in such a way as to allow you to meet your financial goals. You then have the expectation that the advisor will reposition or reinvest assets as necessary to keep your portfolio at the proper level of risk and return, and permit it to continue to grow in the future. There are other equally important roles that do not involve invested assets, such as insurance and estate planning, where an advisor may sell you commission based products. But with invested assets, the devil really is in the details.

Unnecessary Moving of Assets

If an advisor moves assets and unnecessarily generates a fee or commission, he can be subject to criticism and accused of "churning" your assets. You should never see your advisor move your assets from one type of share class to another within the same fund family, since this would generate an unnecessary commission. You are allowed to exchange investments in like share funds within a fund family at no charge, subject to possible short-term redemption fees to discourage market timers. If you feel that your account is being churned without real benefit to you, there are two steps you should take:

1) Ask the advisor to summarize in writing why he is taking the action.

2) Get a second opinion from another qualified financial professional.

If the account is being churned, get a new advisor without delay. If you were harmed financially, file a written complaint with his broker-dealer and the appropriate regulatory agency in your state. Putting a complaint in writing may trigger a formal review of the problem by the compliance people who oversee your advisor. Use it sparingly, only when necessary to get action. The broker-dealer should be willing to make you whole, and appropriately discipline the advisor. This could result in possible sanctions from his broker-dealer that might include a loss of his license, and therefore, in the most extreme case, his job.

Damned If You Do

If the advisor does not reposition and/or reinvest your assets simply because it would generate a commission or fee, you could incur significant losses on your investments, far in excess of the fee or commission that it would cost to move them. By remaining in poor performing investments, you risk diminished long-term performance that could result in losses many times greater than the typical 1% to 5% range of fees or commissions.

Damned if you do and damned if you don't, pretty well sums up the quandary the advisor faces on a regular basis. During the market crash of 2000 to 2002, many of the losses clients incurred could have been avoided. After the previous two years of losses, advisors should have had the courage to say in 2002; "I know that it will cost something to reposition your portfolio, Mr. Client, but I believe it is your best option, and will save you more down the road". Unfortunately not enough advisors took this path. Part of the reason, I believe, is that it would appear that the advisor was profiting from the misfortune of his client. Both clients and advisors need to avoid this self-defeating course of action when the next market downturn inevitably occurs.

If there is one good answer it might be this:

The advisor should review all of the alternatives with you, and disclose the fees or sales charges associated with each option. Then you and the advisor should agree on what is the best course of action for you, regardless of whether there is a benefit to the advisor in the form of a fee or commission. In the majority of cases, a good option will become evident that does not cost you a new commission or a fee. Any new fee or commission should be justified by the proposed course of action, both in the short run, and in its ability to help you reach the long-term goal of the portfolio. In the short run, the goal may be to minimize losses, and that is an acceptable investment strategy.

Mistakes Will Be Made

If the action is taken to correct a mistake made by the advisor in a prior decision, the advisor should be willing to waive or reduce the fee where appropriate and legal. The advisor must have the integrity to admit that a previous decision was a mistake, e.g.; "I recommended that we overweight small cap growth funds, and the ABC fund I selected lost its manager and is performing well below its peers. I now recommend we sell it, and replace it with the XYZ fund. The result will be a commission of 5%, but I think you will be better off within a few years, with the potentially superior performance of the new fund.

As in many other professions, advisors will not be right more than perhaps 70% of the time, so as a client you should encourage him to rectify bad choices or decisions as soon as they become apparent. Your long-term results will improve measurably if you do.

Mistakes Should Be Corrected

Remember that this is a relationship based on trust. If you threaten to take the assets to another firm whenever an advisor makes a mistake, the likely outcome is that an advisor will never admit to mistakes, regardless of the better opportunities that might be available to you. If concerned that admitting to the least little error will cause the loss of assets, he may tend to gloss over small errors instead of correcting them.

On the other hand, if an advisor makes too many mistakes in the management of your portfolio, or other serious and costly mistakes, you should seek the services of a more competent advisor.

No Free Lunches

One factor to consider is that an advisor who provides a high level of service cannot do it without adequate compensation and expect to stay in business for an extended period of time. In some cases, the only way for an advisor to justify the time and effort needed to overhaul a portfolio is to charge a fee, or receive a commission, on the new investments. The key is honest and open discussions between the client and advisor. As a client, don't expect "free" service for an extended period of time.

Fee Aversion Can Be Costly

Lastly, don't begrudge your advisor if they do receive a generous commission on a transaction, when it is the right thing to do for you. An advisor spends years developing a practice, gaining expertise, and generally paying their dues. They earn a good living because, and when, they provide a valuable service.

In my earlier years, I had one client who simply refused to take my advice to restructure a portfolio that she had when I took her on as a client. Over the three years that I tried to get her to implement my recommendations, the portfolio lost almost 40% in value. Eventually I gave up, and the client went out on her own about $150,000 poorer. In our last conversation she was still complaining that I was just trying to get her to pay a 1% fee (about $4,000 per year), even though the recommendation I made would have saved her more than $130,000 after the fee! We have a saying that "You can't save them all." This was the worst, and most costly, example of client fee aversion that I ever encountered. Personally, I viewed it as a failure to persuade her to do the right thing.

There are very few advisors that would trade their professional reputation and integrity for an undeserved fee or commission. In practical terms, the difference in fees between two alternative investment options is simply not that great. Whether your advisor receives a 4% commission for a mutual fund or 5% for an annuity on a $50,000 investment, the $500 difference is not relevant in the context of an annual income of $200,000 or more.

Within a managed account, where the typical fee is 1.0% to 1.5% of assets under management, the repositioning of investments is done at no cost, other than a small ($15 to $20) trading cost. The advisor gains nothing and the client pays nothing by rebalancing or repositioning assets. That is why I favor this type of account (or the core/opportunity portfolio structure) for most clients. It eliminates many of the concerns discussed here.

The Unprofitable New Client

One of the other dilemmas that an advisor faces is that a new client with no assets, who is seeking an advisor to help him or her get started, is seldom financially profitable. The overhead structure of a typical financial services firm is such that the fixed costs of rent, expenses and salaries can amount to more than $300 per client. It is not possible to charge a fee or commission that is sufficient to pay for a client just starting out with no assets. If you did charge a fee that high (ethically questionable in my opinion), you would be overcharging them, at a time when they should be saving as much as possible. The opportunity cost to the client would be extremely high if they were right out of college, and yet this is the time when they need financial advice the most. The answer is to look to the future.

Future Profitability

Most advisors allow their older, and very profitable, clients to subsidize their new, young, clients. This is very evident when parents who are long time clients, with a substantial portfolio, ask the Good Financial Advisor to take on their children. It is a request that is hard to turn down.

In other cases, a decision is made that a new client will become a profitable client in the future, even though they do not cover their costs today. In this case the average revenue derived from the client over a long time will be adequate, even though the initial revenue is well below the cost of acquiring and servicing that client. Of course the Good Financial Advisor takes the chance that when the client does become profitable, after years of service, that they might move their assets to a different firm. It is another risk borne solely by the Good Financial Advisor.

Advice for the Young

I believe that this conflict is the main reason why more people do not have financial advisors when they are young, and could really benefit from getting started out on the right foot. It is a problem begging for a breakthrough solution, such as mandatory participation at work similar to Social Security.

Teaching basic finance to children at the high school level is one answer, but the high school curriculum is already full of equally important courses. Teaching it in college also leaves out a large group of people who need the information. A private market solution is required, and the sooner one is found, the better our collective financial future will be.

Weed Out the Miscreants

If you do find an advisor who does anything inappropriate, report them to their broker-dealer, your state banking commission, the state insurance commissioner or FINRA, as a favor to the vast majority of hard-working and ethical advisors in the business. We will all be better off when they seek another profession or early retirement.

Ask better questions.

You will get better answers.

Chapter 3M – Insight vs. Information

"Those who do not understand the past are condemned to repeat it."

As little as 30 years ago a financial advisor was someone who gave you advice on what stock to buy. He was usually known as a stockbroker or investment advisor. If you were wealthy, you also had an insurance agent that provided advice on some areas of financial planning. Many people simply put their money in a bank and depended on their company pension and Social Security to take care of their retirement. Those days are gone forever.

Quality of Life Planning

Financial planning has become desirable if not necessary to almost everyone today, regardless of their current wealth. The role of a financial advisor has grown to encompass other facets of financial planning. They provide advice in many areas related to investments, such as estate planning, protection planning, and retirement planning.

The term life planning is sometimes now being used to describe the full scope of advice that a financial advisor provides today, although I feel that term is too broad in scope. Nevertheless, in the future, a financial advisor may help you in other areas of your life that involve planning, since many of those are related to your financial situation.

I believe that helping you to achieve a quality of life is the role financial planning will take as the financial advisory profession matures. They will help you find answers to questions such as these:

Should you save a little more or spend an extra vacation with your children?

Is a private college worth the extra cost or should you give your son or daughter a down payment on a home and send them to a less expensive school?

Do I have enough money to gift to my church while I am alive?

Can I afford to change careers?

Should I improve my lifestyle or plan to retire a few years earlier?

Quality of life is not solely determined by the size of your bank account or the type of car you drive.

Therefore, trying to earn the maximum possible on an investment account without regard for risk or goals is a fools' errand. Try to remember this as you read about hot stocks and mutual funds where risk is never mentioned. It also puts 1.0% in fees or expenses in context. Quality of life just doesn't sell as well.

This Is Not Your Parents' Financial Plan

It is becoming more difficult to be your own advisor, and manage all of your finances and risks. Not only have the products available to you become more numerous, but their complexity has increased significantly. Your chances of becoming an expert in any one area have diminished a lot over the past twenty or so years, and they will only get more difficult in the future.

In addition, we are barraged with information from sources that did not exist twenty years ago. However, information alone is not sufficient to guide us, unless we have time to turn it into wisdom. Look at these five levels of cognizance to appreciate why more and more people are letting professionals handle their finances and risks.

Five Levels of Cognizance

The First is receipt and recognition of **Data**. As an example; "In 2005 the S & P 500 Index is 1229.47. This sounds good, but is meaningless by itself without any context or frame of reference. Today we are overloaded with Data from a myriad of sources, and filtering out the junk from the valuable is a daunting task.

The Second is **Information**, or Data with context. As an example; "In the year 2000 the S & P 500 Index was at 1,548.92. You now have a sense of what happened between 2000 and 2005, and a basis for evaluating the S & P 500 Index today. You know that it has decreased over a five-year period, and you are aware of what circumstances accompanied that decrease. We live in an age of information overload.

The Third is **Knowledge**, or Information enhanced by experience. If you had invested in the S & P 500 Index via an index fund in 1996, you understand how that index varies with time. You also realize that you can make money even when your investments go up and down over short periods of time. You understand the volatility of the overall stock market.

The Fourth is **Wisdom**, or the practical use of knowledge. This is the application of knowledge with predictable outcomes gained by working for many years in a specific field. For example, we know that if we diversify our portfolio, one bad stock will not prevent us from reaching a specific investment goal. In the above example of Knowledge we learned that to make money in the market you had to be invested in good times as well as bad. If you tried to "time" the market the outcome could have been disastrous.

The fifth is **Insight**, or the personal understanding of what to do with the data, information, knowledge and wisdom that you possess. This is difficult to attain and sometimes more difficult to retain. What worked in the past may not work well at all in the future under different circumstances. Insight does not come easy or often.

Data is Not Wisdom

In summary, data is nice, but will not help you to achieve financial goals. Do not confuse information and knowledge with wisdom and insight. Some people who attempt to manage their own finances can do harm rather than good, even with the best of intentions. Overconfidence in our ability to apply knowledge is common, as I describe in Chapter 6L on Investor (Mis)Behavior. Do not let it adversely impact your future.

It takes many years of experience to gain wisdom and insight. The Good Financial Advisor, with more than a decade of experience, will provide you with his insight when guiding you towards your long-term goals.

Insight is a rare and wonderful thing.

Chapter 3N – Continuity of Coverage

"Dying doesn't scare me, as long as I'm not there when it happens. "

We all must deal with the fact that one day we will no longer be here, and someone will be left behind to clean up our mess. The Good Financial Advisor can make sure that all you leave behind is a wonderful legacy and fond memories.

Who's In Charge?

In most cases one person is responsible for handling the finances of the family, while the other has little or no involvement in that area. A potentially serious problem exists when the person handling the finances is no longer capable of doing so. This can be temporary, as in the case of a car accident, or permanent, as in the case of dementia or Alzheimer's. As mentioned in Chapter 3E, The Role of an Advisor, maintaining the continuity of your financial plan after your death or incapacity is extremely important to the financial health of those you leave behind.

Trust Is Still the Issue

It is very difficult for a surviving spouse or partner to quickly develop a relationship of trust with a new advisor under those stressful circumstances. In too many instances the remaining person makes quick decisions to their detriment, because there is no one around to provide trusted guidance.

The Good Financial Advisor is the one who will help to ensure that things go right following the death or incapacity of a loved one. This can't be done by just any advisor, but requires someone who is familiar with you, and your financial situation, and can effect a seamless transition.

The Good Financial Advisor as Backup

Even if you manage your own finances, contact the Good Financial Advisor and pay them a fee to meet with you at least annually, and maintain an ongoing awareness of your overall financial situation. This will be money well spent. You can still manage and control your own finances, but you will be ready for the inevitable day when someone else will have to step into the picture.

Don't leave a spouse or partner, or the children, to try to figure out what you were doing, or to attempt to find all of your assets. I have seen stock certificates found more than fifteen years following the death of the owner, or life insurance policies that the survivors were unaware of for years. Check the abandoned property department in your state, if you think anything has been overlooked in the estate of a person familiar to you.

Backup for Your Financial Advisor

Either the retirement, incapacity, or death, of your advisor can also cause a serious disruption in your financial plan, unless another advisor is waiting and ready to assume responsibility for your accounts. Therefore, you should be sure that your advisor has a backup plan in case he becomes unable to service your accounts.

You should already know the person who will assume responsibility for your accounts when your advisor is no longer there to manage them. Ask your advisor to introduce you to his backup early on so you can assess whether he will be a good fit.

When meeting with a potential new advisor, ask what his backup plan is should anything happen to him, or what his transition plan is, and how your account will be managed if and when he decides to retire.

The Good Financial Advisor will plan his future,

as well as help you to plan yours.

Chapter 3O – Client Service Expectations

"After the sale came the regrets; when the joy of being a prospect was replaced by the reality of being a client."

One of the most important and often overlooked aspects of a financial advisor's role is service. Specifically, it is the level of service that is expected, or required, in a given client relationship. Quality service provided on a regular basis is very important to the long-term success of your financial plan. A plan that is left unattended has a less likely chance to succeed than one that is reviewed at periodic intervals.

Nearly all investment accounts should be reviewed with you once per year. Twice per year is appropriate for larger, more complex portfolios.

Your Advisor Should Be Watching

Your advisor should also be watching the investments in your account (not necessarily your specific account) on a regular basis, to make sure that if problems develop, they do not linger too long. If a particular mutual fund or stock needs to be replaced for performance reasons, your advisor should notify you within a reasonable period of time, not wait a year until the next service meeting.

If you notice a potential problem and he doesn't call you, call him. A call to your advisor is a sign that you care, and he will attach greater importance to your service than if you show indifference about your portfolio. Excessive calls for trivial reasons will label you as a high-maintenance client (one who demands frequent unnecessary service), so use the phone only when you need assistance.

An old friend related the story of watching one of his stocks go down in price over the course of a year in which he did not hear from his financial advisor. When he finally did meet with the advisor, he asked him why he did not call when this was going on, to see if some action should be taken. The advisor's answer was "I should have." Because of his honesty, the client stayed with the advisor, but he now knows that advisors are not perfect, and they can sometimes forget to do what they are supposed to do.

Even the Good Financial Advisor can make a mistake, and it is perfectly all right, even desirable, for you to call him when you think something needs attention. If the mistake resulted in a loss to you, the advisor may be obligated to compensate you for that loss. On example of this would be failing to invest funds on a timely basis when the investment subsequently went up in value.

You Pay For Service

Your advisor gets paid to perform account service through various trailing commissions and fees, and you should expect it to be done faithfully when required. An advisor who does not earn enough from your account may reduce regular service to compensate, but you should not let that happen. At the start of the relationship, ask your advisor if he will get enough revenue from your account to provide quality service on a regular basis. If not, you should negotiate an added fee to ensure that you do receive adequate service, or seek out a new advisor who will structure a satisfactory arrangement.

The Service Meeting

The usual service meeting should last about an hour, and might include the following:

- A review of your financial situation and goals to determine if your suitability information is still correct.

- An analysis of the performance of your portfolio relative to those goals.

- A review of risk as described in Chapter 6B.

- A discussion of fees charged for services rendered.

- A discussion of changes since the last service meeting that could affect your financial situation.

- A discussion of what items should be addressed in the future, and when the next meeting should take place.

Service meetings can be more detailed than this, but at a minimum you should review your investment accounts and your basic financial plan. If you do not have a financial plan, the review will by definition be rather cursory, which is why I said in Chapter 2 to get a plan sooner rather than later. Some advisors may schedule meetings at which specific topics are discussed, such as your estate planning needs. However they are structured, make sure you are getting at least the minimum level of service on your existing accounts.

Preparation is Important

Come to the service meeting prepared to talk about your financial situation. It is not confidence-inspiring to the Good Financial Advisor when you show up empty handed, and have not looked at your statement since the previous meeting. The quality of the meeting will depend to some extent on the importance you attach to it, and how well prepared you are to discuss your financial situation. When the market is going up, client service tends to take second place to everything else. When the market goes down, as it invariably will every two to three years, service suddenly assumes a sense of urgency. Never let complacency, or fear, rule your service meetings.

When the markets are down, it is not helpful to complain that you could have done better in the bank. The Good Financial Advisor is painfully aware when short-term results are down, and both of you should remain focused on your long-term returns relative to your financial goals. The ability to focus on your goals, and not be distracted or change course due to an unanticipated development (terrorist attack, war, oil price spike, etc.) will almost certainly lead to success in investing.

Advisor Preparation is Important Too

If your financial advisor is not prepared for the service meeting, don't be afraid to ask why. It is not sufficient for an advisor to say, "Well Mr. Client your accounts are up about 7% since we last met, so it looks like you will be okay in the long run. Just stay the course and we'll meet again next year." This is an inadequate and potentially dangerous approach to reviewing your accounts. The advisor is receiving compensation to review your accounts, and you should expect him to earn it with a thorough review of your holdings and your financial situation. If the advisor is obviously not prepared, discuss it with him and ask to reschedule the service meeting. If it happens again, and your advisor shows no inclination to change his behavior, seek out a new advisor.

After reading this book, you will be able to ask the right questions of your financial advisor, so that the service meeting will be productive and beneficial to both of you. Remember, it is your money, and your future depends on it.

Make your service meeting a priority,

in good times or bad.

Chapter 3P - Almost Ready To Begin?

"A journey of a thousand miles begins with a single step."

In the previous chapters you have learned about the advisor selection process, the role of the advisor, setting goals, developing a financial plan, and enough about the business of being a financial advisor to understand how to work with him or her over time.

I also covered topics of related interest such as life expectancy, advantages and disadvantages of doing it yourself and tips on determining if you really need an advisor.

Making Your Selection – With Care

You should now be armed with sufficient information to make your selection of the Good Financial Advisor and get ready for the journey to financial independence. Now it gets good. Before actually making the selection, read the remainder of this book to determine if the advisor can handle everything you need in a relationship. It will also enable you to discuss the issues that will be important to you in the future, to avoid any misunderstandings down the road.

The Learning Begins Now – And Never ends

In the remaining chapters I will cover information that will help you maximize your relationship with the Good Financial Advisor and the results you get from that long-term partnership.

We will touch on all areas of financial planning, with an emphasis on understanding investment basics, investment concepts and risks. Estate planning, protection planning, college funding, wealth accumulation, taxes, mortgages, and investor behavior (that's you) will be covered from your perspective. Topics will be covered lightly, with an emphasis on giving you the ability to discuss options with the Good Financial Advisor in a way that will allow you to make good decisions on your own behalf.

The Rewarding Journey

It is my sincere belief that the information contained in this book will prove to be invaluable in helping you to reach whatever goals you set for yourself. It should also help you to reduce the stress of worrying about your financial future, since it will be in the hands of someone whom you can trust to serve you well; the Good Financial Advisor.

It won't be easy, but it will be worthwhile. And remember, you are on a journey without end, for you will not know when you reach the final station.

If you stumble,

just pick yourself up,

and keep on going.

Chapter 3Q – Becoming a Client

"The best things in life are not things."

The last step in becoming a client normally involves signing paperwork to open accounts or entering into an agreement to pay for financial consulting. In either case you will be meeting with the Good Financial Advisor and making a commitment that many times includes giving him a check, transferring money from another broker-dealer, or processing a rollover of a qualified plan. Be sure to ask questions at this point to be sure you understand all of the fees, charges, restrictions and limitations you will incur as a result of the transaction. This is the time to be outspoken to avoid problems in the future. Some questions to ask are these:

- What is this transaction costing me, either directly or indirectly?
- What will it cost me to undo this transaction if I change my mind within the next year?
- If you find a better product can you reposition my funds without a new fee or charge?
- How long before I can move my funds without any fee or penalty?
- Are there termination fees to close any of my accounts? What are they?

There are others, but these should prevent you from getting into a situation you cannot easily get out of if something goes amiss. You should already have addressed other issues before this point, such as the questions posed in Chapter 3B on Selecting an Advisor.

Remember, this is your final opportunity to say no if you are not completely comfortable with the person who you intend to do business with, and do not trust them sufficiently to enter into the relationship.

Wise men, and informed clients,

go where angels fear to tread.

Chapter 4 – Retirement Planning

"Plan your retirement to happen early enough in life so that you can be a participant, not just an observer."

That great advice came from a friend who happens to have been my attorney for over 30 years. Heed it, or ignore it at your peril. Personally, I do not intend to ever be just an observer.

When we think of retirement planning, we almost always reduce it to this one concern: How much can we save before we have to quit working. It is not that simple, and the Good Financial Advisor can show you all of the other issues you must confront when developing a sound retirement plan. Protection planning, investment management, tax management, and estate planning are also important parts of your retirement plan.

Fear Not, the Best Is Yet To Come

Before you agonize long and hard over how much income you will have over the thirty or more years of your retirement, let me offer this thought. Remember that when you graduated high school you had no idea how to generate income from age 18 to age 67. You had little or no assets, no social security and job security was non-existent. Fast forward, and somehow you managed to generate income and live for over 45 years, while accumulating assets for retirement.

Now, with social security income (steady and with a cost of living escalator), assets that generate more income, and years of experience, it should not be an impossible task to fashion a lifestyle that matches your income, which you know is predictable and available. Don't let anyone scare you into thinking that retirement is less secure than your working years. It is a time to enjoy the fruits of your labors.

If you didn't live your life by spending every dollar you made, don't worry about trying to live your retirement years that way either. Financial plans that use a rigid forecast of spending to show you that you will run out of money at age 83 (and therefore should save even more) are simply not accurate in the way they depict the flexibility you actually have in retirement.

How Much Should You Save for Retirement?

This is the question that has no correct answer. Ask ten financial advisors how much is the right amount, and you will get ten different answers, all substantiated by their assumptions and analysis. Ask retirees, and their most common concern is running out of money before they run out of time. No one wants to outlive their money, and everyone wants to live another year or two. Yet, simply equating retirement planning to the size of your investment portfolio is also misleading, because many other factors affect the quality of your retirement, and to a greater degree. For a different take on retirement you may find this book interesting: Get A Life - You Don't Need A Million To Retire Well by Ralph Warner.

Save Too Much/Save Too Little

If you save too much for retirement, you are unnecessarily reducing your standard of living now, for a future that may never come to pass. Or, you may be creating an estate, which you will simply pass on to others. If you do so knowingly, that is fine. If you do so out of ignorance of your alternatives, you have let opportunities for you, and your family, pass you by. That extra vacation, or a second home, may be far more satisfying than an oversized investment portfolio when you are 86 years old.

If you save too little, you may never enjoy the leisure that retirement promises after a lifetime of work, or the security of financial independence later on in life. Most of us strive for some degree of financial independence, which (as defined in the Introduction) is usually defined as having enough assets to provide you with sufficient income to allow you to either work or not, depending on your choice. Many people who want (or like) to work become wealthy and continue to work by choice, not necessity. Many people who don't want (or don't like) to work, never seem to reach a point where they can stop and be financially independent. There is a message there, but I will leave it for my next book.

That is why I strongly believe you need a plan and professional help. Your retirement plan is too important to be left to amateurs, without proper training and experience, who may confuse knowledge with wisdom.

Have No Fear

In addition, most people are afraid to see a financial advisor about a retirement plan because they fear they will be told that they cannot ever afford to retire. (This is in addition to the financial embarrassment mentioned in Chapter 3A). They think they will have to work until they die, because they didn't prepare for retirement when they had the time and income. This is usually a groundless fear in my experience. We are all going to retire; some when we choose to and some when we are forced to. It is preferable to do it when it is your choice, and part of your plan.

Retirement Planning – Art Not Science

Retirement planning involves numerous assumptions and long-term projections. Little errors can make huge differences in results. Predictions about the future are loaded with errors that we don't know about, and basing years of your life on them is more art than science. Even professionals can make assumptions that lead to erroneous results if you do not tell them exactly what your goals are. With the wrong assumptions you can create a retirement plan filled with errors that appears to be sound, and deceive yourself that you are the right track. Only when you see the oncoming train will you realize that your plan is not the light at the end of the tunnel. Any plan is filled with limitations, so use caution when basing irrevocable decisions on them far into the future.

Doing It Yourself

Here is my personal true story about doing it yourself that I mentioned in Chapter 2H. Some years ago I went to a dermatologist to have an apparently precancerous lesion removed from my leg. After a close examination, it took the doctor about one minute to scrape off the lesion, and when she finished, I said, "Is that all there is to it?" She looked at me with a smile and answered, "That's all there is to it, if you know what you are doing."

At that, I too smiled. Here was a woman with years of medical school, followed by many years of experience, doing something that appeared to be quite simple. Yet if done wrong it could be life-threatening to me, and I had inadvertently minimized her skills with my ill-timed remark. When you think about doing your retirement plan yourself, think of that dermatologist.

Of all the things you can do for yourself, retirement planning is one of the most difficult and one that carries serious consequences if not done correctly. You do not get a chance to undo mistakes, and you must live with them for the rest of your life.

Don't try to pack your own retirement parachute.

Chapter 4A – What Will You Do In Retirement?

"You must retire <u>to</u> something, instead of <u>from</u> something."

Before you can discuss retirement, you have to define it carefully, because it means different things to everyone.

Some people view retirement as the time when they escape from the job they have been trapped in for many years. Others see it as a time to stop doing anything, when they can sleep late, and lounge around all day. A few view it as a time in their life when they can take on a whole new challenge, pursue a lifelong ambition, or tackle a brand new career. How you view it will determine how you live it.

A Tale of Two Retirees

The story of two retired army generals illustrates this point. One took up golf, and spent most of his time on the golf course. The other joined the Peace Corp and fulfilled a lifelong dream of starting up a school in New Guinea.

Several years later they met and discussed their experiences since retirement. The first general complained about everything. The weather, the fees on the golf course, how he couldn't depend on his fellow players to always show up, his arthritis, how his wife didn't listen to him, and so on. The second general told a story of the challenge of building a school, and how rewarding it was when it was finished. He was truly happy, and hoped he could stay healthy long enough to take on one more project for the Peace Corp.

One general's retirement was repetitive, and without meaningful purpose, while the other general's was the fulfillment of a lifelong dream. Retirement without purpose, meaning, or challenge, may prove to be less than envisioned when you were working at your "daily grind".

<u>Your</u> Retirement Is What Counts

What will your retirement look like? When you plan your retirement, plan the next phase of your life, not years of relative inactivity.

As mentioned in Chapter 2G on Health and Life Expectancy, one frequently reads that people who remain active, socially connected, and have meaning and purpose in their lives, stay healthier, both physically and mentally, much longer than those who have little physical or mental stimulation in their lives. This evidence is compelling, though not yet overwhelming, so you ignore it at your own risk.

What can you do in retirement?

Draw your family tree

Take a walk – make it a hike

Read a non-fiction book

Teach others something that you know

Work a little at something you like

Listen to good music

Play with your grandchildren

Pick a bouquet of flowers

Cuddle with your partner or spouse

Go to a movie or a play

See other people you know

Take up a new hobby

Call someone long distance

Go back to school

Start a new career

Learn to dance

Volunteer somewhere

Travel around your local area

Write a book

Visit someone who can't drive

Call an old friend

Have lunch with your children

Go to church during the week

Learn a new game

These are only a few of the things we could do but sometimes overlook because they are right in front of us. Just do something besides contemplating your inevitable demise. You will be better off for it in every way.

Plan for It Now

The time to figure this out is well before you make those irrevocable decisions to leave your job of many years. Communicate your retirement dreams to your Good Financial Advisor, so he can factor them into your financial plan. Remember that opening quote in Chapter 2A about dreams coming true. Create your own dreams, limited only by your imagination.

What is your to?

Chapter 4B – Retirement Plan Basics

"It is not only difficult to develop a retirement plan, it is hard simply to define one in a meaningful way."

There are many ways to create a comprehensive retirement plan. Some are very simple, some are extremely complex, and most are part of a comprehensive financial plan (or should be). Do not judge a plan by its size or sophistication, and always remember that it is likely to have a bias, depending on who created it. If you have a retirement plan done by a financial advisor, expect to pay a reasonable amount for a good one. Somewhere between $500 for a basic projection of assets, to $2,000 and up for a complex plan, is in the ballpark today, although estate planning for high net worth clients can run into five figures. In addition, you should expect to pay for a periodic update, perhaps every three to five years, to maintain the value of the plan.

The Conservative Approach

Many plans take a very conservative approach by assuming high rates of inflation, low returns on investments, and spending levels that increase forever at the rate of inflation. This results in a need for large amounts of insurance and savings. If the company that created the plan also sells insurance and investments, you should understand that they also want you to buy their products. And they want you to buy as much of them as possible. Look at the assumptions in total to make sure they are reasonable. You do not want to be too conservative nor too aggressive. Either is a problem. Make sure the estimates of insurance and savings needs stand the common sense test.

Too Simple Is Not a Plan

Simplistic plans, similar to those you can get for free off the internet, are usually useless, and can be dangerous if they give you bad advice regarding what your retirement needs really are. Look at the assumptions that went into a plan, and how it generates its results. If you don't understand the assumptions, ask the advisor who prepared it to explain them in detail until you do. If your financial advisor can't explain a plan to your satisfaction, get a new plan, and a new advisor.

Some plans do straight line forecasting, while others use Monte Carlo simulations based on variability of inputs. Either can be effective, you just need to know what the limitations of each are when evaluating the result. (Reread Chapter 2 on plan limitations).

Regardless of its sophistication or cost, no plan can accurately forecast the future more than a few years ahead. Due to changes in you and the world around you, a plan cannot maintain its accuracy and value as a guide for more than a few years. Your health, goals, and prior investment results all affect the future outcome of your retirement plan.

Estimating Income Requirements

Many retirement plans start by taking an estimate of the income you will need in retirement based on your pre-retirement income; such as 70% of your pre-retirement income. These are only estimates, and you should take the time to make your own evaluation of what you will need in retirement. Keep in mind that your needs and associated spending will likely diminish with age, while your medical costs may increase. As you age, you typically drive less, eat less, travel less, and put less wear and tear on your clothing.

The amount of income you might need in retirement is related to your pre-retirement income, but you need to look at the absolute level involved. If you lived on $50,000 per year before you retired, you might need 80% to 90% of that income after you retire, but if you lived on $150,000 per year before you retired, you might need only 50% to 65% of that in retirement.

Most retirement planning software used by financial planners does not account for these decreases. They instead take the most conservative route of assuming constant spending levels regardless of age, to make sure that, no matter what happens, you have enough money. This is done primarily to protect the company that issues the plan from liability related to you running out of funds in retirement, and blaming it on their bad advice many years before. While this conservative approach may assure you of more than sufficient funds if you live to a ripe old age, it can also reduce the quality of your life in your pre-retirement or early retirement years. I can't really blame the companies for taking this approach, because they get sued often, and for a lot, but you must factor it into any advice you receive.

Line Item Spending Approach

The latest approach to estimating income needs is to look at each line item of spending individually to get a more accurate picture of retirement needs over time. Food costs will likely increase with inflation but decrease with age for example. Auto expenses will decrease as miles driven decrease. Clothing costs will likely diminish, but health care will likely increase. If you downsize your house all of the operating expenses associated with it will decrease. Vacations can be budgeted based on what you are able to do at any point. Gifting to children and grandchildren is discretionary and does not have to follow general inflation.

Doing a plan this way requires a lot of work on your part as well as the Good Financial Advisor, but it should yield better results. One main drawback to this approach is the lack of software to create a plan in this manner. It may require multiple spreadsheets to actually formulate a plan like this until some company steps up with commercially available software. It is probably well worth it if your situation warrants this level of analysis.

Retirement Spending Data

A recent study of government data on consumer spending concluded that advisors routinely overstated the financial resources needed for retirement, and failed to take into account that consumer spending dropped significantly through much of retirement. Using the common sense test, how many 85 year olds do you know that spend or do anywhere near as much as they did when they were in their 60's or 70's? Do you think you will?

The best way to answer that question is to do your own retirement spending plan, just as you did before you retired. Allow for the discretionary spending you desire. Build in three nice vacations and gifts for the grandchildren if that is what you want to do. Let the good Financial Advisor build your Retirement Spending Plan into your comprehensive retirement plan.

The Phased Spending Model

The other issue in calculating retirement needs is taking an estimate of a person's basic spending needs on the day they retire, and adding a fixed cost of living adjustment to it for the rest of their life. This does not accurately reflect how people will actually spend their money.

I prefer to have clients look at retirement in 5 year increments, and set spending levels for each increment based on age and desired activity in that time period. For example, if a couple retires at 65, I might recommend that they set 120% of their basic spending needs for the 65 through 70 time period while their health is good and extensive travel is possible. In the age 70 to 75 range, 110% of their basic spending needs might be a reasonable figure if they are still in good health. For the age 75 through 80 time period, 90% of their basic spending needs might be a suitable number. For the age 80 through 85 segment, I might reduce that to 80% of their basic spending needs.

All time periods are adjusted for inflation, but they reflect likely spending and desired activities, not pre-retirement basic spending levels. If phased spending is combined with the line item spending approach you would get a very clear picture of retirement, although at the cost of a lot of effort and expense. This involves a significant amount of discussion with you, and some work on your part. Many advisors might shy away from this approach as too time-intensive, and difficult to receive adequate compensation for the work required. However, no advisor wants to see an elderly client run out of money, especially if they know where their advisor lives. Time spent here will be well worth it.

Protection is a Must

Most retirement plans assume the need for protection against unforeseen medical expenses, known as Long Term Care (LTC) Insurance. This is a complicated type of protection and you should understand it thoroughly before you buy it. Most people with a substantial asset base will benefit from having LTC insurance, but those with small asset bases might be better off without it. I expand on LTC insurance in chapter 8B.

Life insurance is also a part of most Retirement Plans where concerns exist for a surviving spouse or partner and their ability to get by after the death of the first person. When the first person dies, a pension can be lost, or the remaining spouse or partner may need to hire someone to help them with day to day living. Consider it carefully before you assume you do not need any survivor protection. In the estate planning and protection planning sections you will see the need for insurance for other reasons.

Make Your Plan Reflect Reality

Think about your retirement, and make sure that your plan truly reflects what you feel your lifestyle will be at a given age. If you want to go skydiving, do it while you can, and allow for it in your financial plan. As I wrote this book, it occurred to me that I would never go bungee-jumping or mountain climbing in my lifetime. Age, and a 1975 back injury that occasionally revisits, simply won't let it happen. Skydiving has not been ruled out yet, but it may take a large single malt scotch to get me into the plane, and a good push to get me out.

If you wish to be generous to your children or grandchildren, there is nothing wrong with that. Just make sure it is factored into your spending plan. Spend well and live well.

Retirement Expenses Increase with Time

Remember Charles Dickens famous quote from David Copperfield, "Annual income twenty pounds, annual expenditure nineteen six, result happiness. Annual income twenty pounds, annual expenditure twenty pounds ought and six, result misery." This is why a Spending Plan as described in Chapter 2D is critical to your success.

Whatever your retirement plan, you must live within your annual income. Bear in mind that your expenses will double in about 24 years at 3% inflation, and inflation for retirees may be higher due to increased medical expenses. It is for this reason that you cannot ignore the return on your investment portfolio. If it is insufficient to offset inflation your income relative to expenses will constantly diminish with time. Therefore, you must have a plan to increase your income commensurately, or your standard of living will shrink year by year. Your independence eventually disappears, and finally your dignity, as you become completely dependent on the good graces of others.

Income May Not Be Guaranteed

Your annual income may come from various sources: Social Security, a pension, part-time work and income from your investment portfolio. Social security increases with inflation but the increases are fairly small. Pensions usually do not have an escalator, and part-time work depends on your health and the economy. How much income you can expect to get from an investment portfolio without depleting the principal is complicated to estimate. As a general guideline, you can take about 4% to 5% out of a properly constructed portfolio each year, without depleting the original principal and providing for future growth to offset inflation. If you decide to deplete principal you can take much more than that depending on your returns, but you take on the added risk of running out of money at some point in the future if you guess wrong on life expectancy. Thus, the investment portfolio determines in part how much retirement income you will have. I discuss this in more detail in Chapter 7J on withdrawing money in retirement.

It's Hard, Not Impossible

With all of these variables to consider, you should give long and careful consideration to your retirement plan. It may take a year to develop a plan you feel comfortable with, but the work will translate into a better retirement for many years to come. Consult with a professional like the Good Financial Advisor to make sure you understand the impact of any assumptions you make. Start the plan today, because retirement may be closer, and last longer, than you think.

Without a retirement plan you cannot act,

you can only react.

Chapter 4C – Protecting Your Pension

"When there are fewer days ahead of us than behind, and fewer dollars with which to live them, a steady income is a priceless thing."

For those of you fortunate enough to have a defined benefit pension plan from your current or former employment, you should understand what it is, how the distribution options work, and how you can maximize the payment you receive in retirement.

A defined benefit plan, commonly called a pension plan, is one where your company put aside funds for you over your working career, and guaranteed you a certain benefit when you retired. This contrasts with a defined contribution plan, such as a 401(k) plan, where you make contributions on a before tax basis, and the company may or may not provide matching funds.

Your Risk Is Increasing

Today, most companies are trying to eliminate defined benefit plans, where they take all of the investment risk, in favor of defined contribution plans, where you take all of the investment risk. This is another reason you need a financial advisor which did not exist in your parents' generation. In the next chapter I discuss managing your retirement plans.

When you reach the point when you begin taking your pension, in the form of an annuity, or stream of income, you must make a decision as to what form it will take. If you are married, your spouse is entitled to share in this pension, and he or she must agree to whatever option you take, if it is not shared with them for life.

If you are taking your pension early, typically before age 65, it may be significantly reduced. Like Social Security, this reduction is permanent for life, and can make a big difference over your remaining life expectancy. Be sure that taking your pension early is the right decision before making that choice, since it is almost always irrevocable.

Pension Options

There are numerous pension options, depending on your particular plan, and these are the most common forms you will encounter:

Life-Only Annuity – This is a pension that continues for your lifetime, and stops at your death. It does not provide any income for your surviving spouse, and because of that, requires your spouse to sign off on its selection. Before electing this option, be sure that the surviving spouse or partner can get by without your pension when you die.

Joint Life Annuity – This option does provide a benefit to your surviving spouse. This benefit is typically 100%, 66% or 50% of the original pension, meaning that the benefit after your death is reduced to that percentage of the pension when you were living. There is a cost to having your pension continue on after you are gone and that is a reduced initial pension benefit. In effect, the reduced benefit purchases insurance for the survivor, which is then provided in the form of a monthly benefit.

For example, you may be entitled to $2,000 per month as a life only pension, $1,900 per month as a joint and 50% pension, $1,800 per month as a joint and 66% pension and $1,600 as a joint and 100% pension. The reduction in initial monthly benefit is usually permanent, and as mentioned, is a form of insurance for the survivor. Some pensions have provisions that allow the benefit to revert to the life-only level upon the death of the spouse, but these are not common.

Ask your pension plan provider to give you estimates of your pension at whatever retirement age you choose. Review these options with the Good Financial Advisor and decide what best suits your situation. The decision you make is irrevocable in nearly every circumstance, and should be made carefully after examining all of the options. Be sure that survivor benefits, such as health insurance, are not tied to your pension, so that they end at your death, leaving the survivor without coverage.

Insure Your Own Pension

One way to increase the size of your pension is to take out life insurance on yourself for the surviving spouse, and elect the life only annuity pension option. This way when you die, and your pension stops, the insurance pays an amount to your spouse sufficient to offset the loss of pension income. It is a great way to increase your retirement income for life, but it must be done early enough in your working career to make it affordable. Find someone who knows this subject well before you try to implement it yourself. It requires permanent insurance, and it must be taken out early enough in your career to allow time to fund it before you retire. And again, it requires you to sacrifice income before you retire to increase your income after you retire.

Create Your Own Pension

As you will read in Chapter 7E on annuities, you can also create your own "pension" by purchasing an immediate annuity from an insurance company. Since this involves surrendering your principal, do not do it without professional help and a clear understanding of what you are giving up. There are many different options available to you when you annuitize, and it can be difficult to understand the ramifications of all of them. Some guarantee that you receive payments at least equal to your initial investment, and some increase the periodic payment over time. All options other than the life-only one carry a price in the form of a lower overall payment.

Retirement Costs Increase with Inflation

Some pensions have a cost of living escalator, but most are fixed. Be aware that costs will go up steadily in retirement, consistent with inflation, or higher in the case of medical costs. You must have a plan to increase your income over time to meet these costs, or your living standard will shrink steadily and significantly over the years. I mentioned this in Chapter 4B and cover this again in Chapter 7J on Withdrawing Money in Retirement, but it bears repeating. You do not want to reach age 80 in good health but with insufficient assets to maintain a reasonable standard of living. Increasing costs and a fixed income are a dangerous combination, as I described in the previous chapter.

Invest Prudently

This also means that your retirement assets must be invested in a manner that will allow them to outpace inflation over a long period of time. If you play it too safe early on, by using Certificates of Deposit and other fixed investments, you might be impacting the quality of life in your later years. Chapter 6B on Risk covers this in more detail. A good Retirement Plan will help you to decide what course to take, which is why you must have one.

Time and inflation march on.

You must find time to deal with inflation.

Chapter 4D – Managing Retirement Plans

"Too many choices can become no choice at all."

401(k), 403(b), 457, etc. It makes you wish the IRS would give names to these important retirement savings plans, instead of numbering them based on the paragraph that they occupy in the tax code. Nonetheless, they are very important in your retirement planning.

If you are not self-employed, most of you are familiar with one of these types of qualified plans from your employer. (If you are self-employed you may have a SIMPLE IRA, SEP IRA, Single 401(k), Keogh or similar plan). They all share one common characteristic: You are allowed to put money in them from your income on a pre-tax basis, meaning you avoid paying income taxes on those funds until you take them out at a later date (which can be many years later). Other rules regarding contribution limits, eligibility, and portability may vary with the type of plan.

The human resources department of your company should provide you with an explanation of the plan in which you are enrolled. Take time to read enough about the plan to understand how it benefits you. If you are not enrolled, get enrolled. You will be unlikely to get any investment advice on the mutual funds within your 401(k) plan. You can blame it on a rule that prohibits firms who provide the investments from giving advice on which investments to choose. The concern is that these firms would promote their own funds over the funds of other firms rather than give objective advice. Therefore you get no help at all. (This rule is being changed as this book is written). Show your plan to your Good Financial Advisor and get help in setting it up to meet your needs.

No Plan at Work – Make Your Own

If you are so unfortunate as to work for an employer who has no retirement plan, ask them if they plan to put one in place soon. Too many small businesses don't have a plan because the owner is under the mistaken impression that they cost a lot, and he will be forced to contribute big dollars to them on behalf of his employees. Neither is correct, and you can ask your Good Financial Advisor to speak with them, and explain the benefits of a retirement plan. If they do not opt to put a plan in place, see your Good Financial Advisor to discuss available alternatives. You may be able to maximize the contribution to your spouse or partners' retirement plan, and direct your contributions to a traditional IRA or Roth IRA, and accomplish the same end result. Not having a retirement plan at work should not be a reason that you fail to save for retirement.

Matching Funds

Some employers provide matching funds depending on what you choose to contribute. These are free (to you) contributions, and you should make sure you get these matching contributions if at all possible. You may have to remain working with the employer for a certain period of time, known as the vesting period, to keep the funds, so time your career changes accordingly.

Tax Savings Are Important

A key point to remember is that when you save $100 out of your paycheck, it only reduces your take home pay by what your after-tax income would have been. That $100 would only have been about $70 in your pocket after federal income taxes and state taxes are deducted. Therefore, don't inadvertently reduce your retirement plan by 30% or so because you thought you couldn't afford it. When people are starting out in their working careers, they often have little discretionary income left over after making a car payment and saving for a home. They then elect not to participate in their company plan, even when they could get the company matching funds. This is a Big Mistake from a financial perspective, and very costly in terms of retirement savings.

After people have been working for a number of years, and have sufficient cash flow to participate fully in these plans, they are limited by the amount they can contribute, and it is hard to "catch up". Because of the Magic of Compounding (Chapter 6M), everyone should participate in these plans early on, to the greatest extent they can, even though this requires some deferred gratification.

Save Early – Retire Well

The impact of saving early for your retirement is huge as illustrated by these two examples. Frugal Fred saved $6,000 per year starting at age 22 when he began working. Extravagant Ed waited ten years to begin saving for retirement, and then saved $6,000 per year for the next 34 years. Both earned an average of 8% on their account. Fred ended up with more than $2,000,000 at retirement, while Ed had only $900,000, even though Fred contributed only $60,000 more then Ed.

In a second example, Fred saved $6,000 per year for ten years starting when he began working, and then stopped saving altogether to pursue other goals. Ed again waited for ten years to begin, and then saved $7,500 per year until retirement (34 years). Both earned 8% and wound up with the same nest egg at age 65, even though one contributed over four times more than the other. I talk more about these two fellows in chapter 6D on Opportunity Cost.

Invest With Care

When you participate in one of these plans, the guidelines regarding diversification should be followed to ensure you are not taking undue risk. Because it is costly, company plans do not usually have a large number of investment options, and care must be taken to avoid the poorest ones within the plan. It may also be difficult to properly diversify with limited investment options, so the Good Financial Advisor can be helpful in guiding you to the best choices.

In some cases there are simply too many selections for the typical investor to deal with. Here you should ask your Good Financial Advisor for assistance in developing a diversified portfolio that will provide you with safety and growth. Studies seem to indicate that with too many choices, many plan participants just elect the safest option for 100% of their money. For many people this is very costly in terms of reduced long-term growth. You do not want to take excessive risk and you can't play it too safe. Seek out guidance, even if you have to pay a fee to get it.

Rollover Your Plan and Stretch It Out

When you leave one job for another, consider the option of taking your company plan and rolling it over to your own IRA. This usually provides more, and better, investment options, and allows you to stretch out the IRA for your heirs, instead of them receiving the IRA in a taxable lump-sum distribution. The advantages of a company plan are that you can usually take loans from them, while you cannot take a loan from an IRA. Few financial advisors would ever recommend a 401(k) loan except as a last resort, so I view this as a small (if any) advantage. From the perspective of a financial advisor, loans from a 401(k) plan are both costly and dangerous. While you think you are paying yourself back with interest, you are actually losing some of the tax-deferred growth of the plan. In addition, if you lose your job, you must repay the loan immediately, or it becomes a taxable distribution, with penalties if you are under age 59 1/2. This is one of the minefields you should avoid if possible.

Don't Cash Out Your Plan

If you terminate employment for any reason, do not cash out your retirement plan or you will lose the benefit of tax-deferral, pay current taxes, and pay an additional penalty if you are under age 59 1/2 and do not qualify for a hardship exception. You will also be given an option to annuitize the plan, which is almost never in your best interest. The only option which makes sense in nearly all cases is the direct rollover to IRA. Many people leave their 401(k) plan because they feel that it has grown well over time and don't want to risk change. This perception is likely based on the fact that they were contributing to it constantly while they worked, not because of superior investment returns, so look at the plan carefully before leaving your money unattended at your old company. If you need money before age 59 1/2 see chapter 7J on SEPP withdrawals. Consult the Good Financial Advisor before making a final decision, because your decision is almost always final.

Creditor Protection

A company-sponsored plan may have better protection from creditors in the event of a bankruptcy. This last matter has been ruled on recently by the Supreme Court, and it appears that IRA's will be protected up to a million dollars. Consult an attorney regarding the laws of your state if you have any creditor concerns at all.

Manage your retirement plans before they manage you.

Chapter 4E – Retirement Accounts

"Grow old along with me. The best is yet to be".

Individual Retirement Accounts, or IRA's as most of us know them, are the single most important way to save for retirement outside of your qualified plan at work. There are several types of IRA's, each with its own rules and purpose:

IRAs for Individuals

The most common is the **Traditional IRA**, into which you put pre-tax money (up until age 70), thereby saving taxes today. It grows tax-deferred, and you pay taxes on it when you take it out. You must begin taking it out when you reach age 70 1/2, by means of Required Minimum Distributions or RMDs.

A recent addition (1998) is the **ROTH IRA**, into which you put after-tax money. This IRA grows tax-free, and is tax-free when you take it out. Unlike a Traditional IRA, you are not required to take RMDs out of a ROTH IRA at age 70 1/2, and you can make contributions to it after age 70 if you have earned income. This may be the best investment vehicle available today outside of a company-sponsored plan

Both the traditional IRA and the Roth IRA penalize you if you make withdrawals before age 59 1/2 although the Roth IRA allows you to take your contributions without penalty. Check the rules before making any withdrawal from an IRA or a qualified plan.

The **Beneficial IRA** is designed to receive an inherited IRA. It is like a Traditional IRA, but provides a surviving spouse the ability to take withdrawals without penalty, even if they are under age 59 1/2.

IRAs for Small Businesses

There are two IRAs that are designed for small business owners or the self-employed:

The **SIMPLE IRA**, or Savings Incentive Match Plan for Employees, is an IRA designed for small businesses. It has characteristics of a 401(k) plan, with minimal administration and cost involved. It allows all employees to put a share of earnings away pre-tax, and requires an employer contribution as well.

The **SEP IRA**, or Simplified Employee Pension IRA, is designed for self-employed business people. It also allows you to put a percentage of your earnings away, providing you do the same for your employees. Its contribution limits are higher than a SIMPLE IRA. It has essentially replaced the Keogh plan, now seldom used.

The **Single 401(k)** is relatively new, and is available to the self-employed who have no other employees except for their immediate family. It is not an IRA, and provides the ability to save more than either a SIMPLE or SEP IRA in a given year.

Know the Rules

All of these have rules governing how much you can contribute to them in a given year, depending on your age and income. Some require contributions to be made on behalf of your employees. All have rules governing when you can take money out of them, depending on age and circumstances. And it seems that every year, some of these rules change. The important point is that you should find someone who understands these rules, and use whichever plan is appropriate for your situation. If you do not use a plan, you are simply giving tax money to the government that could be used to help your retirement plan grow.

The Stretch IRA

IRA's can be passed on to a spouse or other beneficiary, and the benefits of tax deferral stretched out for many years. The stretch IRA is a very powerful way to pass on your IRA to your children, and should not be overlooked. It can be more difficult to use any other qualified plan to stretch out your tax-deferral for your children, so consult with your Good Financial Advisor when you have a 401(k) or similar plan that you can rollover to your own IRA. It is seldom a wise move to leave your plan at your last place of employment. The one negative thing to consider is the difference in creditor protection in an IRA vs. a trusteed plan like a 401(k). A recent Supreme Court ruling greatly improved creditor protection for IRAs, and it should not be an issue for most people.

Roth IRA Conversion

You can convert a traditional IRA to a Roth IRA if your household adjusted gross income is below a certain threshold (currently $100,000). See your Good Financial Advisor to find out if it makes sense for you to consider this option. You should also consult a tax advisor on this matter to be sure of its effect on your taxes. When you convert a regular IRA to a Roth IRA, the amount of money converted is added to your current income so that you can be taxed on it. This may be more costly than it is worth, so have someone look at it before you decide.

If you are young, or in a low tax bracket, it probably will make sense, because you have sufficient time to allow the tax-free growth of the Roth IRA to offset the initial amount of taxes paid. If you are older and in a lower tax bracket it may make sense to convert your IRA to a Roth IRA for the benefit of your children, especially if they are in a higher tax bracket.

If you don't have an IRA, set one up, or see your Good Financial Advisor for help in getting one established. Remember, with an IRA the government is allowing you to use tax money for decades to grow and improve your retirement. This is an opportunity you do not want to pass up. A great website to visit for IRA information is www.edslott.com. He is one of the most respected experts in the field today,

Without an IRA,

you will pay taxes today.

Chapter 4F – Required Distributions

"Two things in life are certain: death and taxes."

Whoever said that must have had Required Minimum Distributions (or RMDs as they are usually called) in mind. What are RMDs? At age 70 1/2, the government decides it has waited long enough to begin getting back some of the taxes due on your tax-deferred retirement savings plans, and requires you to begin taking money out of them based on your remaining life expectancy. Your first withdrawal is due no later than April 1st of the year following the year you turn age 70 1/2. If you wait until this point your second withdrawal is due by December 31st of the same year and each year thereafter.

Your RMD is based on your age, and the balance in your particular tax-deferred plan at the end of the prior year. Using your age at the end of the year you are taking distributions, go into the IRS table for RMDs (available on www.irs.gov) and select your divisor. Divide your prior year-end plan balance by that divisor, and the answer is the amount you must withdraw for the year.

If you have multiple IRAs, you can add them up to get the total amount of your RMD, and then take the actual distribution from wherever you choose. You can take it all from one IRA or a little from each, as long as the total withdrawn is correct. With all other types of plans you must take the RMD from each individual plan.

Well before this happens, consult a tax advisor, along with your Good Financial Advisor, and determine if waiting to take money out of a retirement plan at age 70 1/2 is your best option. It may be advantageous to begin removing money earlier to smooth out your tax burden later on. This depends on what tax bracket you are in today, vs. what tax bracket you will be in when you take the RMD.

The Stretch IRA Legacy

You can also leave an IRA to a spouse or heirs, who can then stretch out the RMDs based on their own life expectancy instead of yours. This stretch IRA, as I mentioned in the previous chapter, is a very valuable gift for your heirs, since it is in tax-deferred status and remains that way for many years, depending on their age.

The Roth IRA is exempt from RMDs, so you may wish to convert some of your Regular IRA money to a ROTH IRA, to avoid having to take distributions at age 70 1/2. This will allow you to leave the entire IRA to your children, who can then take distributions based on their much younger age. If your tax bracket is lower than your intended heirs, it may make sense to pay taxes now, before leaving them your assets. Consult with your tax advisor to see if a Roth IRA conversion is right for your situation.

Penalties for Missing the RMD

One key point to remember is that you do have to take distributions, or the government will assess a 50% penalty on the amount not taken out. This is current tax law, and your custodian reports to the IRS each year on the amount you withdraw. The best way to do this is to set up a systematic withdrawal to take your distribution out on a periodic basis. If you don't set up a systematic distribution, take your RMD at the same time as your regular service meeting with the Good Financial Advisor. Remember to adjust the amount of the RMD each year based on your balance at the end of the previous year.

Use your RMD to enhance your legacy.

Chapter 4G – Home Mortgages

"Home sweet home or money pit?"

The largest financial transaction many of us will make is purchasing a home, and the next largest transaction is financing it with a home mortgage. When taking on the obligation of a mortgage, carefully evaluate your ability to make the payments, pay the taxes and insurance, maintain the home, and live a reasonable lifestyle. Eating is not optional, and you do not want to shortchange your retirement plans to make the mortgage payment.

Be sure you know the real cost of a mortgage loan after tax benefits are taken into consideration. These can be substantial, because in most cases mortgage interest is deductible on your tax return. The savings in the early years can be significant, and allow you to buy a better house than you thought you could afford.

How Long a Term?

When selecting the term of their mortgage, many people focus on having it paid off at retirement. This is a worthy goal, but don't let it adversely impact your other equally important goals. If you happen to have a small mortgage balance on the day you retire it will have little effect on you lifestyle. Say you owe $40,000 on an old mortgage with a payment of $1,600 per month. Refinance it for the next 15 years at 7% and the payment becomes $351 per month (before the tax deduction for mortgage interest). In all likelihood, your house taxes will be of more concern than the mortgage payment because they increase with time. Remember to refinance before you retire so you will have sufficient income to qualify for the mortgage you want.

Fixed or Variable Rate?

If you can choose between a fixed and a variable rate loan, I would always select the fixed rate loan because it removes interest rate risk. If the variable rate loan interest rate is much more attractive, or you know you will be moving within a few years, take the variable rate loan. Just be sure you can handle the payment increase with the maximum allowable rate increase, in case you stay in your home.

Prepaying the Loan

People are always concerned about whether they should pay off an existing mortgage, refinance it for a different term, or make additional principal payments. There is no simple answer, but here are the things you should consider when deciding on what is right for you.

Before making your home purchase, determine if you have sufficient cash flow to fund your other obligations, such as a Roth IRA, your 401(k) plan at work, and a 529 college savings plan for the children. If not, think twice before shortchanging those areas in order to pay off your mortgage a few years early.

Can you earn more on the money invested elsewhere? If your mortgage costs you 4% after taxes, and you can earn 6% in an investment account, it may be prudent to keep the mortgage in place rather than prepay it.

If you are in a financial bind for any reason, such as an accident, job loss or unforeseen medical expenses, your lender will not give you credit for prepaid principal. In fact, if you are in a difficult financial situation, most lenders will not do a thing for you due to the risk involved. It comes back to that old saying that no one wants to lend you money if you really need it.

Keep in mind that many home foreclosures result from illness or disability of the primary wage earner. Therefore, having money available to carry you through a difficult period is a prudent course of action. Most people should have cash reserves equal to four to six months of expenses. Remember this when you consider what level of disability income protection you should have.

The Home as an Investment

It is not my view that your home is an investment, but it certainly has characteristics of one. To ignore historical real estate appreciation would be silly, if not negligent, when looking at your financial position.

My recommendation is that you purchase as much house as is consistent with affordability and your desired lifestyle. A financial plan would be a great tool to help you make that decision. Buying too much house can eat into your cash flow and significantly affect your ability to accumulate wealth.

There are three advantages to home ownership that tend to enhance its investment qualities:

First, the government subsidizes your loan payment by allowing you to deduct your interest against income. Property taxes are also usually deductible against income. The taxes saved by these two items are pretty large compared to renting a home where none of the payment is deductible.

Second, it is leveraged, since you only have to put a small amount down on the home and borrow the rest. This magnifies any positive return, (although it also magnifies any losses).

Lastly, you pay no taxes on any gains until you sell, and then the first $500,000 in gain (for a couple) is exempt from capital gains taxes. If you stay in a home for an extended period of time, it typically increases in value with inflation, assuming your home and the neighborhood are well maintained.

These three factors combined can produce a substantial amount of equity as you pay off the principal balance of the loan over time.

One thing I have never recommended is taking equity from your home via a refinance or home equity loan to invest in the stock market. The overall risks are unsuitable for most people.

Control Is Important

Before you make decisions about prepaying, or paying off your home mortgage, look at your overall financial plan and see if it is in your best interest, or in the best interest of your lender. Again, you must have a financial plan to make a good decision here.

What I recommend to most clients is that they should take out the longest mortgage they can, and save the payment difference in an investment account. While this would seem to be self-serving, the amount of savings involved is small relative to a typical account. If you then choose to pay off the mortgage at some point in the future, you do it on your terms, not those of the lender. Ask the Good Financial Advisor to evaluate your own specific situation before making a final decision.

Don't rush to give money to a bank.

They have plenty.

Chapter 4H – Reverse Mortgages

"Home sweet home sweet retirement plan."

Reverse mortgages have developed as a way for people in retirement to access the equity in their homes, when other options are not available or desirable. If you want to use a reverse mortgage, you should definitely use a reputable firm that specializes in reverse mortgages, and retain an attorney who handles real estate financing to represent you in the transaction. This is no time to be taking out a mortgage from an out-of-state company or on the Internet.

They Are Complicated

Here is a brief overview of how they work. You must be older than 62 and have some equity in your home. You apply for a reverse mortgage based on your age, interest rates, and the equity in your home above the existing mortgage, if any. Since you do not have to make any payments on a reverse mortgage, income is not required for qualification.

You can take a lump sum, monthly payments, credit line, or a combination of these. The loan is repaid only when you sell your home, move or die. You cannot owe more than the value of the home when it is repaid.

Since this is your money being given to you, it is not income and does not affect the taxation of your social security benefits.

Most reverse mortgages are taken under the Home Equity Conversion Mortgage (HECM) program insured by the U.S. Department of Housing and Urban Development (HUD).

They Are Expensive

These loans can be expensive to take out, with some costing as much as 10% of the loan value or more. Be sure this is the right option for you.

I would ask your Good Financial Advisor to explore all of the other less costly options available to you before you look at a reverse mortgage.

As crass as this may sound, the people who provide reverse mortgages must make a good profit in order to remain in business.

Evaluate the Alternatives

At this point, it is my opinion that a reverse mortgage can, in some cases, be more expensive than alternative ways to access the equity in your home. Study your options carefully before making this decision, and ask the Good Financial Advisor to compare the reverse mortgage with other options to determine which is best for you.

Be slow to undo years of equity buildup in your home.

Chapter 4I – Social (In)Security

"The early bird gets the worm, but the second mouse gets the cheese."

Social Security has been called the most successful government program ever created. It has lifted millions out of poverty in retirement, and provided many benefits to the orphaned, disabled, widowed and sick.

Without getting into the political debate over what reform is necessary to keep the Social Security system solvent and healthy forever, you should understand these issues that relate directly to your financial security in retirement.

When Do You Take Your Benefit?

You will receive Social Security at some level, depending on when you elect to take your benefit. You may take your benefit early, and receive a reduced benefit, take it at your full retirement age and get the standard benefit, or take it later and get an increased benefit. There are pros and cons to each, and your health and financial situation should determine what course you choose. The old philosophy that said take Social Security benefits as soon as you can get them no longer applies in a world where life expectancies are in the eighties and constantly improving.

This is one of the biggest decisions you will make regarding your retirement, so study this issue carefully before deciding on what is best for you. Consult with your Good Financial Advisor, and your tax advisor, to be sure you understand the ramifications of your decision. Visit your local Social Security office if you can, and discuss your options with them. If you are a widow or widower, you may be eligible for benefits at age 60, so check with your Social Security office to see if this applies to you.

Health Is a Key Factor

If your health is poor, or you do not expect to live beyond your normal life expectancy, it is usually appropriate to take your benefit early, even at a reduced level. If your health is good, and you do expect to live beyond your normal life expectancy, it generally is a good idea to wait and take a higher benefit. If you are still working, you could pay taxes on the benefit and possibly lose some of it if your income is too high. Order the Social Security informational booklet for a more detailed look at these issues or go to www.ssa.gov for more information.

Waiting Can Pay Off

Since Social Security is a guaranteed income with a cost of living escalator, the larger it is when you take it, the larger it will grow with time. It may also increase for your spouse if half of your benefit is more than 100% of their own. Look at the benefit statement that is sent to you each year and review your options with your Good Financial Advisor.

There are strategies to maximize your total retirement income between you and your spouse, and you should take advantage of them if you can. Also keep in mind that your decision can affect the income for your spouse after you die.

Make sure you get the cheese.

Chapter 5 – Estate Planning

"We are afraid of the legacy we will leave."

Do you need to do any estate planning? Only if you want to control the disposition of all of the assets you worked your entire life to accumulate, and keep the state and federal government from being your heirs, or the guardians of your minor children.

Estate planning is a process that addresses two important questions:

1) Will I have enough money to live the way I want to live? The operative word here is live. Proper estate planning allows you to live a more comfortable and worry-free life.

2) What will happen to my assets when I no longer need them? There is no mention of death here either. The big question is, when will you no longer need your assets to accomplish 1) above.

Estate planning also helps you deal with these realities of life

1) Mortality is 100%. Sorry to break the news like this.

2) You can't take it with you. No matter where you are headed.

3) You can't leave it all to your heirs. Others want their cut.

4) You will be remembered by what you do. Scary isn't it?

5) When contemplating death, we don't fear extinction. We fear extinction without significance. Our concern is for our legacy.

By now you may have gotten the idea that estate planning provides benefits to almost everyone, regardless of the size of their estate.

Estate Planning is for Everybody

Almost everyone should do some level of estate planning, if not for themselves, for those they leave behind. Estate planning addresses the situation where you, or a spouse or partner, are incapacitated and unable to make decisions regarding your financial situation, health care, or your estate. It also minimizes the costs of probating your estate when you are gone, or eliminates most of those costs through the use of trusts in place of wills. If you don't do some minimum level of estate planning, the state and federal government will be happy to do it for you, and take a large share of your estate in the form of taxes in the process.

Watch Out for 2011

The current estate tax laws are due to sunset in 2010, and no one knows what our government will do to extend them. Consequently, many people are doing nothing, which is certainly not the best way to deal with estate planning. At a minimum, you should see if you have taken advantage of existing laws for avoiding estate taxes through the use of trusts which shelter your unified credit (the amount the current laws allow you to pass through to your heirs without taxation).

Simply leaving your estate to your spouse, or splitting it between your spouse and your children, may leave you with a significant tax liability that could have been avoided with proper planning. This is an area for a skilled estate-planning attorney, not a do-it-yourself job. I have deliberately omitted more detailed information on estate tax planning techniques here, because I don't feel anyone should attempt to do their own estate planning without the proper professional help.

No Will - No Problem – No Control!

If you die intestate, without a will, the state and federal government will create an estate plan for your heirs, and it will probably not be one you would approve.

If you fail to name custodians for your minor children, the court will pick someone to raise them.

If you and your spouse should perish at the same time, you can inadvertently disinherit children from previous marriages.

If you have not properly designated beneficiaries, you may lose large tax benefits on your retirement plans, or an ex-spouse could inherit some of your estate.

If you gift assets before you die, you might lose the step up in basis that occurs at death, and cause your beneficiary to pay taxes that could otherwise have been avoided.

Failing to utilize your unified credit could unnecessarily cost hundreds of thousands of dollars in estate taxes.

This list could go on, but I think the point is made. If any of these situations concern you, see an estate planning attorney at your next opportunity.

Your Legacy is the Key

As I mentioned in Chapter 2A on setting goals, what do you want your legacy to be? Do you want your friends and family to think of you as a successful person, who dutifully took care of his family, and left gifts to friends and charities? Or would you prefer that friends and family think of you as a successful person, who forgot that he was going to die someday, and left a lot to the government, and a mess to the rest.

There are numerous stories of those who failed to have an estate plan, including the Supreme Court justice who did his own, and cost himself hundreds of thousands of dollars. As I said in Chapter 2H, doing it yourself can be detrimental to your financial health, no matter what your occupation. In addition, you have to get around your behavioral issues, discussed in Chapter 6L on Investor (Mis)behavior. These are not easy hurdles to overcome.

Assess Your Estate

In order to determine if you have a need for an estate plan you should take a look at what is in your estate. Remember that the value of any insurance policies you have is included in your estate unless it is held inside an irrevocable life insurance trust. Add up the value of all of your assets, retirement plans at work and personal property to see where you stand today. Then project that value out to your life expectancy and see what you might have then. You will probably be surprised.

Here's a short action plan to get you on track.

- Call your estate-planning attorney tomorrow.

- Call your Good Financial Advisor to meet with your attorney.

- Develop your estate plan.

- Put your estate plan in place.

- Congratulate yourself and sleep well.

Your legacy is secure.

Chapter 5A – Wills, Trusts, Etc.

"You should set up a trust fund," said the financial advisor to the client.
"If I could find someone I can trust I would." answered the client.

Financial advisors are generally prohibited from giving legal advice, but they should inquire as to the type of estate planning documents you have, and how old they are.

Advisors who have an advanced designation, such as the CFP® (Certified Financial Planner), are especially aware of the ramifications of poor estate planning, and will typically look at ways to maintain control, save taxes, and increase the amount of your estate that passes to your heirs. The Good Financial Advisor will usually refer you to an estate planning attorney and accompany you on the initial visit.

However, you should always consult with an attorney on matters related to estate planning, and only an attorney can prepare the proper documents for you. When you consult with an attorney, be sure that you use one who specializes in estate planning on a regular basis. In addition, you should consult with a tax advisor whose practice specializes in estate taxes. It is a complex and constantly changing field, and is best left to specialists.

Most basic estate plans consist of five parts

A **Will** or a **Revocable Living Trust**, to direct the passing of your estate to the heirs. A will is a simple document that is available to the public and goes through probate. The revocable living trust is a somewhat more complex document that is private and does not go through probate. Ask your attorney to explain the finer differences between these two documents.

A **Living Will** to tell others what to do regarding life saving measures when you are terminally ill.

A **Health Care Power of Attorney** to give someone the ability to choose what kind of health care you should receive, when you are unable to make that decision.

A **Durable Power of Attorney** that survives your incapacity, to give someone the ability to pay your bills, and run your affairs, when you cannot do that for yourself.

Specific Medical Directives to try to ensure that doctors and hospitals will honor your specific wishes in the final days of life.

These documents should typically be updated every five years or sooner, depending on changes in your circumstances. When a death or disability occurs, a child is born, a child gets married, you purchase a second home in another state, a change in health occurs, or a divorce takes place, your estate planning documents should reflect that change. Let your attorney guide you here. Updates are usually done at minimum cost, and they are well worth it.

Complex Estate Planning

More complex estate plans may use a number of additional documents to protect against loss of control of assets and unnecessary taxes. I suggest you read a basic estate-planning book to become familiar with the techniques that are available before you meet with your attorney. It will make the meeting much more productive.

If you are unsure as to the complexity of your estate, consult with your Good Financial Advisor or go to the estate planning attorney nearest you and get an opinion. Remember that life insurance benefits are part of your estate unless they are owned by a trust, so your worth at death may be higher than you think. Your Good Financial Advisor should be able to recommend an attorney if you do not have one.

Areas that may require more complex planning

- A child with a disability who may require a special needs trust

- Children from previous marriages to avoid unintended disinheritance

- Minors who need a guardian until they reach the age of majority

- Grandchildren to ensure they receive what you intended to leave them
- The transfer of a home to your children before death

- Non-spousal relationships

- Gay and lesbian relationships, even if covered by a civil union

- Transfers of a small business

- Gifting programs, whether to a charity or others

Trusts

A trust is a legal entity that gives control over assets to a trustee. This allows you to control the disposition of assets after you are unable to do so, or after your death. Some trusts are revocable and some are irrevocable, and you need to know when each is appropriate to use. Only an attorney is qualified to draft a trust. They are not a do-it-yourself item.

In the area of trusts, the issues are many times so complex that professionals can disagree among themselves as to how the Internal Revenue Service will treat a given situation. Trusts come in a variety of types, and are useful in numerous areas of estate planning to protect assets, reduce taxes and control estate distribution. They do have a cost to establish, but are well worth your consideration if your estate is of sufficient size to justify their use. See an attorney who specializes in estate planning and these issues will be capably addressed. You can then concentrate on the other issues that affect you, while you plan to live well for many more years.

Children are evidence of our desire

to perpetuate ourselves.

Grandchildren are proof that we got it right.

Chapter 5B – Caring for Your Children

"We need to make sure we take care of our children. They not only are our legacy to the world, but they may get to select our nursing home."

As I said in the beginning of the estate planning chapter, you can't leave it all to your heirs, but you can make sure your children get what you desire them to have. To do that however, you must have the right estate planning documents in place. Unless you are two adults who have never been married before, with no children from any previous relationships, it is important to see an attorney to ensure that you do not inadvertently disinherit any of your children. This is of particular concern when passing IRAs on through a current spouse to children from a prior spouse.

Uniform Transfer to Minors Act

As to investment vehicles, there is one that pertains to children specifically. This is the Uniform Transfer to Minors Act trust, commonly known as an UTMA (previously known as an UGMA or Uniform Gift to Minors Act), that allows you to make irrevocable gifts to children. These receive preferential tax treatment, and revert to the minor when they reach the age of majority. If you do not want a minor child to suddenly have a large amount of cash when they turn age 18 or 21, an UTMA may not be the way to go.

Trusts Maintain Control

There are others, primarily trusts, that you can use, but they involve more cost to set up. Consult with your estate-planning attorney to see if they make sense for you.

One of the key issues when leaving assets to younger children is whether they are responsible enough to handle them at time of receipt. Think it through carefully before leaving a large amount of assets to any child, no matter how much you love them. The receipt of a large sum of money by a person in their early twenties might create more problems than you can imagine, and if the person is unable to handle that money, it could disappear in a short period of time. A trust can let you control the disbursement of funds and alleviate these concerns.

Equal May Not Be Fair

In considering how to leave assets to your children a constant question is whether equal is fair. Should your financially successful daughter get the same dollar amount as your son who chose to become a schoolteacher? Can you intentionally disinherit a child with whom you have a poor relationship, without impacting that child's future relationships with his or her siblings after you are gone?

These are some of the emotional questions that arise in the estate planning process. Talk things over with your family and these decisions will be easier to make. Your Good Financial Advisor will help in this regard because he is interested in maintaining continuity with your children. Whatever you leave your children will undoubtedly be appreciated.

For your nursing home, your grateful children will pick

Marvelous Meadows instead of Gravel Gardens.

Chapter 5C – Gifting In Your Lifetime

"There is no greater joy than knowing you have made the life of one other person a little better. Such is the happiness that gifting brings."

The government allows us to give a certain amount each year to as many people (friends or relatives) as we wish, without having to pay gift taxes. Currently that amount is $12,000 indexed in increments of $500. For example, two grandparents can give $12,000 from either of them or $24,000 in total, to each of their children and grandchildren without concern for gift taxes. For the financially independent, this is a great way to get dollars out of their estate that will otherwise go to the government in the form of taxes.

Plan Your Giving Well

If you plan to gift, consult with both a financial and tax advisor to determine the best way to accomplish your goal. For example, if you have an IRA and some old stock as the only two gifts you wish to make, and you want to leave something to a charity and your children, leaving the IRA to charity means they pay no taxes on it (charities are exempt from paying taxes). The stock steps up in basis at death under current tax law and therefore your children would pay no taxes on it, except for gains that occurred after your death. Even though your children could stretch out the IRA, it might be worth it to leave stock that they could access immediately, without a taxable consequence. Let the Good Financial Advisor study the best way for your circumstances, before you make the final decision.

Charitable Giving

If you have a charitable intent, you have many options to give to a charity and receive a current tax break in the process. Charitable remainder trusts or lead trusts are a couple of ways to do this, but you definitely will need professional help to guide you through the rules governing how to set these vehicles up properly. The IRS looks very carefully at these gifting programs and an audit should not surprise anyone who gives large amounts in a given year. There are also limits on the amount of deductions you can take in a particular year. Proceed with due caution.

 I kept this section deliberately short because I believe you should always consult with a tax advisor and an attorney before implementing a gifting program. The Good Financial Advisor will provide assistance in evaluating the financial benefits or costs associated with your program.

Being able to give to others while we are still alive

is one of life's greatest pleasures.

Chapter 5D – Estate Taxes

"To my spendthrift nephew who always thought nothing was too good for him, I leave nothing!"

Maybe that is a little harsh, but most people do not want to leave money to that other "spendthrift", our federal government. I commonly hear from clients that…"they already have enough and don't need any more of my money."

Estate Taxes Affect Many

Estate taxes (also called death taxes depending on your political view) are assessed on estates above a certain size at your death at a rate that is very high (above 50% at the margin). Under current 2006 tax law, if you leave more than $2,000,000, you will owe taxes unless you take certain steps to use the credits that are available to you to avoid those taxes. This is an area where a competent estate-planning attorney is a must.

Trusts Are Estate Planning Tools

The way the trusts work in general is to let you leave the maximum amount allowed under current law to a credit shelter trust. This trust protects the credit the government gives to every person for their estate. The surviving spouse is usually the trustee and has complete access to the assets of the trust for health, education, maintenance and support. The rest is left to a marital trust, since you can pass an unlimited amount tax free to a spouse. For unmarried couples or non-spouse beneficiaries, the law is different. Taxes will be due on any amount over the current limit of $2,000,000 in 2006.

Step Up In Basis and IRD

When items are passed through an estate today, the cost basis is stepped up to current value, so that heirs inherit a new cost basis, and are free to sell something without capital gains taxes being due. This is destined to change under the new rules in 2011, and may affect how you wish to transfer assets before you die. Income in respect of a decedent, or IRD, is given special treatment so you do not pay taxes on it twice. If any tax-deferred investment, like an annuity, passes through your estate, you can get a credit for the taxes paid on the deferred income. If you have this type of a situation, be sure to tell your tax advisor to apply for the appropriate credit, since it is often overlooked.

Estate Tax Laws Are Changing

Complicating matters further, estate taxes are going to be reduced until 2010 via larger exemptions, and then revert to the old law in 2011, unless changes in the current law are enacted. No one can plan around this type of political games-playing in Washington, since it was designed to fit a ten year budget projection, not make sense for the American people.

For your own protection, consult an estate-planning attorney and see what your circumstances warrant. If your estate is of any substantial size, the Good Financial Advisor will urge you to put an estate plan in place to protect you and your heirs. When calculating the value of your estate, you must add in the death benefit of any insurance policies you have, unless they are held in an irrevocable life insurance trust.

Estate taxes are high, but not inevitable.

Chapter 6 – Investing Concepts

"Be guided by the facts, not by emotions."

There are many investing concepts that professionals tend to follow. Some are just rules of thumb that may or may not have lasting value, and others are sound guidelines that you would do well to heed. I want to introduce a few of my favorites that I feel everyone should be aware of to assist you in understanding the actions of your Good Financial Advisor and communicating effectively with him.

Choose With Care

If you choose to read more on investing, you will find other investing concepts that may help you, to a greater or lesser extent. I encourage you to do so, because it will help your understanding of the investment process. Try to avoid the fools, idiots and dummies types of books. They tend to reduce everything to meaningless simplicity. They may do as much harm as good for those who wish to become truly educated. Also, try to avoid such simplistic concepts as "Sell in May and go away." This refers to a strategy to avoid the summer slow period, when many market professionals are on vacation. Ignore hemline lengths, and who won the Super Bowl, and stick to sound basics. Given enough time, and a computer, you can come up with any number of meaningless relationships that correlate with the stock market (it's called data mining). In addition, any rule that really works will quickly be followed by so many others that, by definition, it will soon fail to work.

Prudent Man Rule

One of the concepts that some professionals follow in investing is called The Prudent Man Rule, here quoted from Justice Samuel Putnam in 1830.

"All that can be required of a trustee to invest is that he shall conduct himself faithfully and exercise sound discretion. He is to observe how men of prudence, discretion and intelligence manage their own affairs, not in regard to speculation, but in regard to the permanent disposition of their own funds,

considering the probable income as well as the probable safety of the capital to be invested."

It has a nice ring to it in this day of complicated and convoluted laws and rules. Ask your prospective or current advisor if he is familiar with the Prudent Man Rule. If he says no (or worse doesn't know that it exists), you might want to look for another advisor. If he says yes, ask him for a copy of it. If he does not have a copy, keep this book handy. Read it now and then whenever you decide to take a lot of risk with your invested assets. Whenever you invest new funds, reread it first to avoid rash decisions.

Concepts Help You Understand

In order to invest well, you should have an awareness of some of the other common investing concepts that will help you to become a better long-term investor. The concepts discussed in the following chapters are by no means all-inclusive, but they will help you to get started on the road to better investing. There are others that I felt went beyond the scope of this book that would add to your knowledge of investing. As I said in Chapter 1, there are many good books that expand on investing, and I encourage everyone to read them if you are so inclined. The twelve investing concepts that follow in Chapters 6B through 6M will allow you to communicate with your Good Financial Advisor in a way that will improve your ability to work with him, and increase your chances of achieving your financial goals.

Short Run vs. Long Run

Remember that in the short run, the stock market is a voting machine and is swayed by investor behavior, external shocks (wars) and public sentiment (technology bubble) to name a few factors. In the long run it is a weighing machine, and invariably follows the fundamentals of the market. The only two fundamental variables that affect the long-term level of the market are interest rates and earnings. Everything else is noise.

Ignore the noise and invest to win.

Chapter 6A – The Wonder of the IPS

"Learn from the past, live for today, plan for the future"

The Investment Policy Statement, or IPS, is a document that you should receive from the Good Financial Advisor if your portfolio is of sufficient size. It will clearly spell out what she intends to do, and what you hope to accomplish, with your investment portfolio. It need not be long, and may even be a single paragraph. It may be provided orally in the case of smaller or simple portfolios. It should contain the essence of what is needed to direct your Good Financial Advisor, and achieve your goals for the portfolio.

If an advisor declines to provide an IPS when you ask for one, I would seek out another advisor. No reputable financial advisor should decline this request. Writing down what the investment portfolio is all about is just good practice. It avoids a lot of misunderstandings should events unfold differently than anticipated.

A typical IPS might contain the following:

- The assumptions used to establish the IPS: Tax rates, interest rates, inflation rates, historical data, and the like, where relevant.

- The level of risk you are willing to tolerate, and your risk capacity regarding loss of principal.

- The target asset allocation of the portfolio.

- The performance goal of the portfolio, and the benchmarks that will be used to evaluate that performance. Do not be fooled by artificial benchmarks that make it appear that the portfolio is doing well, when it is actually underperforming its true benchmark. Ask your advisor to explain the benchmark she is using, to be sure it represents the IPS goals. Some typical benchmarks would be the Lehman Brothers Aggregate Bond Index, the Morgan Stanley Europe, Australasia and Far East Index (MSCI EAFE), and the S&P 500 Index. If you change benchmarks, it should only be for a good reason, such as a change in your portfolio and its goals.

- The dollar value target of the portfolio when the performance goal is reached.

- The time frame in which the performance goal is to be reached.

- The time frame, if any, during which funds will be withdrawn.

- How the funds will be used. If funds are necessary to maintain a minimum standard of living in retirement, they may be viewed different from funds earmarked to buy a classic red convertible.

- How often the portfolio will be reviewed. This should be annually at a minimum, and more often for complex portfolios. I prefer twice a year for regular portfolio reviews, with additional meetings for other subjects as necessary.

- How frequently the Good Financial Advisor and you should communicate with each other, outside of scheduled service appointments.

- Under what guidelines or circumstances will the portfolio be rebalanced, or restructured.
  Rebalancing means restoring the portfolio to its original asset allocation (or an equivalent updated asset allocation), if circumstances warrant, due to variances in growth between the asset classes. For example, if you started with a portfolio that was 50% equities and 50% bonds, and equities grew by 30% over a three year period and bonds grew by 15% over that same period, you would then have a portfolio that was weighted 53% equities and 47% bonds. It would require selling 3% of the equities and purchasing 3% more bonds to restore the original 50/50 balance.
  Restructuring means revising the asset allocation because of changes in the external environment, goals, risk tolerance/capacity, or timeframe, that makes a revision appropriate. For example, if you retire and want to begin taking income from your investment portfolio, and it is 80% equities because it was designed for growth, you will have to create a new portfolio with a much higher share of bonds in order to generate that income.
  There are no hard and fast rules that guide rebalancing or restructuring. It is essentially up to you and your Good Financial Advisor and his expertise. I expand on this in Chapter 71 on Portfolio Construction.

A complex IPS can contain much more than this, but any IPS should accomplish the same purpose. It should tell you, and your Good Financial Advisor, what to do with the investment portfolio under most foreseeable circumstances.

A well-written IPS benefits you by helping to keep the portfolio on track. It sets expectations, and will likely result in a more satisfying relationship over time by reducing misunderstandings. It can also prevent short-term reactions to happenings in the market.

The main drawback to an IPS is that it does require substantial time and effort on the part of both you and the Good Financial Advisor to develop. In my experience, this is time well spent for both parties. Some advisors may charge for the time and effort spent to revise a portfolio if they are not getting an asset-based fee on the account. This is acceptable as long as the charge is reasonable relative to the effort involved.

Bear in mind that investing should not be viewed in the same context as buying a lottery ticket. You cannot live your life hoping that one great investment will make you wealthy overnight. *And the best time to invest, as well as the hardest, is always <u>now</u>.*

Let the Investment Policy Statement be your roadmap

on the journey to financial independence.

Chapter 6B – Risk and Your Tolerance Of It

"Risk. You can't see it, smell it, taste it, feel it, hear it, or weigh it, yet it is everywhere at all times."

Risk is difficult to measure. Traditionally, it is measured using Standard Deviation, which sounds like a nasal problem. It really is a measure of volatility that tells you how much your investment may go up or down in a given period of time. We don't worry much about the up part of volatility, but when it goes down, people become increasingly uncomfortable. Therefore, you should get familiar with risk and volatility so you can understand your portfolio and how it will vary over time.

Risk Defined

Many people look only at risk as the possibility of loss, but it is more than that. My favorite definition of risk is this:

Risk is the uncertainty of the expected return.

Simply put, it means these two things, <u>measured at the time you need your money:</u>

1) What is the chance that it will be there?

2) What is the chance you got the return you expected?

1) Defines the risk of loss, or return of the principal value of their investment. Everyone worries about return <u>on</u> their investment when they should also worry about return <u>of</u> their investment, which I discuss in Chapter 6C.
2) Means that you have the quantity of money you anticipated when you made the initial investment.

Both of these must happen at the right time, which is when you need your money, not at some later date. If your return comes earlier than needed, be sure to secure it by taking profits and fixing the return.

Before you need your money, the actual return is not too meaningful.

When you need your money, nothing else counts.

Investing vs. Speculating

Look at the definition of an investment in Chapter 7 to make sure you do not confuse investing with speculation, which involves high and generally immeasurable risk.

If you let someone take enough risk with your money, they will occasionally make some for you, or lose it all. Professional athletes seem to learn this lesson well, and often. I have told this story many times in my investing classes.

> *A wealthy businesswoman called in two financial advisors and asked each of them to invest $100,000 for her. "Come back in one year and report on how you have done with my money." She said and sent them on their way.*
>
> *A year later, both advisors returned to her office, and she asked the first advisor how he had done.*
>
> *"I am glad to tell you that I doubled your money over the last year." said the advisor.*
>
> *"How did you accomplish this?" asked the woman.*
>
> *"Well, I set you up in a diversified portfolio, rebalanced it at midyear, and took advantage of solid growth in the areas in which you were invested." He replied.*
>
> *"I am very pleased with your efforts and results", said the woman.*
>
> *She then turned to the second advisor and asked how he had done with her money. "I too am glad to tell you that I doubled your money", said the second advisor.*
>
> *"And how did you manage to do that?" asked the woman.*
>
> *Sheepishly, the second advisor responded, "I cannot lie to you, so this is what happened. I took your check last year, and inadvertently invested it in a cash management account until about a month ago. Realizing that I would be called here in a month, and that I had no hope of making any money for you in such a short time, I decided to go down to the local casino.*
>
> *There I bet all of your money on red at the roulette table and won. That is how I doubled your money."*

These are identical results with extremely different methods. Which advisor do you want handling your investments?

It's About Risk, Not Return

This is an exaggerated story to be sure, but the point is valid. If you do not know how much risk your financial advisor took with your money, how can you fairly judge the quality of the result, even when he makes a positive return?

When an advisor loses money for you, it is safe to say you are not pleased with that result (unless you signed a letter of instruction telling him it was okay to lose your money!). You should be equally curious when the result is a gain, since a high-risk investment approach is more likely to fail one day, with potentially adverse results for your portfolio.

At every regularly scheduled service meeting, it is appropriate to ask these questions regarding risk (See Chapter 3O on Client Service Expectations):

1) How much risk did you take with my portfolio, to achieve the results you are showing me today?

2) Should the level of risk be revised, based on changes since our last review?

The Good Financial Advisor will welcome the opportunity to show you what results he provided, what level of risk you took, and what revisions, if any, are warranted. He will assure you that you received value for the fees you paid.

Types of Risk

Risk and reward are always related in the long run. Therefore, you should have a familiarization with the various types of risk that you face, in order to understand what you can expect from your portfolio. What types of risk are there? Here is my list, in no particular order:

Interest Rate Risk – When interest rates rise, the value of your bonds, or bond fund, typically goes down. When rates are at historic low levels, this should be a concern to everyone.

Reinvestment Risk – When your fixed income investment comes due, you may have to reinvest the money at a much lower interest rate than you had anticipated. This is a common occurrence with certificates of deposit.

Currency Risk – The value of the currency in which your investments are denominated falls, reducing your return when converted back to dollars. This is a serious concern in international investing, but affects every company that does business outside this country. Some mutual funds hedge currency risk, so when the value of the U.S. dollar falls you do not get the benefit or impact of currency translation in your international investments.

Purchasing Power Erosion Risk – When your investments fail to keep pace with inflation and taxes you lose; so while your nominal return is positive your real return is negative. You are safely losing money. Keep in mind that money has no value beyond what it will purchase. This will be discussed in Chapter 6K on the Definition of Money.

Liquidity Risk – You are unable to sell your investment without causing a drop in its price. If you own a large share of a small company, you may not be able to sell a big stock position without causing the price to drop substantially.

Marketability Risk – You discover that there is no market for your investment at any reasonable price. This is typically an issue with private equity investments and limited partnerships.

Political Risk – This occurs when the government decides to do something that is not in your best interest. This can range from massive changes to existing programs, such as Social Security, to simply revising the tax laws to tax something you have that previously was not taxed. Losing property to the State or Federal Government through seizure by Eminent Domain is also a risk, borne mostly by individual property owners.

Country Risk – The government of the country nationalizes the company in which you invested, and pays you nothing for your ownership or other interest. Sometimes this is referred to as geopolitical risk.

Business Risk – When the business you invest in falters because it is made obsolete by a new development or product. Today, the computer business, and technology in general, is subject to significant business risk.

Company Risk – When the company you invested in fails to operate the way it should, either through mismanagement or bad management. Enron, Global Crossing and Tyco are a few of the companies that fit this category.

Industry Risk – You own a great company in an industry that suddenly becomes obsolete, similar to business risk. Think of the fate of buggy whips when cars became popular.

Credit Risk – This measures the degree to which a person or business to which you have loaned money may be unable to pay back the interest and principal you are owed on a timely basis. This applies primarily to bonds, and bond mutual funds, and is a big factor in "junk bonds".

Default Risk – When the party to which you loaned money fails to pay either principal or interest when due, they are in default, and the value of their note decreases significantly. This is a subset of Credit Risk that is very applicable to private loans. When you lend money to a friend or relative, be careful.

Legislative Risk – This is similar to political risk. When laws are passed that affect your financial assets, you can lose money. Declaring your land a wetland, and therefore unable to be developed, is a consequence of environmental protection laws. Changing the tax benefits of owning real estate devastated the real estate market in the late 1980's. You cannot assume that what you have is never going to change.

Mortality Risk (Dying Too Soon) – This is the effect of loss of life on meeting the financial goals of those who survive our passing. It seldom happens, but when it does the effects are tragic and far-reaching. This is why people need life insurance. Everyone knows someone who died very young, and left behind people with no way to make it financially. Don't let it be you. The Good Financial Advisor can estimate what your needs are and how much coverage you need to protect those you leave behind.

Longevity Risk (Living Too Long) – This is a fairly new risk. Many people will live well beyond their life expectancy, and they are not planning for it at all. They will either run out of money, or be forced to make drastic changes (reductions in quality) in their lifestyle in later years, including leaving nothing to heirs. (See Chapter 2G)

Behavioral Risk – This is the risk that you will behave irrationally when it comes to your own financial plan or investment portfolio. Chapter 6L on Investor (Mis)behavior expands on why this is a serious risk for every investor. In my opinion, the odds of this occurring are about 100%.

Event Risk – This is the risk that some unforeseeable event, such as a report on a drug that causes it to be recalled, can impact your investment out of the blue.

The Risk of the Unknown – We don't know what we don't know. And what we do know that is not true can be very dangerous to our financial health. Think about it. (Remember Chapter 2). Unfortunately, we have far too much confidence in our ability to predict the future.

Risk Tolerance vs. Risk Capacity

No discussion of risk would be complete without addressing risk tolerance vs. risk capacity, because the difference is important.

Risk tolerance is your ability to stand the variances you incur in your financial plan or investment portfolio. Your portfolio may drop 20% one year, and it does not bother you a lot because you have a lot of tolerance for risk. However, if you need to preserve your entire portfolio, because you will begin taking systematic withdrawals in the next year, your capacity for risk is very small. In other words, even though you can stand it emotionally, you can't stand it financially. Always keep this difference in mind when you decide on what level of risk you should have in your portfolio.

The Biggest Risk of All

Had enough of risk? There are certainly other risks beyond the scope of this book, but this should give you the idea. If I could sum it up in one line, I would say that in my opinion the biggest risk is this:

The most important risk of all is the risk of
failing to meet your financial goals because
you did not assume sufficient risk.
Therefore, you must have financial goals.

Hint. See Chapter 2A on setting goals. The fact that you are even reading this book means you have a big head start over many others who are still waiting to hit the lottery.

Categorizing Yourself

No discussion of risk would be complete without a discussion of how you should categorize yourself on the risk tolerance spectrum. Many advisors use a risk tolerance questionnaire to determine your risk tolerance. Some of these are good, but most miss the mark, because they simply cannot go deep enough to understand your feelings and concerns. Treat them with skepticism, for they are better than nothing. I will review them in more detail after looking at classifications of risk.

Classifications of Risk

The following classifications should serve as a guideline to determining where you fall on the overall risk spectrum. They are of necessity imprecise, but they should keep you from making the Big Mistake because you took too much or too little risk.

Very Conservative – You want minimal variability in your portfolio. All investments should be fixed, guaranteed, or very low risk. Your primary goal is income, with no concern for growth of principal. You have no equities in your portfolio; it is 100% fixed-income. High grade bonds are usually held in mutual funds, although very short duration, high grade bonds may be held individually. Insured municipal bonds may be included.

Conservative – You want little variability in your portfolio. Some portions of it may vary a small amount, as long as the entire portfolio never drops in value for a given year. You want to keep pace with inflation and taxes, but growth beyond that is not necessary. You have a minimal portion of equities (less than 25%) in your portfolio, and they are primarily high quality equities held in mutual funds. You have no individual stocks. You may own some individual bonds.

Moderately Conservative – You are concerned about preservation of principal, but you can tolerate small annual drops in the portfolio (less than 10%) as the price you pay for modest growth potential. Some income is desirable, but you want growth beyond the rate of inflation and taxes. You have a blend of various types of high quality equities that range between 25% and 45% of the portfolio. You favor a value style of investing. You may own some high quality individual stocks, but they will be less than 10% of your portfolio. High quality individual bonds are fine, especially in a bond ladder.

Moderately Aggressive – You have a goal that requires a reasonable level of growth. You can tolerate a short-term loss of principal because you have sufficient time to allow it to recover. Income is secondary to growth of principal. You have a blend of equities that ranges between 45% and 70% of your portfolio. You have all types of equities, except for speculative asset classes. Value and growth styles are evenly balanced in the portfolio. Individual stocks will usually represent no more than 25% of the equity mix. Bonds will be the more aggressive type, and therefore will be held in mutual funds. You worry in the short-run, but are confident of the long-term.

Aggressive – You require average to above average growth over the long term, and income is not desirable or necessary. No class of equities is excluded from consideration for your portfolio, but speculative types are held to a minimum, and limited to the more aggressive asset classes. Equities make up 70% to 90 % of the portfolio, and it is biased towards growth style investments. Individual stocks may constitute up to 50% of the overall equity mix. Downturns in the market, and your portfolio, look like buying opportunities to you, not a cause for worry.

Very Aggressive – You are reaching for high performance in excess of the market. Equities make up 100% of your portfolio, and every asset class and style is eligible for inclusion. Individual stocks make up at least 50 % of the portfolio, and will include high-risk growth or momentum stocks. Bonds are usually excluded from your portfolio. You are not concerned over loss of principal, and can sleep well regardless of the length, or duration, of a falling market. Growth is your primary concern to the exclusion of everything else. You laugh at danger.

100% Individual Securities Portfolios

There are those who like individual stocks and bonds, and who wish to avoid mutual funds with their operating expenses and tax efficiency issues. They pay a reasonable commission to buy a stock or bond, and then hold it for a substantial period of time before selling it, or allowing the bond to mature. They avoid management fees, trading scandals, hidden expenses, embedded capital gains, and all of the other concerns that are associated with professionally managed investments.

So why wouldn't everyone want to do this? The answer is that unless you have a large enough portfolio so that you can purchase about 50 securities, to ensure that you are adequately diversified, you may incur risk beyond what you can tolerate or have the capacity to withstand. Picking a large number of high quality individual securities is a difficult task in itself. You also must do a lot of work to monitor that portfolio (buying and selling), or the results may suffer. In effect, you must create and manage your own mutual fund.

If you do have a portfolio large enough to warrant all individual holdings, but do not want to monitor it yourself, one option is to hold them in a managed account and pay an asset-based fee to a financial advisor to watch over them. This still eliminates some of the other expenses and tax issues, and keeps you from having to do all the work.

You can also pay an RIA a fixed fee not dependent on the size of the account to watch over the portfolio. This will eliminate any bias at all towards what or how large are your holdings, or when they should be bought or sold.

You will need a fairly large portfolio before these options will make sense from an economic point of view. Assuming each stock position is a minimum of $5,000, you must have about $250,000 to make this feasible.

So Where Do You Fit In?

Everyone likely falls into one of these categories or some mix of them, but there is no "correct" portfolio, so you can have a unique investment portfolio and still meet your financial goals.

If you do not fit exactly into one of these categories it is no cause for concern. Discuss them with the good Financial Advisor and he can tailor a portfolio that is right for you.

Risk Tolerance Questionnaires

Risk tolerance quizzes ask a lot of questions regarding choices you might make under different circumstances. For example, would you prefer an investment with a 50 % chance of returning 12% and a 50% chance of returning 0% or an investment with a 100% chance of returning 6%. They are statistically equal, but have different risk profiles. They also include questions on when you need the money, how long is your investment time frame, what is the money intended to be used for and similar general questions.

I am not a fan of these types of quizzes, because they are simply too tricky for the average person to answer in terms that will reveal their true risk tolerance. In addition, most of these quizzes are designed to find out what your <u>maximum</u> risk tolerance is under <u>ideal conditions,</u> rather than your average tolerance under all types of circumstances. This can lead you to invest more aggressively than you will be comfortable with when conditions turn down (as they absolutely will at some point). To get a better sense of your true risk tolerance ask the Good Financial Advisor how much he feels your portfolio can drop in dollars rather than percentages based on past experience.

Behavioral finance experts argue endlessly about the correct way to determine risk tolerance, so I won't try to settle the argument here. Just use common sense and your gut instinct when telling the Good Financial Advisor how much you can really lose on your statement before you start to lose sleep.

Control your risk, or it will control you.

Chapter 6C – Return <u>of</u> Investment

"I will gladly pay you Tuesday for a hamburger today."

The above quote from Wimpy of the Popeye cartoon series is a good example of risk of return <u>of</u> your investment, since your chance of getting your money back from Wimpy was pretty small. Return <u>of</u> investment is a concept that was all but forgotten in the last bull market when return <u>on</u> investment was all that seemed to matter. I mentioned it as a part of my favorite definition of risk, and it is an essential part of intelligent investing and wealth accumulation.

If you take too much risk with your investments, and lose a significant portion of your principal, you may be unable to recover that loss in a reasonable period of time (i.e. when you actually need the money), if at all.

And, as stated in the previous chapter, taking too little risk can also be dangerous to your financial health, since it may prevent you from reaching your financial goals.

Capital Losses and Recovery

Just as the Hippocratic Oath says that a doctor should first do no harm, a financial advisor should first lose no principal. If you suffer a loss in a given year of investing, it could take years of above average returns to restore the average target return level. Here is an example of what it means to lose 20% in a given year in which your target return is 8%, compared to an investment with a fixed rate of return of 5%.

Matching a Fixed Rate of Return

When you incur a 20% first year loss on an investment that generates a fixed 8% return in subsequent years, it takes nearly ten more years for you to equal a 5% fixed rate of return. I believe this explains why older investors utilize guaranteed fixed annuities, or similar investments, much more so than younger investors do. They intuitively grasp this concept, because they do not have an extended period of time to recover from a drop in the value of their investment.

Matching Your Original Target Rate of Return

If you incur a 20% first year loss on an investment that was targeted to return 8% on average for 10 years, you must achieve a return of about 11.7% for each of the remaining 9 years, just to reach your original target return of 8%.

That is a difficult return to achieve, and unlikely to happen, unless you take on significantly more risk, which puts you back into the higher risk situation where you incurred the 20% loss. This is not a virtuous cycle.

Be Careful – It's Your Money

Do not put your investment at significant risk of loss unless you have adequate time or resources to recover, and still reach your financial goals. If you wish to have some aggressive investments, such as individual stocks, make sure they constitute only a small part of your overall portfolio and they are diversified in their own right. I recommend to clients that these types of investments should not exceed 10% of a portfolio (5% is about right), and they must be able to lose 100% of the investment's value and still achieve their financial goals.

Many great money managers will candidly tell you that one of the main reasons for their success is that they avoided large losses. This is such an easy idea to grasp, yet it is so often ignored. The Good Financial Advisor will always be cognizant of the fact that you did not give him approval to lose your money.

The Good Financial Advisor will address

return of investment in the

Investment Policy Statement.

Chapter 6D – Opportunity Cost

"That red convertible looks so much nicer than an investment account statement."

Opportunity cost in this context is what is lost when one spends instead of saves. Saving, or deferred gratification, is difficult to accept when you are young (and almost as hard when you are old). Yet, if we were to save a little when we are young, and have years to go for our investment to grow and compound, our retirement would be more financially secure.

Try to view all of your discretionary expenditures as opportunity costs and it will help you to avoid wasteful or high cost spending when you develop your Spending Plan (Chapter 2D).

We saw this in Chapter 4D with our two friends, Frugal Fred and Extravagant Ed. Fred chose to defer some of life's pleasures for a few years and secured a sound retirement very early in life. Ed was forced to work and save from age 32 on to secure his retirement. Balance your current and future wants and needs so you can enjoy all that life has to offer.

Two College Graduates

An easy example to illustrate opportunity cost is the purchase of a first car by two 22-year-old college graduates. When your daughter or son graduates from college, they have a choice to either save or spend, and here is what could happen.

Frugal Fred decides to buy a 2-year-old car for $10,000, puts $2,000 down and finances the balance at 8% for 3 years. His car depreciates by $5,000 over the next 5 years and is covered by a 7-year maintenance warranty.

Extravagant Ed buys a new car for $25,000, puts the same $2,000 down and finances the balance over 5 years at 8%. Ed's car depreciates by $15,000 over the next 5 years, and it is also covered by a 7-year maintenance warranty.

Fred pays about $250 per month over 3 years and then owns his car outright. Ed pays $466 per month for 5 years and then owns his car outright.

At the end of 5 years, here's how they compare, assuming equal salaries, and that Frugal Fred invested the additional cash flow he had from purchasing a less expensive car. Fred had about $2,600 extra in years 1, 2 and 3 to invest, and about $5,600 in years 4 and 5. If invested in an account earning 9% per year, Fred had a total of about $21,000 in his investment account, while Ed had nothing.

The $140,000 Car

Ed had a car worth about $10,000 vs. Fred's car worth about $4,000, giving Ed a $6,000 advantage. In total, Fred was about $15,000 ahead because of his wise purchase of a lower cost car. That is a down payment on a condo, or if left until age 67 for retirement, an additional $470,000. Even at 3% inflation, that represents about $140,000 in today's dollars.

That is serious money by any measure, and is the opportunity cost to Ed of buying a new car, instead of a more affordable used car. All numbers are approximate in this example, and I make no value judgments about Ed's ability to impress girls with his new car, vs. Fred's older car. But I definitely want to be Fred forty years from now.

Consumption vs. Savings

It is important to understand that money spent on consumption, instead of savings, has a serious impact on your financial future. You forego the opportunity to build wealth when you spend instead of save. All wealth accumulation was accomplished by spending less than your income. Wishing for a higher income (or hoping to hit the lottery), and spending accordingly, is a strategy that is doomed to fail.

Using reasonable assumptions, the opportunity cost of smoking a pack of cigarettes a day from the age of 18 to 67 is about $1,500,000 as I stated in Chapter 2G. I won't even try to estimate the opportunity cost of a drug or alcohol habit.

Don't lose the opportunity

to enjoy a secure and comfortable retirement.

Chapter 6E – Diversification

"Bet not the farm"

Whoever first stated that you should not put all of your eggs in one basket could have been a hungry farmer who did not want to miss breakfast. Another way of putting it is that the only investors who do not need to diversify are those whose investment selections are correct 100% of the time.

True vs. Meaningless Diversification

Diversification is the fundamental way in which you manage the level of risk in your portfolio, and ensure a reliable and somewhat predictable rate of return. In practice there are a number of ways in which you should be diversified, and I will cover these in this chapter.

Meaningless diversification is one of the most common errors I have found in self-directed portfolios. This occurs when the investor has five different mutual funds that contain about 80% common holdings, and all of it is concentrated in one style, two asset classes and three sectors. In 1999 it was common to find someone with several large-cap growth funds (heavily weighted in technology), that thought he was well diversified. By the end of 2002 it was obvious that he wasn't.

True diversification involves more than selecting funds from different companies or having one equity fund and one bond fund. There are many ways in which a well-structured portfolio should be diversified.

Methods of Diversification

- Diversify between fixed income investments (bonds) and equity investments (stocks). More than anything else, this will determine the overall level of risk in your portfolio.

- Diversify among asset classes based on company size or market capitalization (the number of shares of outstanding common stock times the current price of the stock). There are large, mid and small capitalization companies, and variations on them such as mega cap (very large) and micro cap (very small). Different size asset classes perform in different ways at various stages of the business cycle, and respond in various ways to changes in interest rates.

- Diversify among mutual fund companies, regardless of sales charge breakpoints, unless you have a portfolio in excess of a million dollars. No single fund company has a monopoly on high returns or low risk. Sales charge breakpoints were designed to coax you into concentrating your funds with one company, but a sales charge reduction of 1% or 2 % is not worth the risk of having your entire portfolio in the hands of a single company. I know many good mutual fund companies, but none to which I would entrust all of my money. Each company has its strengths, and you can benefit from their diversification among research and management styles.

- Diversify outside of the USA into international investments. The majority of market capitalization is outside the United States today, and many good investment opportunities are available in foreign countries.

- Diversify among taxable, tax-deferred and tax-free investments. See Chapter 9B for more discussion of tax control. You do not want all of your investment gains and income to be subject to the same taxation.

- Diversify among investments that produce ordinary income and those that produce long-term capital gains. See Chapter 9A on tax deferral for more details

- Diversify among sectors of the economy, such as technology, energy, and consumer goods. Based on some recent studies, sector diversification may be more important than asset class size diversification in determining risk and return. I believe this may be the most important form of diversification in your portfolio in a market downturn.

- Diversify among investment styles such as value and growth. See Chapter 6I.

- Diversify among lower-risk and higher-risk investments. Enough said on risk already in Chapter 6B.

- Diversify among interest rate sensitive and interest rate insensitive investments. When interest rates go up, as they almost always will when the government decides to raise rates to slow the economy down, you do not want all of your investments to follow.

- Diversify among short-term and long-term investments. You do not know the future.

There is no Perfect Portfolio

Will you always be able to create the perfectly diversified portfolio? Probably not, but in trying to do so, you will tend to avoid the horribly concentrated portfolios that can devastate your long-term returns.

Remember that a truly diversified portfolio will always have some investments going up while others are going down or lagging. If all of your investments are going up at the same time and rate, or going down identically in a true bear market, you probably do not have real diversification. The technical term for this is positive correlation and you should question the Good Financial Advisor when this occurs.

The Good Financial Advisor will discuss these elements of diversification with you as you go through the Investment Policy Statement, and may use a software program to evaluate your portfolio to ensure that it really is diversified.

Even when you diversify well,

you should still keep a close eye on your baskets.

Chapter 6F – Asset Allocation

"Let a man put a third of his wealth in land, a third of his wealth in assets, and a third in the coin of the realm."

That was good advice then and now. Asset allocation is the process of diversifying a portfolio among various types of asset classes, in order to reduce portfolio risk, and enhance risk-adjusted returns.

Today, most financial advisors use some variation of asset allocation modeling to design a portfolio for you, typically using computer software from various sources. Asset allocation is not designed to produce the highest absolute return, but rather tries to create an optimal portfolio on the risk vs. return "efficient frontier" curve, giving you the highest return at a certain level of risk.

Two Investors

Look at this comparison of two hypothetical investors to see what asset allocation can do regarding risk and return. Both investors are the same age and risk tolerance, and each had $30,000 to invest.

The first investor placed all of her assets in a guaranteed product, such as a certificate of deposit, and kept it there for twenty years, getting an annual return of 5%. This was a "safe" investment that required little monitoring.

The second investor divided her assets evenly among four asset classes, with these results:

- One class went bankrupt and all of it was lost. This was a hot stock tip from a friend at work.

- One class got a return of 5% similar to the first investor. This was a CD at the local bank, which just kept renewing every 5 years.

- One class got a return of 8%, in a diversified portfolio of mutual funds, 60% equity and 40% bonds.

- One class got a return of 12%, in an individual stock portfolio of high-quality, blue-chip stocks.

After the failure of her first investment, the second investor got help from a financial advisor to set up and manage her mutual fund and stock portfolios. This is how they compared after twenty years:

The first investor had about $79,600 at the end of 20 years.

The second investor had the following results:

- From the failed investment, nothing.

- From the 5% investment, about $19,900.

- From the 8% investment, about $35,000.

- From the 12% investment, about $72,300.

Total: $127,200

The diversified portfolio produced about 60% more after 20 years, even though 25% of it had failed.

It's an Art, Not a Science

Asset allocation is not an exact science, and aspects of it are hotly debated today among investment professionals. Yet it does seem to reduce risk and produce more predictable returns. One concern is that if historical data is used, it can be incorrect in setting the direction for the future. This is particularly worrisome when it pertains to bonds and interest rates. The other concern, when selecting the asset classes in the correct proportion, is that those classes that have performed the best in the past five to ten years may not represent the best opportunities over the next five to ten years.

One of the worst mistakes investors make is "driving while looking in the rear view mirror". Studies have shown that picking last year's best performing mutual fund invariably leads to below average performance in the future. That is why you see the constant reminder that "Past performance is no guarantee of future results." on nearly every piece of literature designed for use by the retail investor.

What Model Should You Use?

Ask your Good Financial Advisor if he uses asset allocation modeling to design a portfolio, and what determines the specific asset allocation he recommends for you. He should consider your risk tolerance, how much you can afford to lose, your required or desired level of return, your investment time frame, and costs as they relate to the size of your portfolio (since it is impractical to have twenty asset classes in a $25,000 portfolio). The asset allocation he selects will likely determine the returns you get over time, assuming the fees are normal, and the quality of the investment selections is acceptable. If he does not use asset allocation to construct your portfolio, ask him what method he does use, and listen very carefully for the answer. Flying by the seat of your pants is not the way to go here. (See Chapter 7I on Portfolio Construction)

Tactical Asset Allocation

Tactical asset allocation is something you may hear about, and it is essentially a form of market timing. This is discussed in the next chapter. It consists of moving large amounts of the portfolio from one asset class to another, in response to changes in market conditions. I am not a proponent of this approach, because it has not been proven to work. Motion is not the same as action.

Asset allocation remains one of the most controversial issues in financial planning today, but properly used it can limit your risk and provide fairly reliable long-term investment results. As discussed in Chapter 9 on Tax Management Philosophy, and Chapter 7I on Portfolio Construction, asset allocation should also consider the location of assets relative to taxable and tax-deferred accounts.

The Good Financial Advisor will have an asset allocation model appropriate for your needs, and be able to explain it to you when developing your Investment Policy Statement and constructing your actual portfolio.

Watch your assets,

and your asset allocation.

Chapter 6G – Market Timing

"Do not let the perfect be the enemy of the good."

Market timing is a controversial method of asset allocation at the extreme, about which many books have been written, and numerous arguments waged. Those arguments will not be settled in this book, but you should have an understanding of what it is, and how it could affect your investment portfolio.

In the most basic form, market timing means moving your investments out of the equity market, to cash or its equivalent, when you think the overall market is going to drop in value. You then wait until the market looks more favorable, or appears to be heading up, and move your investments out of cash and back into the market, into whatever investments you choose. In simple terms, you must make two correct decisions in order for this to work. Good luck!

It sounds good, but so far, no one has ever been able to accurately determine when the market will go up or down. Typically investors move their money out of the market after it drops (selling low), and wait until the market is heading back up to reenter the market (buying high).

It can also mean moving assets from equities (stocks or stock mutual funds) to fixed income (usually bonds or bond mutual funds, money markets or CD's), depending on the direction of the market, interest rates, economic growth or other events which affect the market. This is equally difficult to do, and I have yet to find someone who has claimed to do this on a consistent basis.

Buy and Hold Is Not Set and Neglect

You may hear some advisors talk about a "buy and hold" investment approach. This does not mean "set and neglect", "set and forget", or "park and pray", three of the common slang versions of that strategy. Buy and hold should mean that you buy for the long-term, and hold until there is a good reason to sell, not because you are trying to time the ups and downs of the market.

Experience is Not Favorable

In my 36 years of investing, I have not found a simple or easy answer to this issue. My experience has been that moving in and out of the market does not work, because we never know what really lies ahead with any degree of certainty. Even if you miss a downward move, you inevitably miss the following upward move too. Remember, the market has a long-term bias upward. In a given period of time, your success will be the result of a few large upward moves of the market. If you miss them, you lose. Many charts are put out by investment firms showing what your results would be if you miss the best 10 or 20 days out of a ten year period, and the results are dramatic.

Keep in mind that those same investment firms also want you to keep your money invested with them, so they have a bias towards having investors stay the course through any kind of market. When you move out of investments to cash, certificates of deposit, a bank, or under your pillow, they make little or no money on those assets. The Good Financial Advisor has the same bias since he makes little or no money unless you are invested with him, except when he is paid on a fee-only basis. In that case, it is difficult to justify a large fee to watch over assets held in a certificate of deposit or money market account. In the end, the best course is to stay invested in an appropriately constructed portfolio.

Meeting Investment Goals Is Key

The relevant question to ask yourself is this: Given your investment goals, can you achieve them if you are not invested in the market? If not, then going to cash may adversely affect your future. Therefore, make sure that your investment portfolio is sufficiently diversified so that you can weather short-term drops in the market. Do not take on more risk than you can comfortably handle when the going gets tough, which it always will at some point. Downturns in the market occur every 2 to 3 years, and you should be positioned to withstand them, emotionally as well as financially.

Changing Your Portfolio

If your financial advisor suggests that you move a large percentage of your portfolio because of a drop that has already occurred, be wary that you are not simply selling low, or in the worst case that he is churning your assets. Only major, and unforeseen, events should cause someone to make large, or sudden, changes in an investment portfolio.

On the other hand, your Good Financial Advisor may have sound reasons to recommend changes. If major events such as these occurred it might be appropriate to respond with portfolio revisions:

- War. It can affect world trade, government spending priorities, and business confidence.

- Tax law changes. Who knows what Congress can think of that will adversely impact you?

- Inflation Rate Changes. It can be harmful whether the outlook is inflationary or deflationary.

- A government policy shift by the Federal Reserve or congress. Someday they might decide to balance the budget, fix Medicare, or make Social Security solvent.

- Sudden and significant economic upheaval from a major terrorist attack.

- Fundamental changes in currency valuations. If China devalued its currency we would all be affected.

- Similar types of large scale, outside influences that we cannot anticipate.

These events will be rare, when they occur at all. Even if there is a small cost associated with portfolio changes, the benefits should far outweigh those costs. Those who refused to sell in 2000 at the height of the technology bubble, because of capital gains taxes that would be due, saw the value of their investments drop by far more than the taxes that they would have paid.

The better you understand what the impact of moving in and out of the market is, the more likely you are to achieve favorable long-term investment results. Market timing is very difficult to do well, if at all, and is potentially harmful to your long-term investment success. Use it with great caution and at your own risk.

Individual Investors vs. the Market

A Dalbar study showed that from 1985 to 2004, individual investors got a return of 3.7% from the market, while the average return of the S & P 500 index was 13.2% over that same period. Technically, this is explained by comparing time-weighted returns to dollar-weighted returns. Time-weighted returns measure the performance of an investment assuming you invested all of your money at the beginning of a period and remained invested until the end of that period. Dollar-weighted returns measure performance based on when your dollars were invested and over what time period. The only plausible explanation for the above results is that the individual investor bought high and sold low throughout that period, by moving in and out of their investments.

In my opinion, this one statistic shows the unquestionable value of having an unemotional and competent professional to aid you in difficult times. The above difference in returns overshadows all of the talk about fees, expenses and sales charges used by the do-it-yourself crowd. They have never refuted this study, most likely because they can't. Check out the Quantitative Analysis of Investor Behavior on the Dalbar website, www.dalbarinc.com, for more information.

The Downturn of 2008

As this book went to press, the latest market downturn that began on October 9, 2007, had brought the S&P 500 index down about 42% as of October 10, 2008, a significant drop to be sure in only a year. However, about 20% of that drop occurred in the ten days from September 26 to October 10, 2008, faster than anyone could anticipate or act to avoid.

The downturn was caused by the housing bubble/mortgage crisis/credit crisis, and if history is any guide, it will be followed by a recovery and the market will eventually go on to new highs. The patient long-term investor with a well structured portfolio need only let time and the Magic of Compounding take its course.

If you needed an example that shows the futility of trying to time your exit from the market (stocks and bonds boths went down), this was it. It is equally difficult to time your entrance back into the market, and as of October 20, 2008, the market had risen over 9% off its low.

Anyone can sail the ship when the sea is calm.

The Good Financial Advisor will make sure you can also

weather the inevitable storm.

Chapter 6H – Dollar-Cost Averaging

"Diving off the low board five times is not the same as diving off the high board once, but it sure is a lot easier on the nerves."

Dollar-cost averaging (DCA) is a risk management technique that is used to remove emotion from the investment decision process. It works like this. You invest a given amount of money, at specified intervals of time, regardless of what is going on in the market or the world. When the price of stocks, bonds, or mutual funds is lower, you will buy more of them. When the price of these investments is higher, you will buy less of them. In a very volatile and declining market, your average cost might be less than if you simply invested all of your money at one time. In a steadily rising market DCA will provide no advantage at all, and will result in lower performance than lump-sum investing.

DCA arrangements usually call for regular monthly contributions to an investment account, or are used to fund an investment portfolio over a specified period of time, such as a year at quarterly intervals. Using the DCA technique allays the fear that investors have that they might invest a large sum of money on Tuesday, and find that on Friday the market has dropped 25%, or the fear that you are investing all of your funds at a market top. Based on historical experience, these fears are wildly overblown.

Dollar-Cost Averaging may Reduce Performance

There are many financial advisors, myself included, who believe that better results will be obtained over time by lump-sum investing. This is because the long-term trend of the stock market is upward, and a DCA technique nearly always yields poorer results than investing the money in a portfolio as soon as possible. Studies have been done that show this, yet DCA continues to be a popular method of investing for many people, most likely because of behavioral reasons. The potential reduction in performance from dollar-cost averaging should not be large enough to affect your ability to reach your financial goals.

DCA vs. Lower Risk portfolios

One of my concerns is that too often DCA is used as a technique to get you to assume more risk than you are really comfortable with, so that your money gets invested, period. Remember that an advisor typically does not get paid unless the money is actually invested in something besides cash. I believe a better technique is to use a lower risk portfolio to minimize your concern over risk of principal loss, and invest the funds in a lump-sum. In a properly structured portfolio, you can always increase the level of risk or aggressiveness of the portfolio at a later date without incurring any added costs.

Do not let Dollar-Cost Averaging place you in an investment portfolio that has more risk than you can handle, or you could wind up with the worst of both worlds. That is selling out of an investment (out of fear of incurring further losses) that you took too long to get into in the first place (out of fear of future losses). The net result would be that you bought high, when you thought you were buying low, you sold lower because you incurred losses beyond what your risk tolerance or capacity could stand, and you waited until the market recovered before considering whether to reinvest (buying high again). That qualifies as a Big Mistake.

If your advisor recommends DCA to you, ask him to explain his rationale in light of the issues discussed above. If his rationale is sound, go ahead, but if he has no rationale except that this is a good way to get your money into the market, perhaps you should rethink the level of risk in the investment itself. In a long-term investment, the results in any given year will make little difference in your ability to reach your financial goals.

DCA vs. Market Timing

Historically, there have been few periods of time when a DCA strategy would have improved your results. If it makes you feel more comfortable than lump-sum investing, it may be right for you, as long as you understand its limitations. DCA comes dangerously close in some respects to being a form of market timing, especially when prolonged for an extended period. However, if you were to DCA over a very long time, such as your entire working career, there is a benefit to be had from overall risk reduction, versus lump-sum investing. A systematic retirement plan contribution is an example of this. The argument for or against will not be settled here or soon, but you should be aware of both sides of it.

In Chapter 7J, Withdrawing Money in Retirement, I mention that taking systematic withdrawals from your portfolio carries some of the same risks as dollar-cost averaging money into a portfolio. DCA in reverse can lead you to sell low when the market is down. Whether you are putting money in or taking it out, it requires paying attention to the volatility of your portfolio. The sequence of negative and positive returns in a portfolio affects the overall return of that portfolio when you are taking withdrawals. Therefore, portfolios must be designed with withdrawals in mind.

Check the height of that diving board

with the Good Financial Advisor,

before you take the plunge.

Chapter 6I – Growth vs. Value Investing

"The only time to buy things at a favorable price is when no one else wants them."

Growth and value are the two distinct investment styles most widely used in the investment world today, although there are variations that creep in now and then such as growth at a reasonable price (GARP). There is also deep value, momentum investing and many others, but generally you will see the most impact from how you choose between these two styles.

A Bias Towards Growth

Clients have a bias towards seeing their accounts grow, and may select growth styles because of the name, instead of their goal for the portfolio or their tolerance for risk. Financial advisors also have a vested interest in seeing a clients account grow, and therefore may be unwittingly biased towards a growth style. Over the years, either style has performed within 1 to 2 percentage points of each other, with value slightly ahead overall, so whether you favor growth or value, you should be able to achieve any reasonable portfolio objective.

Balance Growth and Value

I believe you should strive for a balance between value and growth in your portfolio. Since both styles perform relatively similar over time, this approach would seem to reduce overall portfolio risk, regardless of which style is in favor at any one point in time.

As to specific style risk, growth would seem to carry a somewhat higher risk profile, all other things being equal. As one value manager told me, the value manager makes money from a price-earnings ratio of about 7 to 13, while a growth manager makes money from a price-earnings ratio of 13 to 20.

With value stocks you usually have a larger margin of safety, because of their inherent characteristics. Value investors believe the market has become too pessimistic regarding a stock's future value.

Growth investors believe that continued high rates of growth are worth a lot, and are willing to pay higher prices to get stocks with high growth potential.

Growth and Value may Be Identical

In many instances, growth and value investments are so similar as to blur the distinction between them. There are numerous articles written by some of the best money managers of today describing identical stocks as both a value and growth selection. This is similar to why the perception of a half-full glass of water depends on whether you are the person who intends to drink it or the person who is pouring it. As long as you are well diversified, you should be able to achieve your financial goals with either style.

There is value in growth,

and growth in value.

Chapter 6J – Historical Performance

"<u>Nothing</u> is a guarantee of future performance."

Chasing hot performance or last year's winners is a sure losing strategy. Every study I have ever read on this subject, warns about picking last year's hot investment for the year ahead. When Dalbar released their study of mutual fund performance vs. individual investor results from 1985 through the end of 2004, the results were eye-opening. As mentioned in Chapter 6G on Market Timing, the average investor underperformed the market by a significant amount over the past ten years. The only reasonable answer as to why that could occur is that investors bought high and sold low on a regular basis. This also is a big argument against the do-it-yourself using an index fund crowd, because people tend to misbehave, as I describe in detail in the next chapter.

Past Performance is no Guarantee of Future Results

There is a reason that most of the sales literature you see contains the words, "Past performance is no guarantee of future results." Because it is true, due to that word "guarantee". And most studies have shown that if you invest based solely on past performance (chasing last year's best fund), as many do, your results will be substantially less than average. Yet, past performance is one of the best indicators of potential future performance when you look at the right information.

Consider this when looking at past performance. Do you really want the absolute best performing fund of the prior year? Wouldn't you like to know how that fund outperformed the other thousand or so funds in its category? Was it due to pure genius on the part of the portfolio manager, concentration in a hot sector like energy, dumb luck, adherence to prudent diversification, a few great stock picks, or leverage using borrowed money? If you don't know you should find out. The chances of repeating performance of that magnitude are small, and if and when the fund regresses to the mean you will get hurt by the losses in your portfolio.

Fund managers are the Key

One of the few good indicators of future performance is the past performance of the people managing the investments or fund. However, you need to understand how the performance was derived to see if it is likely to continue in the future. Experienced investment managers, with excellent long-term records, are more likely to give you good results going forward than those with poor records. Remember those two financial advisors in Chapter 6B.

Some recent studies indicate that the record of the fund manager is much more important in determining the future performance of a fund, than the actual record of the fund itself. This makes good sense to me, and I would consider it well before simply investing in a fund without a record backed up by its manager. It is impossible to ignore the long-term records of some of the great money managers, who have outperformed their benchmarks for a decade and longer. The fact that many money managers can outperform the market is proof in my eyes that mispriced assets exist, the Random Walk Theory notwithstanding. The big question is how do you find them? As of this writing, a rating service is emerging that rates the fund managers instead of the fund. Keep watching for the results of their studies.

Index Fund Performance

My aversion to Index Funds is that they eliminate any possibility to select these mispriced assets. They eliminate the chance to outperform, by offering what appears to be a minimal chance to underperform in a specific asset class.

Since asset allocation is more important to long-term performance than fund selection, the argument that you can outperform by simply choosing index funds is hard to make. Asset allocation is much more important to your long-term results. In addition, if your financial goals do not require you to even match the market performance to achieve them, then you are just taking on excessive risk with passive investments. Read more on this in Chapter 7D on Index Funds.

Fund Size Makes a Difference

One other issue that you should be aware of is the size (as measured in dollars of assets under management) of a fund relative to its historical performance. Funds that performed well when they were smaller, say ten years ago, may not be performing as well today when they are significantly larger. However, their 5, 10, 15 and 20 year performance records will be heavily influenced by their earlier favorable performance. There is an entire body of thought that argues against mega-sized funds, and one look at Fidelity's Magellan Fund will show how a fund becomes nearly unmanageable when its size becomes too large.

Watch the size of the funds you are invested in. All things being equal, a smaller fund may have less risk in a down market, and better potential performance overall. I would keep an eye on it, because I have talked to fund managers who have told me that it is nearly impossible to sustain a high level of performance when the fund becomes too large. As proof of this, fund companies will close funds and refuse to accept any more money when they believe a fund becomes too large to manage.

Bulls vs. Bears

You will hear the term Bull Market, which signifies a stock market that is going up because everyone is bullish or optimistic, as the time to get in and make money. You will also hear the term Bear Market, which signifies a market that is going down because everyone is bearish or pessimistic, as the time to get out before you lose your money.

Having read about market timing I hope you understand that bulls and bears both create a lot of b—s—t (More on this in Chapter 7G). If you have an investment plan, and are well diversified, you are very capable of riding out the ups and downs of the market. In the past 20 years, clients who invested well, and stayed invested, did significantly better than those who bought and sold based on bull or bear markets, as evidenced by that Dalbar study mentioned in chapter 6G. Historically, the market has been on a steady upward trend for its entire existence. It is unlikely to change tomorrow.

Forget the bulls & bears - Soar with the eagles!

Chapter 6K – The Definition of Money

"Things are not always what they seem to be, and a dollar isn't what it used to be."

If you want to understand what the end game of investing is all about, it helps to understand what the real definition of money is, versus what it appears to be.

Money is only a measure of purchasing power. Currency is the paper the government issues to represent money, in order to facilitate financial transactions. Don't confuse protecting the face value of your currency, with its actual purchasing power. Here is an example that will help illustrate this point.

Purchasing Power Is the True Measure

Assume that today it costs $20,000 to buy the sedan of your choice, a Whizmobile with just the right options. You have $20,000 to buy the car but you want to wait three years because your current car is still running well. You decide to put the money in a 3 year CD paying 2.5% per year until you are ready to buy the new car.

During the next three years, inflation is about 3% and car prices track inflation, so the cost of that Whizmobile is now about $21,855.

Meanwhile, you have had to pay taxes each year on your CD earnings at a rate of 25%, so your CD has increased in value to just $ 21,146. You are now short, by $709, the amount you need to buy your car, even though you put your money in a guaranteed investment.

You have not lost any "money", since its face value has actually increased, but you certainly lost purchasing power. Your money will no longer buy the car you wanted, just three years later. This is an example of purchasing power erosion risk, and shows why a CD is usually not a good long-term investment.

Another way to look at it is, if someone offered you Ten Thousand Kronayen for your car, would you sell it without knowing what the Kronayen were worth? Not likely, until you knew what the Ten Thousand Kronayen could buy in terms you could evaluate. (Since Kronayen do not exist, having been made up for illustration purposes, you made a good decision.)

Beware of Losing Money Safely

Always evaluate your investments in terms of the overall inflation rate of the economy, and the taxes you will have to pay on the earnings, before you determine that the investment is "safe". Safely losing their savings is an experience that has befallen many investors. It is not what you earn on your investments that is important, it is what purchasing power you maintain after taxes and inflation that counts.

When you look at the value of your portfolio, look at it in terms of what it can buy, not its numerical dollar value. Even 3% inflation can seriously erode the purchasing power of your money with time (Purchasing Power Erosion Risk). You will read about the Rule of 72 and the Time Value of Money in Chapter 7, where this is discussed in more detail.

A dollar <u>is</u> what it used to be.

Just paper!

Chapter 6L – Investor (Mis)Behavior

"Conclusions are drawn based on reason. Decisions are made based on emotion"

There are books written on the unpredictable behavior of investors that go well beyond the scope of this book. Suffice it to say that behavior is an important factor in how we do as investors, and you need to understand how your behavior can impact your financial future.

Here is the essence of what I believe you need to know about behavior in general, to help you avoid the types of behavior than can be harmful to your financial health.

In economic and financial analysis it is assumed that people are rational and consistent, even when it is fairly obvious that investors are many (if not most) times not rational in their investment decisions, nor consistent in their behavior, even when they think they are. You are probably not a rational investor or financial planner.

Behavioral Characteristics

There are a number of generally accepted characteristics of investor behavior that you should be aware of when making decisions for yourself. It is beyond the scope of this book to explore these in detail, but a brief note on each will give you the general idea.

Narrow Framing

People tend to look at investments individually, rather than at their entire portfolio, their asset allocation, or the total risk they are taking. Looking at specific stocks or sectors can lead you to make bad decisions on your own behalf. Remember that in a truly diversified portfolio, some asset class has to be performing below average, in the opposite direction of the best performing asset class. If every part of your portfolio goes up and down at the same time, and in roughly the same proportions, you probably are not very well diversified. You want assets that are not correlated with each other.

Disposition Effect

People tend to sell their good investments and hold on to their bad investments. You should do the opposite, but it is more gratifying to say I sold and made a profit, than to say I sold and took a loss. What you paid for an investment is not relevant to whether you should sell or keep it, but many people let emotion affect this decision. Don't reward yourself by selling a winner and patting yourself on the back, when you should be selling a loser, and taking the punishment for making a bad investment decision. Letting your winners run is a hallmark of great portfolio managers. And, if you really have a sell discipline (Chapter 7), you will sell your losers before they do significant harm to your portfolio.

Home Bias

People like to invest in things they are familiar with, such as companies in their home state, or companies that make a product that they use every day, in the mistaken belief that they know more about these companies than others. This also affects International vs. Domestic investing decisions by biasing you to this country, even when better opportunities exist outside our shores. It is important to keep an open mind regarding your actual knowledge of investment opportunities.

Loss Aversion

Why do people sell their investments after they have gone down in value? It seems logical to buy things that have gone down in value, but we have a fear of loss that kicks in at some point, and overrides our sense of logic. Many investors project performance by assuming that if they lost 20% in the previous two months, in eight more months they will have nothing left.

An advisor can help remove the emotional aspect of investing, and prevent panic selling at low points, a large source of poor investor performance. In time you can learn to avoid selling at low points, and instead, look for buying opportunities, even though a sell discipline is the one thing missing in most investor's bag of tricks. People are inherently risk averse. They hate losses much more than they like gains, and that leads to irrational investment decisions.

Regret & Hindsight Bias

Hindsight bias means that you tend to view outcomes as more predictable after they actually happen, than before they occur. Things that do not occur seem less likely to have occurred before. We make the outcomes conform with our beliefs today, not what we were thinking beforehand. Before you say, "I knew that was a good or bad idea" think back to a time prior to the decision, and see if you are right, or just revising your view of events.

Regret is the feeling we have when an outcome is bad. We feel more regret from an action that causes a loss, than a lack of action that turns out to be a missed opportunity. Therefore, we tend to delay investing when we are concerned about possible losses. Investors who delay for a couple of years in a rising market will then rationalize that inaction by assuming there is no sense investing now, because the market is due for a fall.

Anchoring

This refers to using an artificial point of reference when making a judgment about something. As an example, using a benchmark of 1,200 for the S & P 500 will lead us to think that it will be higher in the future than if we use a benchmark of 600. The number becomes the anchor. When looking at your portfolio, don't get hung up on beating the market or an index, when your long-term goal is what is relevant. The benchmark in your Investment Policy Statement is important, in order to keep you focused on the proper goal.

Mental Accounting

In its most simple definition, this is what happens when you begin playing with your winnings, or the house money as the casinos call it. People also tend to treat different investments in different ways, rather than looking at their overall portfolio. In company 401(k) plans, people may view the stock of their company as safer than other equity investments, sometimes leading to an overweighting in their company stock.

Media Response

You must be able to distinguish news from noise. Listening to radio, and watching TV daily, can be detrimental to your investment success, because people tend to be overactive. They buy and sell too often, and miss long term trends and the benefit of compounding. They also incur too large a tax bill, because of the less favorable treatment of short-term capital gains. Learn to filter out the noise, and use only the information that pertains to long-term investment success. Don't buy the stock of the day, instead buy the stock of the next decade.

Optimism & Overconfidence

We have an unfounded belief that good things will happen to us, and bad things will happen to others. We are also overconfident with respect to our abilities and knowledge of the world around us. This leads us to believe that we can predict the future with far more certainty than is actually possible. If you doubt this, ask yourself how many people will admit that they are average or below-average drivers. Nearly everyone feels they are an above-average driver, and we know that is not true.

People tend to invest when they are overconfident or comfortable, and that is typically when the market is very high. They also tend to sell their investments when they are concerned or uncomfortable, and that is typically when the market is low. This is a recipe for investing mediocrity at best. You should place little confidence in anyone's ability to predict earnings, interest rates or the direction of the market.

Herding

People tend to follow the crowd. If everyone is buying a stock, it doesn't matter how overpriced it is, they want to be in on the action. This is why I recommend that you ignore advice from general media outlets, and tips from friends, coworkers and neighbors. Just look at what happened to tech stocks in the year 2000 through 2002, to see this effect in action. In the field of investing it is fine to be a contrarian, just don't stand in front of the herd and yell for them to stop. For a look at the manias of the past read Charles Mackay's book "Extraordinary Popular Delusions and the Madness of Crowds." It is an eye-opener.

Naïve diversification

The number and type of choices that you have when picking a portfolio affect your decision on how to diversify that portfolio, and allocate the assets in it. You need an understanding of asset allocation, and modern portfolio theory, to help you to avoid this problem. The most common error of this type is concentrating in the stock of your own company when it is offered in your 401(k) plan. If your 401(k) plan offers many more equity choices than fixed income choices, you will almost always overweight equity choices in choosing where to invest your contributions. The opposite holds true as well.

Emotions Affect Investing

The behavioral traits that rule us when we make decisions are often not within our control. Greed, fear, laziness, arrogance, and impatience are the ones I feel do the most harm. You must work to overcome these if you are to become successful in managing your finances. If you cannot, get an unemotional partner, like the Good Financial Advisor. The Good Financial Advisor can help reduce or eliminate the effect of these behavioral tendencies, simply because she is dispassionate towards your portfolio. Many times, the right course of action is to do nothing, and a voice of reason can help you stay that course. There are many ways to go astray when investing on your own, and they may not be your fault, or even under your control.

Goals, Goals, Goals

As mentioned in Chapter 2A, one of the most significant mistakes that investors make is failing to tie their investment goals to their financial planning goals. An example is the investor who says, "I want to make as much money as I can", when asked what his goal is for his portfolio. My first response is to tell him that we will invest his entire portfolio in emerging markets in Russia. This usually elicits a response like, "I don't want to do that, because it's too risky." I then advise the client that I think they really mean that they want to make as much as money as they can, at an acceptable level of risk. The discussion then goes to evaluating how much risk the client is really able to handle, consistent with his financial goals.

Greed & Fear vs. Goals and Facts

To minimize the impact of behavior on your financial future it is essential that you replace the two strongest basic emotions of greed and fear that are hardwired into us at birth. The most well known of our emotions is the fight or flight response that kept our primitive ancestors alive, and it lives on in the way we fight our disbelief that we picked a poor investment, and then flee that investment (sell) when it is down in value.

Greed and fear are comparable and the best way to reduce or eliminate their effect is to replace them. Replace greed with goals, so that you are not chasing an elusive performance level that is either unrealistic or unachievable. Educate yourself and replace fear with facts, so that you know to remain invested during the normal up and down movements of the market.

This is a primary benefit of engaging The Good Financial Advisor, since she knows the facts and has no emotional attachment to your portfolio. In my experience, as mentioned in Chapter 3E, managing your "behavior" is the single most challenging, and important, role The Good Financial Advisor can play in helping you to achieve your goals. By replacing greed and fear with goals and facts, your chance of achieving your goals is measurably improved.

Behavioral Finance

The field of behavioral finance is emerging as perhaps the most important area of study if you wish to excel in investing. While it may be a little dense and dry for many, it is helpful to people to explain why we behave so badly at times with our investments.

I will not go into great depth here except to say that this is a rapidly developing field with potentially significant impact on the way we conduct ourselves when managing our investments, planning for the future or protecting what we have. It appears that we are nowhere near as rational as we believe and seldom able to control our emotional responses to difficult situations. How else can we explain the historical tendency to buy high and sell low?

Why wouldn't you want someone on your side to help control your "misbehavior"?

Risk, Risk, Risk!

Every investor has a risk tolerance profile. It will influence your behavior under different circumstances. Your risk tolerance profile will determine, to a large degree, how your financial advisor manages your investments. Be sure to be candid with your advisor as to how much risk you believe you can handle, and what your goals actually are, not what you think they should be.

Many mutual fund companies have risk tolerance questionnaires that you can use to try to determine what your risk tolerance is. Be very skeptical of most risk tolerance quizzes you find. They are usually too simplistic, and can give answers that are far from the truth. Nothing can replace a conversation with the Good Financial Advisor.

As my mother often reminded me,

behave yourself!

Chapter 6M – The Magic of Compounding

"Give me a lever long enough and a place to stand, and I will move the world."

Compound interest is financial leverage and truly is one of the great instruments of financial planning and investing. It means that each period, typically a year, you add your earnings from the prior period to the old principal and calculate your next year's earnings on the new higher principal balance. Take the following quiz to see if you appreciate the real power of The Magic of Compounding.

1) You invest $4,000 when you graduate college at age 22 and earn an average return of 10% until you reach the retirement age of 67. Your account is worth approximately:

   A) $59,600
   B) $95,200
   C) $147,300
   D) $320,700

2) You invest $5,000 each year from the time you graduate college at age 22 and earn an average return of 10% until you reach the retirement age of 67. Your account is worth approximately:

   A) $636,000
   B) $945,000
   C) $1,478,000
   D) $3,774,000

3) Your wealthy grandparents offer to give you a penny at graduation and double that gift each year. You would get two pennies in year two, four pennies in year three and so on. How big would your account become in thirty years, even if it was kept in a safe and earned nothing?

        A) $194,000
        B) $857,000
        C) $1,785,000
        D) $10,737,000

Example 1) is similar to a gift of the initial funding of a Roth IRA. Example 2) is similar to how you might save in a company 401(k) plan, ignoring inflation. Example 3) is just for fun unless your grandparents are dotcom billionaires. Without using a calculator or computer how many did you guess right? The correct answer in each case is D).

I referred to The Magic of Compounding at the end of Chapter 2C and will again in Chapter 7 on Investment Basics under the Rule of 72.

It's not magic.

It's just math.

Chapter 7 – Investment Basics

"An investment operation is one, which upon thorough analysis, promises safety of principal and an adequate return. Everything else is speculation."

There are several basic investment concepts that are helpful in guiding your investment decisions. The first and most important is a clear definition of an investment.

Investing Defined

You need at least two things to be a successful investor. (There are others but we won't try to address all of them here). You need money, and you need a definition of an investment that will help you make "good decisions". If you have not read a book like The Intelligent Investor, by Benjamin Graham, you should. It is a good way to learn from the real professionals. The definition of investing that Benjamin Graham used is that shown above in Italics. If every investor had followed this or a similar rule, the results of the three years from 2000 to 2002 would have been markedly different.

Certainly we should stop using the phrase, "playing the market." I often chide clients that I do not play with their money. If you do wish to play or speculate, set aside a small portion (5 to 10% at most) of your total assets, and don't mix these with your invested assets portfolio. The key here is that you must be able to lose 100% of your speculative assets, and still reach your financial goals. Again, the need for goals is very important in order to be able to make this judgment.

You should also resist the impulse or urge to "try something for a while." If you are not willing to invest in equities for at least ten years, you probably should not be investing in them for ten minutes, according to a saying attributed to Warren Buffett. It is very difficult to trade in equities on a short-term basis and make a profit. Trading costs alone take a big piece of your money, not to mention that you must make many little decisions to earn a profit, and if any of them are wrong, it could lead to large losses. Ask any day trader how easy this is, if you can find one still in business.

Here are a few more basic investment concepts that should assist you in making good decisions.

Rule of 72

It helps to understand how changes in return affect the time it takes to achieve a given result. The Rule of 72 is a good guide to help you understand the relationship between time and return. The Rule of 72 states that if you take your return, or interest rate, and divide it into the number 72, the answer is the approximate number of years it takes to double your investment. For example, if you make 8% on an investment it will take about 9 years for it to double in size. If inflation is about 3%, it will take about 24 years for costs to double.

This will start you thinking of the large, long-term, difference between safe investments, that return 6% and take 12 years to double, and more aggressive investments, that return 9% and take only 8 years to double. For someone who has 24 years to invest, one investment doubles twice, while the other doubles three times, thereby producing twice the amount of dollars as the lesser return. This is what is referred to as the magic of compounding, and magic it surely is for those who begin early and allow time to work for them, as I illustrated in Chapter 6M.

Time-Value of Money

The time-value of money tells you that a dollar received next year is worth much more than a dollar received ten years from now. Remember this when you are tempted to buy a stock of a company that promises profits a number of years into the future. To properly evaluate the worth of future dollars, you need to discount them, at a rate equal to what you could earn on them if they were invested over that same time period. The discount rate should be in the vicinity of 10% to 15% in my opinion, to compensate you for the risk you take as well as the return you should get.

Marketability and Liquidity

Marketability means that there are people out there willing to buy what you have to sell. Some things have no marketability, such as a minority share of a family owned partnership. Who would want to own a piece of something over which they had no control and could not easily resell in the future? Don't buy things that do not have a ready, willing, and able group of buyers waiting to buy it from you.

Liquidity is a different beast. It is the ability to sell what you have quickly without affecting the market price. For example, if you owned a large stock position in a small company, it might be difficult to sell the entire block of stock in a hurry, without reducing the price. There may not be that many buyers out there who want to own a large single position in that small company.

Marketability and liquidity are two key points to consider, whether you are a buyer or a seller, and I mentioned them in Chapter 6B on risk.

When an advisor recommends an investment, ask him if either marketability or liquidity is an area you should be concerned with in the future. REITs that are not publicly traded fall into this category, as well as start-up companies, penny stocks, and limited partnerships. When investing in very large mutual funds, liquidity may affect their performance, because of the difficulty in selling large stock positions in a short period of time.

In addition to the items mentioned above, there are two others especially worthy of mention here.

A Buy Discipline – You definitely need one.

When you purchase your investment, you should have some idea of what the upside and downside is, to the best of your ability to make that assessment. I like to have a potential upside that is three times the size of the potential downside so that the risk/reward ratio is favorable. Keep in mind what Yogi Berra said, that "predictions are tough to make, especially about the future."

Purchasing a stock is viewed somewhat differently than purchasing other products. When buying anything from appliances to tuna fish we tend to want to buy them when they are at low prices. With stocks, we prefer to buy them when the price is high, after a run-up in their price. As I said before, you are probably not a rational investor.

Many investors, when they feel an investment is a sure thing, get the urge to <u>B</u>UTT it. That means <u>B</u>ack <u>U</u>p <u>T</u>he <u>T</u>ruck and buy a lot of it. Concentrating your investments, as opposed to diversifying them, is a recipe for disaster. Even if you have several winning investments in a row, the next one can go bad and wipe out the gains from the previous good ones. Don't BUTT, it's too much like a BET! Do your homework on the investment you are thinking of buying. Spend time reading about it until you have a basic understanding of what it is and what it does. Make your buy decision an informed and considered decision, that after thorough analysis promises safety of principal, and an adequate return (That was worth repeating).

A Sell Discipline – You need one even more.

Knowing when to sell, or when not to sell, is probably the single most important decision in the investment process. Wall Street is very good at telling you when to buy, but terrible at helping you decide when the correct time to sell has arrived. Remember that you only have a paper profit until you sell the investment. Taking a profit is the only sure way to make a profit.

After you sell, you must then find a suitable replacement investment, so selling involves work. When you decide to sell, you must have a market for what you are trying to sell, and it must be liquid.

Of these two, the sell discipline is by far the most difficult to develop and maintain. When we buy, the excitement of realizing a future gain is a good feeling.

We see riches ahead, and little downside risk, because we are confident of our ability to select a winner. When we sell, and especially so if we have a profit, we are giving up a winner. Our heart tells us it will continue to go up, and we will miss another big gain. Reread the previous chapter on behavior to see why this is just in our minds.

And after you sell, since the long-term trend of the market is biased upward, you will usually see the investment you sold go higher. This is okay, as long as the investment you selected to replace the sold one also goes up.

Never look back with regret, as long as you followed your sell discipline. Many people experience myopic aversion when it comes to a losing investment. They do not want to sell until they see that they are at least even with their purchase price. This is another behavioral problem, and is a sure way to lose more money.

Keep in mind that preserving your capital is a fundamental part of growing it. It is not as exciting in the short run to be sure, but over the long term it is very fulfilling.

Here is a good start at a sell discipline. Consider selling when any of these happen:

- The fundamentals of your investment change for the worse. A drug is not approved, profits turn to losses, an accounting scandal hits, the company president is indicted, and similar adverse items, should be immediate red flags.

- The future prospects of your investment have dropped, and there are better investment opportunities available to you. Personal computers have essentially become a profitless commodity, and their future prospects are probably limited.

- You have too much exposure to one asset class, or one type of investment, perhaps because it has grown so rapidly compared to your other investments. You must walk a fine line between letting your winners run, and taking a profit here. Think about risk when making your decision.

- When evaluating an individual stock, one sell discipline that you might consider to minimize losses is this; sell anytime you experience a 20% loss relative to the initial purchase price within a year following the purchase. Reconsider the stock only after a 10% move, either up or down. If you have owned the stock for more than a year, follow the sell discipline described above using your current start of year price, to avoid giving back too much of your gains.

You Ain't perfect

Recognize your behavioral limitations because you almost certainly have some.

- You will not always be right in investment selection, nor is it necessary to be a successful investor.

- Learn how to spot a mistake, since you will make some, perhaps many. Learn from them.

- Correct your mistakes as soon as you see them. Do not agonize.

- Never fall in love with an investment. It can lead you to make bad decisions.

- Remain flexible, because everything changes all the time. What works today, may not help at all next year.

Get a second opinion from the Good Financial Advisor whenever you need help with the basics.

Chapter 7A – Fees and Expenses

"Cost is only an issue in the absence of value."

No matter how many times we hear this, some people still feel that the less they pay for something, the better the deal, when in fact just the opposite may be true. Ask yourself, how would you shop for the following items?

- Heart Valves

- Parachutes

- Defense Attorneys

On a serious note, do you drive the cheapest car available? There is a difference when quality counts. Never confuse the real difference between what something costs, and what it is worth to you.

Fees and expenses are the price you pay to have others do what you either cannot, or choose not to, do for yourself. Having said that, fees and expenses should always be fair, reasonable, and fully disclosed.

Fees and Performance Are Related

What is a reasonable or fair fee is open to debate, but a financial advisor has to earn a fee sufficient to cover his overhead, expenses, salary and a profit commensurate with his experience. If an advisor provides exceptional advice, service and investment results, he can (and should) charge a larger fee, consistent with his superior results. Otherwise there would be no incentive for an advisor to do any more than provide minimum basic service. Nor would there be a reward for the talented financial advisor who excels at his profession.

Investment Expenses

Make sure you ask about the fees and expenses associated with any investment you make. The Good Financial Advisor will not hesitate to explain them to you, since the lower your costs, the better your investments are likely to do, all other things being equal. The better you do, the more satisfied you are with your advisor, the more your assets grow, the more income your advisor earns, the more referrals you will provide, the better service you receive, and so on. Do you see the "everybody wins" pattern here?

Core (Hub) and Opportunity (Satellite) Portfolio

Portfolio construction has a bearing on fees and expenses. The use of a Core (or Hub) and Opportunity (or Satellite) portfolio structure (Chapter 7H) can minimize initial and ongoing costs.

If you invest 100% of your money in a portfolio of class A shares your up-front sales charge could be about 5%, depending on the funds you select and the type of fund. (Fixed income funds usually have a lower initial sales charge.) You would have no further sales charges in the coming years unless you had to reposition a fund to another fund family and pay a new up-front commission.

If you put all of your money into a managed account with a 1% annual asset-based fee, you would have no initial sales charge, but an ongoing charge that continues indefinitely. You pay this charge on all of your assets whether you reposition them or not. With the Core/Opportunity portfolio you take about 30% of the portfolio (Core) and put it into class A funds that typically cost less than 5%, say 3.5%. You put the remaining 70% of your money into a managed account (Opportunity) at 1%. The amount in the Core portfolio is determined by the structure of the portfolio.

With this structure, your initial year total sales charge is about 1.75% and your ongoing charge is 0.7%. The savings over time can be significant. You still maintain the ability to reposition funds, yet you do not pay an ongoing fee on Core funds that may not be moved for a decade. That 3.5% initial sales charge amortized over ten years is a lot less than 1% per year. In addition, your advisor accepts less up-front revenue in exchange for an ongoing revenue stream that compensates him for client service. This tends to eliminate the concern over how to pay for quality long-term service on your account.

If you advisor recommends a single portfolio, question him as to why the core/opportunity approach would not yield better results. If the size of the portfolio is sufficient, it is almost always to your benefit to use the Core/Opportunity approach.

The Type of Fee Is Irrelevant

If a financial advisor has consistently provided you with excellent service, and above average results, do not be concerned over his fees, even if they are a bit higher than average. Worry more about the quality of advice you receive than the fee structure by which the advisor is paid.

I also want to state again, that whether you pay commissions, fees, or a combination of these, it makes no difference. Only the end result is important. As I said in Chapter 3H, I do not believe that the integrity of your advisor depends on the method by which they are compensated for their services. This argument continues on in the minds of the anti-advisor crowd, but I have yet to see hard evidence that it has real substance. Bad apples are still bad apples, regardless of how they are paid. Character and integrity do not go away because a commission is earned.

Focus On Results – Not Costs

When evaluating investment options, always look at the end result, not just the expenses. If a portfolio manager has consistently returned an additional 2 to 3% in return over his peers, his expenses are more than justified. All performance figures are net of fees, so if a fund manager outperforms his peers by 3% with 2% higher fees, he has actually delivered 5% better gross performance, before the fees are taken out. This is impressive, and deserves your consideration. High fees, not supported by superior results, are a drag on long-term performance, and should show up in poor long-term relative returns. When you see this, avoid that investment like the plague.

The financial services industry is the only service profession where people constantly criticize the members for making a good living. You always read about high commission products, high expenses, excessive fees and the like. You seldom read about results that are achieved by the professionals who receive those fees. I would point out that the financial advisor does not set the commissions on the sale of a product. The manufacturers set commissions. I don't believe those manufacturers would pay one basis point (1% = 100 basis points) more than necessary to get their products sold. When you hear about high or excessive commissions, don't blame your advisor, since they are not under his control. In fact, it is illegal for him to reduce them by rebating some of the commission to you. The financial services industry will have achieved true professional status when successful financial advisors are sought after for the quality of their work, in the same manner as successful attorneys or money managers, without regard for fees.

Reaching Your Goals Matters Most

Lastly, remember that the most important thing is for you to reach your financial goals, not to achieve the maximum possible return in a given asset class. Otherwise, the best strategy would always be to take the most risk you could for a given investment, in order to get the highest possible return.

As I said in Chapter 3H, when your account is going up in value at the rate you anticipated, no fee will look excessive. When your account goes down so much as a penny, no fee will seem reasonable, since you will feel that you are paying a fee to lose money.

Once you have established your financial goals, never lose sight of them. If you wind up paying 1% to 2% in total fees to make sure you really achieve your goals, it will be well worth it.

Think hard.

What <u>do</u> you shop for at the lowest price,

regardless of value?

Chapter 7B – Stocks and Bonds

"Neither a borrower nor a lender be, but if it is necessary to do either, lend only to a good borrower and borrow only from a good lender."

You should have a fundamental understanding of the difference between stocks (equity) and bonds (fixed-income), in order to relate your tolerance for risk to your Good Financial Advisor. It is also necessary in order to understand the basic investment strategy you wish to follow in terms of risk and return. In my opinion, you do not have to know any more than the basics about stocks and bonds to be successful with your investment portfolio if it is in the hands of the Good Financial Advisor.

Stocks/Stock Mutual Funds or Equity

Stocks and bonds are each investments in a firm that have a claim on the cash flow of that firm. However, the differences between them are significant because they involve both risk and return.

When you own a share of stock, you have an ownership position in a firm, and are said to be "long" the stock. This contrasts with the situation where you have sold a stock "short". This is where you borrow a security, sell it, and promise to return it in the future, when you hope it will be cheaper. Short selling is not for amateurs, since it carries unlimited risk. Stocks you own can only drop in value to zero, but stocks you are short can go up in value indefinitely. When a short seller buys back the security he previously sold, it is referred to as covering his position.

Stocks may or may not pay a dividend, and are usually bought for their potential for capital appreciation related to the growth of the firm. Since the tax rate was reduced to 15% on dividends (same as a capital gain), dividends have been more in demand from investors. Dividends today are usually in the 1% to 3% range, but the trend is to increase them because of their favorable tax treatment.

There are several types of stock: Common stock is the most widely used, and is the basis for most equity mutual funds. Preferred stock and convertible stock are used to a much lesser degree, and if you decide to invest in them, get help from someone who is experienced in their use.

Bonds/Bond Mutual Funds or Fixed-income

A bond is an investment with a face value (typically $1,000), a coupon or stated interest rate that it will pay each year, and a maturity date, when it is due to be repaid. There are many additional variations on this, but they are beyond the scope of this book. You can find books that explain other features of bonds, but they are not necessary to understand the basic role of bonds in your portfolio.

When you own a bond, you have loaned the firm money in hopes of getting it back with interest. Bonds pay interest income, and seldom generate significant capital gains or large losses. They normally go up in value as interest rates go down, and down in value as interest rates go up. If you buy a ten year, $1,000 bond today paying 7% ($70.00 per year) and next year rates go up to 8%, so the same bond purchased then pays $80.00 per year, your bond is worth less because it pays $10.00 per year less for the remaining 9 years.

When purchasing individual bonds it is usually advisable to set up a bond ladder that contains bonds of varying maturities. This does not eliminate risk, but it can minimize reinvestment risk. I caution you against thinking a bond ladder eliminates risk, since some advisors may present it simply as a way to get you to invest, similar to dollar cost averaging. Ask the Good Financial Advisor to explain the pros and cons of a bond ladder before investing. Many times, a quality bond mutual fund will provide the same returns, at lower risk and lower cost.

One note when purchasing individual bonds is worth mentioning. They are sometimes sold with a markup in price rather than a commission. Do not be fooled into thinking that you bought them at no cost when you may have paid a large markup. Ask your advisor what the markup is when no commission is shown.

Risk and Reward

In the event of a problem, the bondholder has first claim on the assets of the firm, and the stockholder gets whatever is left after the bondholders have been satisfied. This is essentially what defines the lower risk of the bond vs. the stock. However, the bondholder agrees to settle for a fixed amount of interest and return of principal, no matter how much cash flow the company generates in a given year. The stockholder, in return for having no claim on anything except what is left, gets everything that is left after the bondholder is repaid. Risk and reward are thus always related.

Municipal and High Yield Bonds

There are numerous types of bonds, such as corporate bonds issued by companies, government and state bonds, international bonds, mortgage bonds and inflation adjusted bonds.

Two types are worth special mention: Municipal bonds and high yield bonds. Municipal bonds are federal tax-free and are used to provide relatively safe and steady income. They yield a bit less than other types of bonds because they are tax-free. Municipal bonds from your own state may be free from state taxes as well as federal taxes.

High yield bonds are sometimes called junk bonds, and offer higher yields due to the lower creditworthiness of the issuers. These carry additional risk relative to more creditworthy bonds, but the yields can be substantially higher.

Bond Ratings

Bonds are rated from AAA or Aaa to C (as to credit quality) by agencies such as Moody's Investors Service and Standard and Poor's Corporation. Any bond rated below BB or Ba is non-investment grade, and carries with it significantly more risk of default than higher rated bonds. Before you purchase any individual bond issue, check its rating. No matter how tempting the yield may be, a low rated bond can lose some or all of its value in the event of a default or bankruptcy. You can minimize this risk by investing through bond mutual funds.

Reinvestment of Dividends and Interest

Whether in stocks or bonds, or mutual funds of either, the question of whether to reinvest dividends must be addressed. Traditionally, advisors recommended reinvesting dividends, capital gains and interest income for several reasons: It was convenient, it got the money reinvested instead of spent, it avoided commissions on the reinvestment, and it improved returns through compounding. This was in the days when most portfolios consisted of a single mutual fund that was rarely changed.

Times Have Changed

Today, it seems more advantageous in many cases to use the dividends, interest, and capital gains to continuously rebalance your portfolio. With low transaction costs, or none if you are in a managed account, this helps avoid incurring capital gains by avoiding the sale of profitable positions to rebalance your portfolio, or when you require cash from the portfolio.

By constantly sweeping interest and dividends to a cash account, you tend to reduce portfolio risk over time until the next review. You can then decide, along with your Good Financial Advisor, what is the best way to handle those funds. Bear in mind that the financial advisor may receive commissions on the reinvested dividends, unless they are held in a managed account.

Reinvestment May Not Be the Best Approach

I am squarely in the do not reinvest camp for most accounts, since in today's investment world, I never see professional portfolio managers purchase stocks through a dividend reinvestment plan. Why should you? Only in smaller core portfolios of investments that will rarely be rebalanced, such as U.S. Government bonds, does the automatic reinvestment of interest and dividends seem advantageous.

One place where reinvestment seems to be the preferable way is with small equity accounts, such as a Roth IRA. In these accounts, the amount of dividends, interest and capital gains is too small to be meaningful in terms of rebalancing. You usually invest money annually in these accounts, and that is the money you can use to rebalance or restructure the account.

There is a split within the industry as to whether it is better to automatically reinvest or not, and it will not likely be resolved soon. Discuss it with the Good Financial Advisor and choose the option that best fits your needs.

Stocks and Bonds vs. Mutual Funds

From the investor's point of view, individual stocks and bonds have a big advantage over mutual finds. Unless held in a fee-based account, they have no annual fees or expenses associated with them. A portfolio of individual stocks and bonds will likely have a higher risk profile than a similar portfolio of mutual funds, but the tradeoff will be lower expenses, which can potentially save 1% to 2% per year. With the individual stock and bond portfolio, there will usually be an initial sales charge to purchase them, and a sales charge to sell them at some point in the future.

If they are held for many years, these charges should be a very small amount relative to the overall return. This does raise the question as to how the financial advisor will be compensated to watch over the portfolio over that time period, if there is no asset-based fee being paid. Ask your advisor how he can afford to watch over your stocks and bonds without a service fee in those circumstances, since benign neglect is not what you want to have happen.

Buying and Selling Are Not Free

Whether you see it or not, there is always a cost to buy or sell a security. Sometimes it is a commission and sometimes it is a markup that is hidden, so ask your Good Financial Advisor what you will pay to buy and sell before you agree to the transaction. If the cost seems too high, ask him to justify it in light of the anticipated return of the investment. There is no such thing as a free (or no cost) purchase and sale of a security. If someone tells you that, a red flag should go up immediately.

Investment Analysis

There are three types of analysis that dominate the field of Wall Street types who purport to analyze stocks, bonds, and the direction of the markets. Your Good Financial Advisor may use one of these techniques and you should be aware of their basic methods.

The first is Fundamental Analysis or the study of basic information about the markets, such as price/earnings ratios, price/book ratios, price/sales ratios, debt/equity ratios and related financial information.

The second is Technical Analysis, or the study of past activity by looking at charts of prices, trading volume, cash flow and similar characteristics, under the presumption that investor sentiment can be determined by their previous buy and sell decisions.

The third is Quantitative Analysis, or the study of earnings momentum, relative price strength and the like, to try to predict where prices are headed.

All three methods have their proponents and detractors, and there are pros and cons for each. No one method has proven to be reliable on a consistent basis, although some methods are riskier than others. "What Works On Wall Street" by James O'Shaughnessy is an excellent study of methods of analysis and how they can be used to select investments. If you find a method and stick to it, that may be better than throwing darts at the Wall Street Journal stock section.

If you want to know more about stocks and bonds, there are many good books that explain in depth the differences between them, and how each should play a part in your portfolio. One book will not make you an expert, but it may lead to some insight as to how the world of stocks and bonds operates.

Let the Good Financial Advisor

guide you through this minefield.

Chapter 7C – Mutual Funds

"A rock thrown through a window of 100 panes leaves 99 unbroken."

An open-end mutual fund is an investment in which you and thousands of other people pool their money and turn it over to a professional money manager to invest. The manager then buys and sells stocks and/or bonds in accordance with the objective of the fund. Mutual funds allow small investors to participate in the equity market in a diversified portfolio. They continuously issue new shares or redeem existing shares at their Net Asset Value or NAV. Mutual funds have been criticized for having high, hidden expenses, and for not lowering expenses as assets under management increased, which reminds me of this story of a meeting between an advisor and a client.

> *The prospective client and the financial advisor were discussing the fees associated with the client's proposed new investment portfolio.*
>
> *"In the interest of full and fair disclosure, I want to tell you about the fees and expenses you will pay if I manage your money in the way we discussed." Said the financial advisor*
>
> *"First, there are sales commissions that I receive on a one-time basis for investing your money. Then there are what we call 12(b)-1 fees that I receive for servicing your account. There are also transaction costs for trading the stocks in your mutual fund that go to a broker. There are management fees to the people who actually manage the fund, and in addition there are expenses associated with the operation of the fund."*
>
> *At this point the client interrupted and said, "Wait a minute. I see a lot of other people getting paid here, but I don't see anything in it for me."*
>
> *"Well" said the advisor, "You aren't doing any of the work!"*

Despite their drawbacks, mutual funds have made it possible for millions of small investors to participate in the stock and bond market who would otherwise have been excluded from this form of investing.

Mutual Fund Share Classes

Mutual funds that have sales charges are called load funds, and usually come in three classes, designated A, B, and C. (There are other classes for institutional use that are outside of the scope of this discussion.) The Good Financial Advisor will explain the reason for using whatever share class he recommends.

Class A – Pay Once Up Front

Class A designates a fund with an initial sales charge assessed on the amount you invest. These typically range from 2% to 5.75%. If you invest large amounts of money, the sales charge on an A share is reduced via what are called breakpoints. Be sure to ask your advisor if you qualify for a breakpoint reduction. You will probably have to invest more than $50,000 with a single fund family to get a breakpoint reduction. It may not be advisable to put all of your money with one fund family just to save a small amount in initial sales charges. Always keep in mind that diversification for safety is important, and over a twenty-year period, a difference of 1% in an initial sales charge is not going to make a significant change in your ability to reach your financial goals. If it will, your goals need to be revised.

Class B – Pay for a While Over Time

Class B designates a mutual fund with an ongoing sales charge, usually about .75% per year for 8 years. If you sell a B share too soon, there is a declining contingent deferred sales charge (CDSC) that makes up for the lack of an initial sales charge. After a fixed period of time, a B share automatically coverts to an A share and its expenses are reduced.

B shares were introduced as a response to no-load funds for those who did not want to see their initial investment reduced by an up-front sales charge. Unfortunately, they were sometimes used to avoid breakpoints on large investments and therefore increase the commission to the financial advisor. This practice is currently being investigated and corrected by the mutual fund companies. B shares were also improperly sold as no-load funds by some financial advisors who presumably were afraid to charge for their services. As of this writing, some mutual fund companies have stopped selling B shares, and it is not unlikely that they will cease to exist at some point in the future. I would avoid B shares, except in the instance where you are over 70, and plan to take Required Minimum Distributions. Some companies waive the surrender charges on B shares under that situation, and you could wind up with lower costs than on an A share.

Class C – Pay As You Go for Liquidity

Class C designates a share with an ongoing annual charge that goes on as long as you own the fund, with a contingent deferred sales charge in year 1 only. These shares are usually bought by investors who want or need liquidity, since they could be more expensive than A or B shares over the long term.

However, they can be a good substitute for a managed account, since they provide adequate liquidity after the initial year surrender charge goes away. For accounts too small to qualify for a managed account, the C share is the next best way to construct a portfolio with investment flexibility, and may prove more popular in the future because of the desire to be able to reposition a portfolio to rebalance or take advantage of new products, without incurring a sales charge.

No Load-No Help Funds

No-load funds do not have an initial sales charge associated with them, although they may have redemption fees under certain circumstances. No-load funds do have internal expenses which can be higher or lower than those in load funds. If you buy a no-load fund directly from the manufacturer you are on your own, since they do not provide any help from a financial advisor before or after the sale. Financial advisors acting as Registered Investment Advisors (RIAs) may sell no-load funds and charge a fee for managing them.

Mutual Fund Expenses

All mutual funds have expenses, and the total expenses are as important as whether they assess a sales charge. Even though fund returns are net of expenses, it is hard to overcome a high expense ratio over the long haul. That is one reason that exceptional fund managers, who consistently deliver above average performance over long periods, are hard to find. Remember that when you select a mutual fund, you are selecting a fund company and fund manager(s), not some nameless entity.

Also, expenses are related to the cost of operating a fund. International funds, as an example, are normally more expensive to run than domestic funds. Bond funds are usually less expensive to run than equity funds. Funds that spend heavily on research, and provide superior results, earn every penny they charge. Funds with high turnover have higher trading costs than funds with low turnover. Remember the relationship between cost and value in Chapter 7A.

When Returns Are Low, Expenses Count For More

All of this attention to costs has much greater importance in a low return environment. A 2% increase in expenses, which translates to a similar decrease in performance, can be significant when it reduces a return of 8% to 6%, and affects your ability to reach a certain goal.

Focusing too heavily on costs ignores the fact that many people need help when investing, in order to set up a proper asset allocation based on risk tolerance, age and financial goals. They may also need emotional support in a down market, or guidance to stay away from inappropriate investments. There is a cost for this help, and as long as it is reasonable and proportionate, investors should accept a lower return, in exchange for having someone else do all the work, and allowing them to have greater peace of mind.

Mutual funds trade at Net Asset Value or NAV, which is the price of their individual securities at the close of the market. Load funds sell at the Public Offering Price or POP which includes the initial sales charge. If it is a closed-end fund, it may sell at either a discount or a premium to its NAV.

Mutual Fund Selection Criteria

When it comes to fund selection, ask your advisor these questions regarding why he recommended a particular fund:

- How long have you used this particular fund?

- Is the fund family well known and of high quality?

- How long has the manager been in charge of the fund?

- Was it selected because of the manager's record?

- Was it selected because of the record of the fund itself? Does it have 5 and 10-year performance numbers?

- Is it an open-end or closed-end fund?

- If it is a closed-end fund, is it selling at a discount or a premium to its NAV?

- If it is a new fund, why are you recommending it?

- How large is the fund in terms of assets under management? Is it so large that it may have difficulty in continuing its past performance?

- How do its standard deviation and Modern Portfolio Theory statistics compare with its peers?

- Are its expenses in line with its peers?

- Is its turnover low? (Lower turnover usually translates into lower expenses and reduced trading costs.)

- Are your commissions any higher or lower on this fund compared to similar funds? If there are similar funds available why did you pick this specific fund?

- Are there any incentives that accrue to you that are tied to the purchase of this fund?

- Have you or do you receive financial or other support from the manufacturer of this fund?

- If this fund turns out to be a poor selection, will we be able to move these monies to another fund or investment without incurring any penalties or new charges?

If you don't get satisfactory answers to these questions, a red flag should go up. Your advisor may not have done as good a job as he should when selecting the fund, or its choice was driven by other than your best interests. In any case, you should know what the primary reason was for selecting a given fund. The Good Financial Advisor will not attempt to impress you by selecting a lot of hot funds with high ratings. Instead he will try to construct a portfolio that will deliver consistent, dependable performance that will allow you to reach your financial goals. Remember, the financial advisor is selling his advice, not a product. The product is only the method by which the advice is implemented.

The Fund Manager Counts

Keep in mind that you should select the fund manager that has a good record, not the fund that has a good record. I also prefer to look at a fund with a five-year track record under that fund manager, or where the fund manager has a five-year track record managing a similar type of fund.

Recently, there has been a lot of focus on rating the fund manager instead of the fund (Chapter 6J), and I think that in the future all funds will be rated that way. Don't be taken in by a fund with a great rating (5 Stars for example) since the predictive value of prior ratings is minimal at best

Fund Size Can Affect Performance

Be aware of funds which are extremely large in terms of assets under management, since they may have great difficulty in continuing the track record that was developed as they became very large. Some studies have shown that large size is a handicap to performance and especially so when the market turns down and liquidating huge stock positions is required. You will be better off with smaller funds that are more manageable in up or down markets. Mutual fund companies close funds when they become too large. By refusing your money they are telling you in no uncertain terms that size impacts performance.

Mutual Fund Wholesaler Support

Mutual funds are supported by their manufacturers though wholesale representatives. This person visits with the financial advisor periodically and updates her on information regarding their family of funds. They may also provide financial support to put on seminars or other events for clients on behalf of the advisor, in hopes that the advisor will use their funds.

Ask your advisor how many fund families he uses and why. If he uses only those who provide extensive financial support, and not those that are the best in their class, it may affect your investment results.

With over two dozen top tier fund companies and many smaller ones, you should be concerned about any advisor who uses just two or three fund families. This applies even to those who use index funds or exchange traded funds. There is a practical limit as to how many individual funds an advisor can be familiar with on a regular basis, but there is no excuse for not using the best funds available. Be especially wary of the advisor who uses only one fund family, since there can be little justification for limiting your choices in that manner.

Behavioral Considerations

The Efficient Market Hypothesis states that all relevant information about a stock or bond is priced into that stock or bond immediately, and therefore no mutual fund can outperform the overall market. Read "A Random Walk Down Wall Street" by Dr. Burton Malkiel for an articulate statement of this premise. Not everyone believes in the efficient market. It is an argument that is ongoing, and has as many opponents as proponents.

My own simple view of it is this: At any time, there are exactly the same number of buyers and sellers in the market, assuming that there is a market for a given security. Buyers do not buy because they think a stock will go down in value, and sellers do not sell because they think a stock will go up in value, so other things govern the movement of the market besides perfect information, such as risk perception and individual needs.

In addition, investor behavior is not always rational, as behavioral finance theory has shown based on past experience. That is why, I believe, that the market is unknowable in the short run to anybody. As I stated in Chapter 6J, mispriced assets exist, despite the random walk believers, and many money managers have outperformed the market for extended periods of time. Finding them can be rewarding.

Funds of Funds

A fund of funds is a mutual fund that uses other funds as its investment selections, usually from the same fund family. They set up and manage an asset allocation and typically rebalance quarterly or annually. These are an excellent way for the small investor to have a professionally managed and well-diversified portfolio. A financial advisor just cannot afford to provide the same level of management on a small portfolio. Be aware that there are usually increases in expenses associated with a fund of funds, but as long as they are minimal, the result should justify their use. You also want to be sure that the manufacturer that makes the fund of funds has a wide selection of high quality funds to construct the desired asset allocation.

Closed End Funds

Closed-end mutual funds and unit trusts are funds that issue a specific number of shares, similar to how a company issues stock. These share then trade on a stock exchange and can sell for more (a premium) or less (a discount) than the value of the assets in the fund itself (net asset value or NAV). Unit trusts are self-liquidating in some instances, typically when they are made up of bonds. Use caution when purchasing closed-end funds as they are sometimes sold at a premium to NAV instead of with an up-front sales charge. After their initial offering, closed-end funds typically sell at a discount to NAV.

The Prospectus

Almost everything you ever wanted to know about a mutual fund is explained in its prospectus. Unfortunately, the prospectus is a lengthy, detailed, and difficult to understand document. It is laughable to see ads by mutual funds companies that tell you, "… information about the fund is contained in the prospectus. Read it carefully before investing." It is difficult to read a prospectus at all, never mind read it carefully, whatever that means. This is another example of nearly useless advice, and we can only hope for plain-language, easy-to-read prospectuses in the future. Write your congressman or representative and tell them to try to read a prospectus. Then maybe they will help us to put clear understandable language in these documents.

My short recommendation is to deal only with high quality fund families with a long-term record you can rely on. Avoid trendy funds, or funds that concentrate too heavily in a specific area (thereby reducing the value of diversification that a mutual fund is supposed to provide). Remember technology funds in 1999.

The Good Financial Advisor will explain your options,

so you can make "good decisions" on your own behalf.

Chapter 7D – Index Funds

"The secret to investment success is to buy stocks that go up in value, and then sell them for a profit. But if they don't go up in value, don't buy them."

Index funds are mutual funds that attempt to mimic a particular index of stocks or bonds such as the S & P 500 Index or the Dow Jones Industrial Average. A small group of people, accountable to no one, and not necessarily good money managers, determine the stocks or bonds that make up a particular index. Whether you want them to also determine the return you receive is the issue surrounding Index Funds.

Passive vs. Active Management

Index Funds and Exchange Traded Funds (or ETFs as they are popularly known), have gathered a larger share of the money coming into investment portfolios in recent years. This trend seems to be increasing, primarily in my opinion due to the rising stock market since October 2002. Their main selling point is a very low cost structure, and some large mutual fund companies have made further cuts in their costs in the last year.

Both Index Funds and ETFs track, or attempt to match, some index of stocks or bonds, which is why they are referred to as passive. Some track stocks on a capitalization-weighted basis and others track stocks on the basis of fundamentals. But no one attempts to actively manage the individual holdings on a daily basis, they simply follow the holdings of their index. There are some ETFs that are trying to manage an index in a sense (semi-active instead of passive) by selecting only some of the holdings of that index, but they are too new at this point to determine their long-term performance. However, this trend is gaining momentum, and will probably increase significantly in the near future. Variations of index funds will proliferate as they become more widespread, but until they have performance records you can evaluate, beware the faddish nature of these newer offerings.

ETFs can be bought and sold like a stock, usually with a commission, at any time during the trading day. Index funds, like mutual funds, can only be sold at the end of day closing price.

Indexes are not purely passive groups of stocks. They are assembled to reflect some particular aspect of the market, such as utility stocks, or small cap stocks. Their primary purpose is not to go up in value, but rather to accurately depict some part of the overall market. Look at the biotechnology index in recent years for evidence of that. They periodically review their holdings, and change them as they deem necessary to continue to reflect their underlying index.

As an example, the S & P 500 Index removes stocks that it feels no longer represent the industry, or portion of the broad market, they should, and replaces them with other stocks that are more representative of the overall market. In this regard, its record is one of replacing stocks that have fallen markedly in value, and bringing into the index stocks that have grown rapidly in recent years. Sort of a buy high and sell low approach.

In a rising market, index funds tend to outperform actively managed funds because they have no cash (are fully invested), while in a falling market, their lack of cash hurts performance, and actively managed funds gain an edge. All things being equal, the actively managed fund should provide lower risks than an index fund by more careful stock selection, although this issue is the subject of much disagreement.

The Advisor Bias

Financial advisors may have a bias against ETFs because it might tend to diminish their perceived value in your eyes. After all, if following an index is all he does, you can do it yourself. This of course neglects asset allocation and all of the other issues that surround portfolio construction and management, but it remains a concern for advisors. One way for index funds or ETFs to add value to your portfolio is to use them to increase broad market exposure in the Opportunity side of a Core & Opportunity portfolio.

Set and Forget Doesn't Work

The idea that all you have to do to be a successful investor is to buy an index fund and forget it is not a safe or productive strategy. The place where they can add value today is to give you broad exposure to a particular sector of the market (technology for example) at low cost. Since they have relatively short performance records, it is difficult to judge their value in the long term over various market cycles. Recent studies seem to indicate that active management produces results at lower risk, a desirable result. The big test will come in the next market downturn.

Risk Is Still an Issue

I therefore remain completely unconvinced of the superiority of index funds because of my bias towards lower risk. They also remove any chance you might have to outperform a segment of the market by investing with the great money managers of our time. I think their greatest contribution towards investing will be to force mutual fund companies to reduce their fees, something they have been reluctant to do in the absence of serious competition, and which I think is long overdue.

In an interesting recent development, one of the biggest manufacturers of no-load index funds has recently decided to sell its low cost ETFs through brokers. No load with a load. That is an interesting development. This follows the trend in the past few years for more companies to sell their funds through brokers and advisors, because people seem to prefer to buy them that way.

Ask your Good Financial Advisor to explain the pros and cons of index fund investing. Please bear in mind that it is net performance that counts in the end. Losing money in a low cost investment vehicle is not the way to reach your financial goals.

Don't be passive,

even if you like passive investing.

Chapter 7E – Annuities

"What if I run out of money before I run out of time?"

An annuity is one of the most complicated investment vehicles available, yet it can be valuable when properly used. It is also one of the most highly criticized investment vehicles, largely because it pays seemingly high commissions to the agent who sells it. However, when compared to other revenue sources over a long period of time, an annuity is less profitable to an advisor in many cases.

Since insurance companies are not in business to make their agents wealthy, the only logical reason that an annuity pays the commission it does is that it is difficult and costly to sell. Once sold, the agent can expect no more up-front revenue (commissions) for many years, if ever, and minimal trailing commissions. The commission does not usually come off the front end, like an initial sales charge on a mutual fund or stock however, so to the uninformed it may appear that there is no charge to purchase an annuity. Remember what I said about free investments. They do not exist.

Definitions of Annuities

Let's get some definitions of what we are talking about to clarify the subject a little.

An <u>annuity</u>, according to the dictionary, is a stream of income received over a period of time. We commonly see these as the pension our parents received after a lifetime of work for one company.

An <u>annuity</u> as used in financial planning is an investment contract issued by an insurance company. They are normally deferred annuity contracts, meaning that the stream of income does not start until (or if) you decide to annuitize the contract. You do this by giving the value of the contract back to the insurance company in return for its promise to pay you for a period of time. If they are immediate annuity contracts, then the stream of income starts right after you take out the contract.

The Parties to the Contract

There are three parties to an annuity contract. The first is the owner, the second is the annuitant, upon whose life expectancy the annuitization is based, and the third is the beneficiary. One person is usually both owner and annuitant with a second person as the beneficiary.

Some annuities terminate upon the death of the owner and some on the death of the annuitant. Be sure your contract is properly structured in this respect so it does not inadvertently terminate when one party dies. Upon the death of the owner, a spouse beneficiary can continue an annuity. All other beneficiaries must accept payment of the contract and pay taxes on any earnings. Ask your Good Financial Advisor to explain the contract so you can structure it to meet the right goal.

Annuities Are Tax-Deferred

The feature that distinguishes an annuity from other investment vehicles is that the earnings from an annuity are not taxed until you take them out, or the contract ceases at the death of the owner or annuitant. With an annuity you can defer taxes on earnings until you die, or until you actually withdraw the money. Like most tax-deferred investments, you may owe a 10% federal tax penalty for withdrawals before age 59 1/2. Remember that when you leave an annuity to a child, they will pay taxes at their income tax rate, which could be higher than yours. See your tax advisor before leaving large amounts of annuity income to the next generation.

Fixed and Variable Annuities

Annuities come in two general types, fixed and variable.

Fixed annuities provide a guaranteed rate of return that usually varies each year, and the insurance company guarantees your principal. They are generally seen as risk free, as long as the insurance company behind them is in good financial shape.

Variable annuities are not guaranteed as to principal, and your money is invested in a variety of investment options in the annuity contract. Your earnings are a function of how well the underlying investments perform. One unique advantage of a variable annuity is the ability to move money between investments within the annuity, without incurring any tax liability on gains.

Both annuity types have a place in a well-structured portfolio for people whose tax situation warrants deferring current income taxes.

One Drawback to Annuities

A downside of annuities is that all earnings from an annuity are taxed as ordinary income, even if they are long-term capital gains. You should ask your tax advisor if this impacts you sufficiently to make an annuity unattractive from a tax perspective. Today long-term capital gains rates are 15% and ordinary income rates can run as high as 38%.

Fees and Surrender Charges

Even though annuities have distinct advantages, they come with a price. Nearly all annuities have substantial surrender charges in the initial years of the contract. They are typically in the 7% to 10% range over the first 7 years, but vary significantly with the type of annuity you purchase, with some as long as 15 years. A few annuities have no surrender charges, but higher internal expenses.

Most annuities have annual administrative charges in the $25 to $40 range, though these are many times waived if the investment is more than some minimum level, such as $25,000. Variable annuities have an added charge called a Mortality and Expense (M & E) fee that can be in the range of 1% to 1.7%, to cover risks incurred by the issuing insurance company. They also have expenses to manage the underlying investment accounts inside the annuity. These can be in the range of 0.5% to 1.5%. As stated before, they also convert all income to ordinary income, which is taxed at higher rates than capital gains.

Additional features that an annuity may offer can also come with a price. Guarantees and lock-in features typically add .15% to 1.00% to the cost of an annuity. Make sure that you don't add so many features to the annuity that the anticipated performance of the portfolio selected within the annuity can't support all of the features and still provide an adequate return. A variable annuity, with a conservative fixed income portfolio, cannot bear 3% or more in internal costs. In fact, few portfolios can. In no case should you pay an added management fee on top of the other fees to have someone manage the subaccounts.

Repositioning a Fixed Annuity at Maturity

You should not let a non-qualified fixed annuity automatically renew at maturity if there are other annuities with better rates available. Ask your financial advisor what choices you have regarding repositioning the funds. You can use a 1035 exchange to avoid taxation on the earnings in the existing contract, but you will likely incur a new surrender charge. If you transfer within the same company there may not be a commission generated for the financial advisor. Otherwise, he will receive a commission on the transfer. As long as it is in your best interest to do so, this should not be an issue.

Repositioning a Variable Annuity at maturity

When a variable annuity matures you should consider repositioning it if there are better investment options available to you in another annuity. Again, you can use a 1035 exchange to avoid taxation on the gains in the old annuity, but you will incur a new surrender charge on the new annuity.

Do Not Exchange Annuities Lightly

One area where in my opinion abuse exists is in the transfer of annuities when it is not in your best interest. In general, do not exchange your annuity unless you can quantify the reasons to do so. You should either be able to get lower costs (a lower M & E fee for example), or better investment options (the old annuity was a poor performer).

Avoid any exchange where there is a surrender charge unless the new annuity can offset that charge in one year or less without any gimmicks. Avoid any bonus offerings from the new annuity provider, since they are almost always accompanied by higher expenses and long surrender charges. They may also require you to annuitize the new contract to obtain their benefits, a restriction you should avoid.

If you do not completely understand the new annuity, don't buy it. The Good Financial Advisor will explain the new annuity in terms you can under-stand.

Annuitization

When you annuitize, you give up the right to the principal value of the contract in return for a guaranteed stream of income, so this decision should not be made unless you are sure it is right for you. Annuitization provides income for life in most cases, and should be done when you want to use up principal in your investment portfolio over your remaining lifetime, even though you don't know how long you are going to live. You let the insurance company take that risk, and if you live longer than expected you get more from the annuitization than expected. If you die soon after you annuitize, the insurance company pays less than antici-pated.

Annuitization Options

There are many options available when you annuitize. You can choose fixed annuitization where your payments are fixed, or variable annuitization where your payments can go up or down based on the performance of the underlying investments. You can specify that the income go to two people, called a joint and survivor annuity. This is typically how married couples take their income stream. You can also specify certain terms to guarantee a minimum amount of income is paid regardless of whether you live past the first month of annuitization or not. This is usually used to provide a minimum amount for your heirs.

Fixed annuitization provides a fixed rate of return and should usually not be done when interest rates are too low. This would be like buying a CD with a low rate of return and a lifetime maturity date. Ask what the internal annuitization rate is before you decide. If it is too low relative to other investments of equal risk, look at your alternatives.

Variable annuitization provides payments that vary with the performance of the investments within the annuity. They may go up in value or they may decrease. You take some risk as to investment performance in exchange for the opportunity for your annual payments to increase with time. Compare these two options in light of your future income needs before making a decision.

Before you annuitize a contract, consult with the Good Financial Advisor and review other ways to accomplish the same goal, which should be steady income. If you are not sure, get a second opinion. Annuitization is almost always an irrevocable decision.

You may be able to sell your annuitization in a secondary market if you want to recover a lump-sum of money, but the price will usually be steep. Do not attempt to do this without professional help. Those who would buy your annuity are sophisticated and knowledgeable, and are trying to earn every dollar they can.

Exchanging Your Annuity at Maturity

As I said, do not exchange annuities lightly. Every year insurance companies are developing new annuities with new features. Some of these features are very good, and others are of little value (to most people), but all come at a price. The Internal Revenue Service allows you to exchange your annuity for a new annuity via what is called a 1035 Exchange, with no tax consequences.

When your annuity matures (so that there is no surrender charge to reposition it), exchange it only when it is to your advantage. Be sure the costs and features of the new product are clearly better than the one you are replacing. You will likely incur a new surrender charge when you move your old annuity, and will be unable to access the funds for a substantial period of time. Ask your advisor to explain the advantages of the new annuity contract before you agree to move your existing contract.

If you cash out an annuity, the earnings will become taxable ordinary income in that year. Check out your tax situation before doing this to avoid any unwelcome surprises.

When In Doubt Ask Questions

Whenever you invest in an annuity contract, these are some of the questions you should ask. You can also check out www.annuityfyi.com for additional information.

- Why am I investing in an annuity, as opposed to an alternative investment such as mutual funds or tax-free bonds?

- What advantage does this annuity have that I cannot get in an alternative investment?

- What made you select this annuity in particular? Was it the manufacturer? Is the manufacturer strong financially?

- Do you receive any special incentives, either monetary or other, to sell this particular annuity?

- Does this annuity have any specific features that I could not get in another annuity or investment?

- What is the Mortality and Expense (M & E) fee of this annuity? Is this higher or lower than average? Are there other annuities available with lower costs?

- What is the total internal expense charge of this annuity, with all features considered?

- Are the total internal charges reasonable, relative to my anticipated return?

- What is the surrender charge schedule?

- Can I take 10% of the value out of this annuity each year without a penalty?

- When is the first time I can get out of the contract without a surrender charge?

- Will I have to annuitize this annuity to realize any of the benefits it provides?

- How does this annuity compare to others, regarding the selection and performance of its subaccounts? How long has it been in existence?

- Considering the effect of this annuity, will I have the right proportion of my overall portfolio in annuities? What is that proportion?

Use annuities in an appropriate manner and they can enhance your long-term chances for investment success. By deferring the payment of taxes, you are using the money that you would otherwise give to the government each year to increase your future earnings. One area where I believe annuities work well is in the high-yield fixed-income portion of a portfolio. You can utilize a low-cost variable annuity to invest the higher yielding part of a non-qualified portfolio, to avoid paying taxes each year on long-term money that you may not need for many years.

Watch the Overall Portfolio

Be wary if the percentage of your portfolio your advisor suggests should be in annuities exceeds 15% to 20%. Unless you want a large part of your investment portfolio in a guaranteed product, it is unwise to tie up too much of your money in annuities. There are many alternatives available that will give you the same result with less cost and more liquidity.

The Lifetime Advantage

Annuities are the one investment vehicle that can allow you to spend some or all of your retirement nest egg exactly over your remaining lifetime, even when you have no idea how long you will actually live. It is usually done gradually and only later in life.

In general you should not annuitize a large portion of your total assets at once. It is preferable to annuitize gradually, as your income needs dictate. I expand on this in Chapter 7J, on withdrawing money in retirement.

Annuities also have an advantage at death in that they avoid probate and pass directly to a named beneficiary. The beneficiary is responsible for payment of taxes on income in the annuity.

<u>Never</u> is a good time to run out of money.

Chapter 7F – Certificates of Deposit

"Insurance against principal loss is not insurance against purchasing power loss."

Certificates of deposit (CDs) are fixed income investments, typically sold by banks as a safe but low-yielding investment. They are usually a guaranteed or insured investment, and have a specified rate of return and maturity date.

Drawbacks

CDs have two main drawbacks. First, they normally do not pay enough to keep up with inflation and taxes, so whatever the return, your purchasing power is eroded. Look back at the definition of money in Chapter 6K. Part of the reason for their lower return is that they are usually FDIC insured, and you pay for that insurance.

Second, the interest you earn is taxable in the current year, whether you need it, use it, or simply let it grow.

Although not a huge drawback, they almost always carry a penalty for early withdrawal.

Certificates have a limited, yet important, place in a portfolio. They are there for those who cannot sleep well with any other investment. They also provide a sum certain at a point in time, when that is the overriding consideration in an investment. Only when interest rates are abnormally high will CDs have any substantive value in an investment portfolio.

Watch Those Renewal Dates

Keep your eyes on the maturity dates of your CDs. The institution that sold it to you will usually renew it for another term if you do not request anything else. On a five year CD, you will be locked in for another five years. You can "ladder" your CDs by purchasing them at different maturities, but you should still maintain flexibility by keeping the longest maturity as short as possible.

Be very skeptical of unusually high CD rates on brokered CDs. These can be high risk, uninsured investments, and you may not know it until it is too late. If the rate seems too good to be true, it is. This is a very competitive business, and rates should not vary substantially in your area. If the CD you are intending to purchase has a rate that seems too high to be true, ask the bank or institution that is selling it to explain why.

A Fixed Annuity Can Be an Alternate to a CD

The Good Financial Advisor will show you how a CD fits into your portfolio, and explore alternatives that may provide equal benefits with higher returns. In many cases, a fixed annuity can be a good substitute for a CD, if you are over 59 1/2 (to avoid federal tax penalties on withdrawals). It too is guaranteed, and you do not have to pay taxes in the current year. In my experience, a blend of CDs and fixed annuities works better than either by itself.

Remember the definition of money.

CDs are <u>C</u>onstantly <u>D</u>iminishing in purchasing power.

Chapter 7G – Options, Hedge Funds, Etc.

"Bulls and Bears create lots of B—s—t."

If you can't understand what you have, you probably should not have it at all. There are many investments that serve a unique purpose and also have a place in your portfolio. If you wish to understand them in detail, there are numerous good books available that explore them in detail. In this book, I only want to introduce a few of them to you, and make you aware of their potential place in your investment portfolio, if recommended by the Good Financial Advisor.

Real Estate Investment Trusts – These invest in various types of real estate and are a way you can participate in diversified investments in large properties. They are usually structured to pay a generous dividend, but can be illiquid and overpriced at times. They are long-term investments only, and should be a relatively small (5% to 10%) piece of your portfolio.

Limited Partnerships – These invest in real estate, oil wells and similar creative products. Your returns are limited to what the general partners think they have to give you to get their hands on your money. Avoid them unless the general partner is your sister (or a closer relative). Reread Chapter 6B on risk, regarding marketability.

Options – These are contracts that give you the right (but not the obligation) to either buy (a <u>Call</u> option) or sell (a <u>Put</u> option) a specific security. They require much smaller investments than purchasing the underlying product, and therefore can produce outsized returns if/when you win.

In my opinion, the only option strategy that has an acceptable risk profile is selling a Covered Call on a stock that you own. Even this strategy is not guaranteed to improve your long-term returns, since you may give up a large potential upside for a small option premium. One option is to avoid options altogether, since most people lose money with them. They are speculative at best, except when being used as portfolio insurance, and should be left to professionals.

Hedge Funds – These unregulated mutual fund variations are quite popular now, since they supposedly attempt to provide absolute returns. That is, they attempt to make money in both up and down markets. They are very expensive (high fees), and in my opinion their record to date is not good relative to the risks they take.

Commodities – Unless you are an end user or a trader, these are best invested in through a mutual fund with a long record. Pork bellies are for eating.

There are many other unique products such as futures and derivatives that go well beyond the scope of this book. Some are fads that will eventually be gone, and others are for sophisticated portfolio strategies that are not usually viable in retail investor's accounts. When you have more than a $100,000,000 to invest, opportunities will expand.

Watch Where You Go

Should you utilize any of these types of products, tread carefully. It is difficult to understand their real risks and their potential returns. The subprime mortgage market meltdown in 2007 is an example of how even the most sophisticated institutions in the world did not really understand the risks of the investments they made. You should tread very carefully here. There are many good books written on each of these and it would behoove you to get them and read them until you have a basic understanding of the investment in which you are entrusting your money.

Even when you do understand these products, be sure to ask your Good Financial Advisor for a clear and concise explanation of the specific product and why it belongs in your portfolio. If you don't get one, reconsider the investment and the advice. I do not believe that any of these products are necessary for a successful, long-term, investment program.

When you walk with the bulls and bears,

watch where you step.

Chapter 7H – Managed Accounts

"The only certainty is uncertainty."

Managed accounts are those where a fee is charged based on a percentage of the assets in the account. Sales charges are waived, so you can use stocks, bonds, A share mutual funds, or even no-load funds in these accounts.

Managed Account Advantages

These are sometimes called wrap accounts, because all costs, fees, or charges are wrapped up in a single fee that is disclosed to you. These accounts usually allow you to trade freely without incurring new sales charges (although you may pay some small trading costs), and the actual fees are plainly visible on your statement.

In my opinion, this is the future of advisor-based investing when used in the Core/Opportunity or Hub/Satellite portfolio approach. It is better for both advisor and client in nearly all cases, because it eliminates the need to move money to generate revenue for the advisor, and it provides flexibility without sales charges to the client. The latter should improve long-term performance, by facilitating portfolio revisions when necessary.

The managed account structure is difficult for an advisor new to the field to implement, because it greatly reduces the initial revenue of the advisor relative to a commission-based account. I personally believe it is the way most investments will be managed in the future, due to its simplicity and flexibility. It eliminates the question as to why a commission is generated (since there are none), and provides lower (in the short run), but steadier, revenue to the advisor to pay for ongoing service. In short, it looks like everybody wins, providing the fee is appropriate, and the advisor provides the required service.

Managed Account Disadvantages

The possible downside to a managed account is an ongoing fee that is unnecessary because the investments in your account require minimal or no active management. Short-term government bonds is an asset class that typically does not yield enough to warrant an ongoing asset based fee, nor does it benefit significantly from active management. The term to describe managed accounts that are not managed, i.e. neglected by the advisor through lack of regular service, is reverse churning, and it is being closely watched by regulators as managed accounts increase in popularity. Don't confuse reverse churning with a lack of change in your portfolio. A well constructed portfolio may go several years without need of change in a stable market environment. What is required is that the financial advisor review it regularly to make that determination. He should not simply tell you that you are in it for the long haul and let the portfolio go unattended.

The Good Financial Advisor will not put inappropriate assets in a managed account, and will review the portfolio on a regular basis. Watch closely to be sure that is the case.

Core and Opportunity Portfolio Structure

Some financial advisors structure hybrid portfolios, placing some investments in a Hub or Core Account, upon which commissions are paid, while the remaining investments are held in a Satellite, or Opportunity Account, which only charges an asset based fee, and waives all sales charges (See Chapter 7A).

The Core or Hub account usually contains income investments which have lower commissions than equity investments and therefore do not warrant an annual fee since they are unlikely to be moved for a long period of time. It also contains long-term equity holdings that are unlikely to be moved for extended periods of time and also do not warrant an ongoing management fee. These holdings represent the core of any good investment portfolio. The Opportunity account (named because it provides the opportunity for above average growth) contains all of the other investments, many of which will be sold or repositioned on a regular basis. This is the structure I prefer, for its low overall cost, and maximum flexibility.

Separately Managed Accounts

Separately Managed Accounts are a different product yet. They consist of a portfolio of securities (stocks, bonds or both), that is held for the account owner as part of a larger pool of similar securities. They provide some tax advantages, since unlike mutual funds, you do not inherit embedded gains or losses when you purchase them.

Depending on the fee, they also can be less expensive than mutual funds, since they eliminate certain expenses. The minimum investment in these accounts is usually quite high, typically $50,000 to $100,000, and you need to invest in several to get proper diversification, so ask your Good Financial Advisor if they are suitable for you. It is important to look at the manager of the account to determine their long-term performance record. You are relying solely on them for your future performance.

Key Points about Managed Accounts

*   Their fees should be reasonable based on the size of the account and its complexity. Usually the fee is based on a sliding scale related to the amount of assets in the account. Any fee over 1.5% should be justified by the Good Financial Advisor.

*   The account must be serviced by the advisor at least annually, or it is difficult to call it "managed". Twice per year service is preferable on large portfolios.

*   The investments in the account must be expected to provide a return sufficient to warrant the fee. (In a low rate environment, short-term government bonds returning 1.75% don't work if the fee is 1.5%).

*   They must complement your overall portfolio in terms of diversification. You must have an account of sufficient size to avoid excessive concentration in the managed account.

The Good Financial Advisor should structure your portfolio using the most appropriate account types available. This will give you a cost effective, flexible and efficient portfolio, which will allow you to achieve your long-term investment goals with minimum risk.

Managed accounts are manageable.

Chapter 7I – Portfolio Construction

"If you desire wealth, think of saving as well as earning".

After all of the other items that go into an investment portfolio regarding quality product selection are considered comes the creation of the portfolio.

It is the construction of your portfolio that separates the ordinary from the extraordinary investment advisor. The Good Financial Advisor who can also create an excellent portfolio is an exceptional person. An average or good portfolio will allow you to achieve the financial goals you want, but the excellent portfolio will achieve them at lower risk, and possibly in a shorter time frame. Strive for excellence.

Considerations for Your Portfolio

These are the items your advisor should consider when setting up your portfolio:

- Your level of risk tolerance and risk capacity

- Your investment time-frame

- Your required or desired return

- Your goal in dollars at a future point in time

- Your income generation need

- Your tax situation, current and future

- Your health

- Your ratio of qualified to non-qualified assets

- Where your assets should be located for optimum tax-efficiency

- Your liquidity needs

- The types of accounts to be used

- The fee structure

- The percentage of Core vs. Opportunity Investments if this type portfolio is used

- The asset allocation best suited to your needs. This encompasses many of the other considerations, and is the single most important influence on overall portfolio risk and long-term performance

These considerations all go into how a portfolio is constructed. This is a very time-consuming task, and therefore financial advisors try to standardize portfolios as much as possible. But it is the initial structure of the portfolio that will determine, to a great extent, its performance and risk profile over time. It will also dictate your initial and ongoing costs of management.

Equity vs. Fixed-Income Ratio

The ratio of equity, or stocks/stock mutual funds to fixed-income or bonds/bond mutual funds is the single largest determinate in establishing your portfolio. At the most conservative end a portfolio will be 100% fixed-income, and at the most aggressive end it will be 100% equities. If your portfolio is much different from where you feel your risk tolerance stands, ask the good Financial Advisor to explain how it compares to your classification of risk in Chapter 6B.

Every Portfolio is Unique

Because portfolio construction is an art, few portfolios will be the same from client to client, and a financial advisor will seldom produce the identical portfolio, as little as a few months later. (The exception to this might be firms that use a limited number of standard portfolios). The differences will be small and subtle, but meaningful in that they reflect the latest information available. Unless the differences are of great magnitude, older portfolios can wait until the next service period for adjustments, if any are required. Usually, differences reflect the closing of mutual funds, the availability of new funds, significant change in the fortunes of an individual stock or sector, major governmental policy changes, or external events.

Get It Right the First Time

It is at this point that you should question your Good Financial Advisor on every aspect of how your particular portfolio is right for you. If you started with an Investment Policy Statement, you can continue from there. Don't skimp on time invested at the inception of the process. Little else is as important as establishing the right portfolio, since you may be depending on it for many years to come. If you do it right, you will wind up with a **SWAN** portfolio.

$\underline{S}$leep $\underline{W}$ell $\underline{A}$t $\underline{N}$ight

and

watch your assets grow.

Chapter 7J – Withdrawing Money in Retirement

"Will I outlive my money, or will it outlive me?"

Our greatest fear in retirement is running out of money before we run out of time, as I expressed in Chapter 7E on annuities. We do care what happens to people in retirement, since they become society's burden when they run out of money. Our tax structure may someday be revised to reward saving instead of consumption, so that poverty becomes a rare occurrence, but for now we have to play the hand that's dealt us.

The Retirement Nest Egg

The essence of retirement savings is that we put money aside all of our working lives to accumulate a nest egg, and then do everything we can to try not to deplete it in retirement. There are two different ways to view that retirement nest egg, and each has its merits and drawbacks.

Principal Depletion

If we decide to spend it all over the remaining life we have (which we cannot possibly know), we can live at a higher standard of living than if we decide to preserve the principal, and live only on the income. This is referred to as principal depletion, when used in a financial planning context. Annuities are one way to spend principal exactly over our remaining lifetime, through annuitization.

Principal Preservation

If we decide to spend only the income (or gains) from our investment portfolio, then the rate at which we withdraw money each year will determine how long we can do that and still keep the principal intact. Bear in mind that we normally want the income that we derive from our portfolio to increase with inflation. Therefore, if you expect to maintain a constant standard of living, you must allow for inflation when calculating withdrawals. This means you must withdraw less than you earn.

If we do not spend any of the money, out of ignorance as to how long it will last, then we in fact have created our worst nightmare, by living without it, as if we never had saved the money at all. The Good Financial Advisor should not let this happen.

The Rate of Withdrawal

The withdrawal rate at which you have little chance of ever running out of money, can be, and is, subject to vigorous debate. Current studies put the rate at between 4% and 6% each year, depending on the assumptions you make regarding portfolio growth and volatility. I am in the 4% to 5% camp until I see convincing proof otherwise, because of the unknown and significant impact volatility of returns can have on your results.

Portfolios Must Be Designed For Withdrawals

What is certain is that the portfolio you invest in must be constructed to allow for withdrawals. When you reach the point at which you wish to begin taking money out of your accounts, ask your Good Financial Advisor if he has taken withdrawals into consideration when designing your portfolio. Some portion of your portfolio must be established with low volatility and safety in mind, not for growth. Specifically, some portion of the portfolio must be in stable and liquid investments, similar to short-term government bonds so you can be assured of taking money from a growing, not shrinking, account. You will typically be taking money from the bond portion of your Core Portfolio, if you have a hybrid portfolio setup.

Monitor Your Portfolio

When taking withdrawals, monitor the growth of your portfolio annually, to determine if you are taking too much or too little. Also, remember what I said about life expectancy in Chapter 2G, so that you don't plan on too short a withdrawal period. Withdrawing money in retirement is similar to Dollar Cost Averaging in reverse. The same benefits described in Chapter 6H work against you when taking money out of an account.

Withdrawals Before Age 59 1/2

If you have to withdraw money before age 59 1/2, there is usually a 10% federal tax penalty unless you take it in the form of Substantially Equal Periodic Payments (or SEPP) withdrawals, also known as 72(t) payments. Taking a SEPP withdrawal is complicated, and should be done with the help of a professional. Due to their complexity, your tax advisor and financial advisor should both be involved in helping to properly structure these payments. Just be aware that you can access your retirement money before age 59 1/2 without penalties, if you do it in the correct manner.

You may have spent 30 to 50 years putting money into your retirement plans, and you could spend nearly as many taking it back out. Do it carefully, and you will be able to enjoy all that life in retirement has to offer.

Save with care.

Spend with even greater care.

Chapter 8 – Protection Planning: The Basics

"If I die too soon, maybe life insurance is a good idea. I just haven't set a date yet."

Life insurance is protection against dying too soon. Investments are protection against dying too late. You need them both, and the Good Financial Advisor can keep you from worrying about whether you have too much, or too little, of either one.

Do not fall into the trap of thinking that the only thing that matters to your financial health is how much you accumulate in the form of invested assets. Without adequate protection, assets that took years to build up can disappear in months. Twenty years of asset accumulation can be wiped out with a single illness or car accident. The death of the primary wage earner can wipe out half a lifetime of savings in a few short years.

Disability Income Protection – Get It First

The first item that needs protection from unforeseen illness or an accident is your income. Disability Income protection is one of the least used, and poorly understood, types of insurance there is. We tend to protect all other assets except our income, yet everything we hope to own or enjoy in the future depends on a steady flow of income into our household.

Many people have disability income protection at work, but it usually replaces about 60% of your income, which is not always adequate on which to live. Review your actual coverage to see if it can support you in the event of a prolonged illness, or permanent disability, and supplement it with an additional private policy if necessary. A private policy stays with you during a job change, and unlike employer provided policies, it is not taxable as income when received because you purchased it on your own.

Life Insurance – Get It Next

The second item that needs protection is everyone else but you, should you fail to come home one day. Life insurance is also a critical item in a good financial plan, and the next chapter covers it in greater detail.

Property/Casualty Coverage

Although coverage of your home and car is usually taken for granted, do not forget to review these every few years to see if they are still appropriate for your situation. Underinsurance is dangerous, and two things you should watch out for are sufficient liability insurance in the event of an accident (a million dollars today would not be too much), and sufficient coverage on the appreciated value of your home to rebuild it in the event of loss. This last item is especially important if you live anywhere in the country where floods, hurricanes or forest fires could affect you. See your property/casualty insurance agent for a complete review. It is very inexpensive to maintain proper coverage of your home and property.

First Things First

In my opinion, you should establish your protection plan before you try to implement an investment plan. Most people do it the other way around, and some never get to the protection portion of their plan. Consider how you would feel if you lost a significant portion of your investment account because you failed to protect it.

Ask your Good Financial Advisor to lay out your protection options, and then make an informed decision. On a personal note, everyone knows someone who died early in life and left others in a bind, or became unable to work at his or her chosen occupation and led a life of frugality or worse. Think carefully before you decide to skimp on disability income protection or life insurance.

Stay safe, be well, and,

protect your future.

Chapter 8A – How much protection is right?

"But if I don't die, then all that money spent on premiums will be wasted!"

Just like fire insurance on your home is wasted if it doesn't burn down, medical insurance is wasted if you don't get sick, and car insurance is wasted if you don't have an accident, life insurance is wasted if we don't die. But life insurance is necessary in today's world. This is a quick summary of the common mistakes we make when it comes to purchasing life insurance:

We buy too much at the expense of our current standard of living

We buy too little at the expense of the possible future standard of living of those we love and leave behind

We buy it from the wrong person or online and get the wrong policy

We buy term when we need permanent coverage

We buy permanent when we need term coverage

We pay too much by purchasing a policy that is too expensive

We underfund a cash value policy, causing it to lapse in the future

We name the wrong beneficiary and fail to correct it in periodic reviews

We forget to name a beneficiary and the death benefit goes to our estate

We forget to change a beneficiary and an ex-wife gets the benefit, instead of your family

We forget to name a contingent beneficiary after the primary beneficiary is gone

We name a minor as the beneficiary and forget about a guardian

We select the wrong owner causing taxation when the policy is transferred

We insure the wrong person to the detriment of the survivors

We forget to insure our children to guarantee them coverage as an adult

We put the policy in our estate and make the death benefit taxable at the estate level

We structure it so that the death benefit is taxable as income instead of tax-free to the beneficiaries

We let it lapse before the need for it is gone and then are unable to replace it

We wait to get it until we are too old and it is very expensive, or simply unaffordable

We wait to get it until we are sick and it is unavailable at any price

We die without it and leave our survivors with little or nothing but a bleak future

Other than these issues, life insurance is easily purchased to protect your loved ones from your early demise. Be sure to get competent help when buying any policy.

Evaluate Your Needs

The first thing to do is find out what you really need for coverage. The Good Financial Advisor will develop a complete needs analysis for you to determine the type and amount of coverage you need.

Rules of thumb about multiples of income, and similar approaches are just that, and a more sophisticated approach is called for today. For example, unmarried partners may have different needs than married couples, even with the benefit of a civil union. Couples with children have much different needs than those without dependents.

When calculating your needs as a survivor, these are the basic areas to look at:

- Survivor income needs – If you are not working, can you? Do you want to go back to work?

- Children's daycare cost through age 13 – Someone has to take care of them while you work.

- College funding costs – You may be unable to set college funds aside with only one income.

- Mortgage and debt payoff – You may not be able to make the payments on one income.

- Retirement asset replacement – The second pension, 401(k) plan, etc., is gone or severely reduced.

- Final bills such as medical expenses – They can be substantial depending on circumstances.

- Burial expenses – These are not cheap anymore.

- Charitable intent – Did the deceased want to leave something to a church or charity?

- Legacy desires – Did the deceased want to help a special person after they were gone?

How Much Coverage Is Right?

For a gut check on how much coverage is right for you, ask yourself this question:

If a drunk driver killed your spouse or partner, would you sue (or settle) for the amount of protection you currently have on their life? A more sophisticated approach is to look at the discounted present value of all the future income lost (or expenses required to be incurred such as daycare). If my experience is typical, people usually think of life insurance in the $250,000 range and believe the value of that life to be in the million dollars plus range. What is your gut check telling you?

If income or cash flow is a limiting factor, err on the side of too much death benefit in a lower cost policy, rather than a lower death benefit in a cash value buildup policy. The four primary types of policies you will find are: Term insurance, whole life insurance, universal life insurance and variable universal life insurance. All but the term insurance usually have some element of cash buildup associated with them. Each has its merits and drawbacks, and should be explained to you by someone competent in the area of insurance.

Remember to continuously reexamine your need for coverage, since it normally tends to diminish over time as you build up assets and net worth. You may be able to reduce coverage in the future and redirect the cash flow to a worthier purpose. The Good Financial Advisor should look at your coverage vs. needs periodically.

Group Term Insurance

Group insurance obtained from your employer is usually inexpensive, but should not be relied on as a main source of coverage. First, it goes away when you leave your job, unless you have the ability to convert it. If you can continue it, the cost will likely be based on your current age and health, and may be expensive. Second, if forced to retire due to illness you may be left without the ability to obtain any coverage. Use group term as additional, not primary coverage.

Inflation Affects Death Benefits

Keep in mind that the policy you buy today may not pay off for twenty years. At that time the death benefit will be only half as valuable in terms of purchasing power due to inflation. The definition of money also applies to insurance benefits. A million dollars today will be worth only about $550,000 after 20 years of 3% inflation.

Check the Company

Because a policy may not pay off for twenty years, you must be reasonably sure the company will around to pay its claims when that day comes. Check the rating of the company that you plan to purchase a policy from to ensure that they are well rated by A.M.Best, Fitch, or Moody's. If not, ask the Good Financial Advisor for their rating. He will seldom do business with any but a top rated company.

Protect Your Insurability

Regardless of how much you purchase, remember that buying life insurance early protects against it becoming unavailable because of health reasons later on in life. Even if you buy term insurance, make sure it is convertible to permanent insurance without evidence of insurability.

Life Settlements

Since life insurance is something you own, a market exists for life settlements, where you sell your policy to someone else for value (formerly called a viatical settlement). If your circumstances warrant, you may find a buyer who will pay you for your policy and make future premium payments in exchange for the death benefit when you die. This will typically be when you are terminally ill and need money today, not after you die. Be very careful if you elect to do this, since the people buying your policy know more than you do about life expectancy and how to value future cash flows. I would consider it only as a last resort, and do it only with competent assistance.

It's Not for You

Most people do not like insurance because it forces us to contemplate our own mortality, and its benefits go to others when we are gone. But it is still one of the most important pieces in a good financial plan. Without it you do not really have a complete plan, just a hope that all goes well for a very long time.

Life insurance.

Don't leave home or this world without it.

Chapter 8B – Long Term Care Insurance

"If I get sick, I'll just get some pills and end it all. If, of course, I can remember where in hell I put those pills."

Let's start off with a short quiz:

List your five most valuable assets.

How many of them are insured?

Which ones are not insured?

Why not?

If you are like most people, you have insured your <u>house</u>, <u>car</u>, <u>health</u>, and your <u>life</u>. You most likely have not protected your <u>invested assets</u> against the unforeseen costs of long-term care for a chronic illness. That is the job of Long Term Care (LTC) insurance.

Difficult to Contemplate

Even thinking about becoming ill in our old age is difficult, never mind taking an action that contemplates it happening to us. Yet, about 15% of us may experience some form of illness that will require care at home or in a facility. Medicare does not cover long-term care, other than for a short time and in a small amount. Medicaid does cover long-term care, but it is means tested, and requires you to meet stringent financial eligibility rules by spending down your assets until you have little left.

Complicated and Costly

Long Term Care (LTC) insurance is complicated and can be costly. There is a story about an old man who wanted to go to Ireland before he died, but was afraid to fly, so he asked God to build a road across the Atlantic for him. God replied that building a road that far was a tough job, and could He perhaps grant the old man some other wish. The old man then asked God to explain Long Term Care insurance to him. God replied, "To what port in Ireland do you want that road to go?"

Yes it is a complicated product, and it is made worse by the difficulty in understanding when and how you will actually need it. Many, if not most, people will not use long-term care coverage until they are over 80 years old.

Here are a few of the variables that can affect your need for long term care:

- Does your family have a history of illnesses that could cause you to need long term care? (Arthritis, Diabetes, Osteoporosis, Emphysema, Alzheimer's, or Stroke?)

- What type of illness will you experience? Will it be lingering, or will it cause your speedy demise? We all hope to die in our sleep while in relatively good health in our late nineties, but that is not realistic

- Can your spouse or partner care for you? Do they want to? Can they even lift you if necessary?

- Is your dwelling place suitable for someone who is not 100% healthy? If you live on the second floor and there is no lift or elevator, how will you get up and down the stairs?

Evaluate the Policy Carefully

When looking at a long-term care policy, the list below contains some of the things you should expect to get. Be sure to review these with the Good Financial Advisor to make sure the policy you are looking at is suitable for your needs. Avoid policies with exclusions that could keep you from obtaining coverage, or a lack of front-end underwriting. Go with a company that is experienced and has a strong financial rating, so they will be around to pay a claim in the future. Be sure that the company cannot drop you or raise your premium easily. If you are offered a group policy at work, compare it carefully to what you could obtain on your own.

A policy should provide homemaker services, respite care, training for caregivers, reimbursement for improvements to your home, as well as all of the other standard features good policies offer. Be sure to note how the benefit is paid, since a daily benefit might not be as good as a monthly benefit. Be mindful that companies are changing and adding features to policies all the time. Do not assume that the policy you decided not to take a year ago is the same one you will be shown today.

Affordability is Important

The most important issue is affordability of the policy. You must have the ability to pay the premium for the remainder of your life, without negatively impacting your standard of living. This means that you should have a substantial net worth that includes a large base of invested assets. One guideline for this is that the LTC premium should not exceed 1% of your invested assets. Since most policies have fixed premiums, this is a reasonable guide as to whether your policy will be affordable over a long period of time.

Don't Wait Too Long

When should you consider purchasing LTC coverage? There is no right age, but at age 50 you should begin evaluating it, and purchase it if you can afford it. At age 60 to 65 you should seriously consider it, and purchase it before you become uninsurable. Unlike life insurance where companies have enough actuarial experience to rate your health, and sell you a policy even if you have an illness, LTC is too new and has insufficient historical data behind it. Therefore, most companies will either accept or reject you, with nothing in between. At age 70 and beyond, LTC is very expensive and the likelihood that you can purchase it diminishes markedly.

See an Eldercare Attorney

Before making any final decisions, consult with an attorney who specializes in eldercare planning to make sure you understand your situation and your options. Before purchasing LTC insurance, review the pros and cons of the policy with your Good Financial Advisor, who may also be the person selling you the policy. Deal only with a strong and reputable company.

Good Health is Critical

Most important of all, take good care of your health to minimize the chance that you will actually need long term care. Stay physically active and maintain your weight at normal levels. Watch your diet and get regular physical exams. Numerous studies indicate that the more active we are the healthier we stay. Physical activity also seems to promote mental well-being.

Nothing today will absolutely stop the onset of dementia or Alzheimer's disease. We cannot yet cure arthritis or diabetes, and old age carries with it a deterioration of our bodies that no medicine can prevent. Assume you will live to a ripe old age and take care of yourself accordingly.

Like life insurance,

you also hope your LTC premiums will be wasted.

Chapter 9 – Tax Management Philosophy

"As an American I am proud of my country and happy to pay my income taxes to keep her strong. But, I could be just as happy if my taxes were a little less!"

That famous saying has been attributed in one form or another to many famous people, but it rings true for almost everyone. Taxes affect all of us in different ways. Have you also noticed that when you put these two words together, **THE**, and **IRS**, that it spells **THEIRS**?

Here is what I believe the essence of your tax management philosophy should be.

Defer taxes when you can and when it makes financial sense.

Avoid taxes when you can legally do so.

Minimize taxes to the extent it is allowable.

Never pay any more or any less in taxes than the government requires you to pay.

Remember that acronym: **DAMN.** That is what you will say if you don't develop a tax management philosophy of your own. Without a tax management plan, you are unnecessarily handicapping your ability to accumulate wealth.

More importantly, if you don't have a plan to reduce or minimize your taxes it will be harder to achieve your financial goals. So make it part of everything you do to look at the best way to achieve your financial goals, with a minimum tax bite. When your portfolio is constructed, the asset allocation should consider the optimal way to distribute your assets among tax-deferred, tax-free and taxable investments to reduce taxes overall.

Harvesting Tax Losses

One particular item to be aware of is harvesting tax losses in your non-qualified investment portfolio. When you have losses, consider selling before the end of the year to use the loss to reduce your current year taxes. Under current tax law you can use up to $3,000 of long term capital losses to offset current income. If your losses exceed $3,000 you may be able to sell other investments with a gain, and avoid paying taxes on that gain.

Engage a Tax Advisor

Find a tax advisor and use her to implement your tax management philosophy, and make sure your tax advisor and the Good Financial Advisor talk to each other regularly.

Consult your tax advisor on your own tax situation, and let the Good Financial Advisor guide you in harvesting the losses. Then keep in mind the time value of money discussed in Chapter 7. If you allow tax losses to sit for years, their value is reduced by whatever you could have earned by investing the proceeds of the harvest.

Don't Let Taxes Drive Your Decisions

Also, do not be afraid to pay taxes on the gains in an investment. Taxes should be a consideration, but not the primary driver, in an investment decision. Remember that you don't have a gain on an investment until you take it.

Watch the AMT

Another issue you should be aware of is the Alternative Minimum Tax or AMT. Depending on the structure of your portfolio, this tax may affect you if you have sufficient income and other tax preference items. The AMT will affect many more people in the coming years, so be mindful of its potential impact on your taxes.

Self-employed Can Benefit

If you are self-employed or own your own business, be sure you have taken advantage of the tax breaks that are allowed. Too many people overlook legitimate deductions that could save them money at tax time. If you do not have a company retirement plan, see the Good Financial Advisor about setting one up. It might save you substantial dollars in retirement savings as well as being an attraction for hiring new employees.

The Future is Unknown

Although predicting the future is hard to do with accuracy, keep this thought in mind: At some point we must make Social Security and Medicare solvent as well as balance our budget. This must happen in the next decade or so to be meaningful. In what direction will tax rates have to go to accomplish this? Lower, the same, or higher? If you said higher we are in agreement. Therefore, deferring taxes today, at low rates, may leave you in the position of paying taxes later at higher rates. The tax-free Roth IRA will look very attractive if this is the case. Regardless, you should strive for diversification (Chapter 6E) and balance in taxable, tax-free, and tax-deferred accounts if possible.

Smirk when your friends tell you,

they got killed at tax time.

Chapter 9A – Tax Deferral

"Tax deferral is just one more way of using Other People's Money."

The government recognizes that payment of taxes is something that people would like to minimize if they could. They have therefore made available many ways to defer the current payment of taxes, and you owe it to yourself to take advantage of these when you can.

Tax Deferral Aids Wealth Accumulation

Annuities, life insurance, municipal bonds, IRA's, Qualified Retirement Savings Plans, and long term capital gains tax treatment are all ways that you can reduce, defer, or in some cases avoid, paying taxes during your lifetime. If you are paying taxes and your neighbor is not, you are at a big disadvantage in accumulating wealth for retirement, or any other purpose.

Tax Deferral Can Be Costly

Tax deferral comes at a price in some cases, and therefore you should have balance in the way your assets are structured, to avoid being at the mercy of the next tax law changes. The ability to manage your marginal tax bracket, especially in retirement, can be very valuable.

For example, a variable annuity converts all earnings or capital gains to ordinary income when they are withdrawn. If you need money after 2 years, you should have a regular, non tax-deferred, account from which to get it, so you can get long-term capital gains tax treatment on the earnings.

If all of your money is in IRA accounts, you must begin taking Required Minimum Distributions at age 70 1/2. This will increase your taxable income, and may force you into a higher tax bracket. Roth IRA's have no Required Minimum Distributions and therefore give you greater control over your taxable income in retirement.

Remember that you do not know what the tax structure will be when you eventually begin taking money out of tax-deferred accounts. If rates are higher or surtaxes are added, you can be at a disadvantage relative to paying taxes today.

Some Benefits Are Easy To Realize

Life insurance passes to the beneficiary tax free in most instances. If placed in a trust, it also can pass estate tax free.

Municipal bonds are Federal tax free in most cases, and usually state tax-free, if they originate in your home state.

Stocks held for long periods of time avoid taxation until you sell and realize a gain, and then the gain is taxed at the more favorable long-term capital gains rate.

This is not a complete list, but it should demonstrate that you have many ways to improve your ability to accumulate wealth, or retain what you have saved, if you take advantage of existing tax law. Ask the Good Financial Advisor to explain your options, and see a tax advisor on a regular basis.

Never underestimate the value of a tax break.

Chapter 9B – Tax Control at the Margin

"Remember that our government runs
on your taxes."

The way our government is structured, it tries to expand its share of our income all the time, always finding some good use for our tax dollars. (When have you ever seen a government program eliminated?). Given this propensity to take more and more taxes, the future liabilities of Medicare and Social Security, and our need to control our national debt, you have to believe that tax rates, and the number of ways taxes are taken, will only increase over your lifetime.

Therefore, looking out into the future when you are retired, while it is impossible to see what the tax environment will be, one can assume it will not be more favorable to you. It behooves you therefore to structure your invested assets so that you can minimize any impact of potential tax law changes on your financial health.

Avoid the Next Higher Tax Rate

Your marginal tax rate is what you pay on your next dollar of income, as opposed to your average tax rate, which will be much lower. With regard to tax control at the margin, you should attempt to distribute your invested assets in such a manner as to have sources of retirement income that are taxable as ordinary income, taxable as long-term capital gains, tax deferred, and tax free. With four types of income available to you, it will allow you to select a source of income that will minimize the taxable consequences in a given year. This should have been done years before when your portfolio was constructed.

Tax Control at the Margin

Tax control requires you to balance your savings and assets, to the extent possible, between annuities, IRA's, qualified retirement plans (401(k), 403(b), SEP, SIMPLE, etc.), CD's, bonds or bond mutual funds, stocks or stock mutual funds, cash value life insurance, real estate and commodities, etc., all of which have different tax treatments. At your annual or semi-annual reviews, the Good Financial Advisor will review your position relative to taxation.

You cannot know what tax rates, or even the structure of the tax code, will be in the future. Insulate yourself from any potential reduction in your income to the extent that you are able by implementing a tax diversification strategy today. Engage a tax advisor and encourage him to communicate with your Good Financial Advisor on a regular basis.

Buy your tax advisor lunch.

Chapter 10 – College Funding Planning

"A mind is a terrible thing to waste, and so is the first ten years of your working life spent paying off student loans."

The cost of a college education has risen at rates faster than inflation for many years, and now represents a major expense, even at the less expensive schools. In spite of that, nearly everyone wants their children to go to college, primarily for the prospects of a better job. Before sending your son or daughter to any school of their choice regardless of cost, evaluate the opportunity cost to do so.

College Tuition Is an Opportunity Cost

The amount you spend on college represents an enormous opportunity cost, and the following is an example of why you should carefully evaluate what you plan to spend on college for your children.

If you give a child a gift of $10,000 in each of their four years of college, and allow it to grow tax-deferred at 9% until they are 67 (when they plan to retire), they will have an account worth more than $2,400,000. Even when you discount it back to today's dollars at an inflation rate of 2.5%, it is more than $750,000. Like that famous saying goes, that is real money, and it is all because of the magic of compounding over a long period of time.

In deciding how much to pay for college, remember that tuition costs can vary by over $25,000 per year, but the actual value of the education received may not be that different, with few exceptions. When you plan how you will fund your children's college education, look at the big picture. It may be worth finding a less costly school, and using the difference in tuition to help fund your child's retirement plan, or first home, or startup costs for their business. If the child has W-2 earnings, you can use a Roth IRA to take advantage of their low tax bracket. This will give them tax-free growth for over 45 years, if left untouched until retirement.

Take Advantage of Existing Savings Plans

Whatever you decide, utilize the ways available to you to set aside college funds in the most advantageous ways. Some of these are 529 College Savings Plans, Coverdell Education Saving Plans and prepaid tuition plans. The 529 plan now provides tax-free earnings if used for higher education, and offers a big advantage over conventional savings where earnings are taxable. Examine this option with care, since it has many other benefits vs. other savings plans, and allows you to control the assets.

Watch Out For Schemes

Avoid those who tell you they have a scheme that will increase your ability to get financial aid by repositioning assets. Most of these do not work, and usually consist of moving assets to an annuity, or some similar action that really does not help you. Colleges have become much more sophisticated in evaluating your finances than in years gone by. Transferring assets to a retirement plan vehicle to hide them is unlikely to fool a college into giving you more financial aid. Your level of income is more likely to govern the amount of aid you might receive or your expected family contribution.

Do Your Homework

There are a number of websites that will explain in detail all of the options that you can use. Some good ones are www.savingforcollege.com, www.efc.org, www.collegesavings.org and www.fafsa.ed.gov. The internet has made it possible to do extensive research on ways to fund a college education, and you should take advantage of it to the extent that you can.

Look at the available websites (there are many others), and use other sources of information that you can find. Your high school's college placement office is one of the best sources for assistance. Don't decide until you have all of the facts you need to make a "good decision". Ask your Good Financial Advisor to review these with you to see which make the most sense for your situation.

College tuition money is a terrible thing to waste.

Chapter 10A – College vs. Retirement Savings

"Hobson's choice or a no-brainer?"

Remember these simple, and sometimes overlooked, facts regarding saving for retirement, and saving (or paying) for a college education.

Your Children Have More Time Than You Do

Your children have a full lifetime ahead of them to pay off college loans. You have a much smaller time period to fund your retirement plans. Don't make the mistake of putting too much of your retirement money into their education, and shortchanging your retirement. You don't want to be thought of as a tightwad because you would not pay for your children's college education, but you also don't want to become a burden on them in retirement either.

Retirement Plans Must Be Funded Annually

You have only specified time periods to fund retirement plans. Once a calendar year has passed, your chance to fund for that year is typically gone forever except for the modest catch-up provisions for those over 50 years old.

You can only put limited amounts of money into your retirement plans in a given year, further restricting your ability to fully fund your retirement.

You Can Borrow For College - Not For Retirement

You can borrow to pay for college, but you cannot borrow to pay for retirement. You can extend the financing of a college education for a number of years. It is perfectly appropriate for your children to extend the repayment of college costs for a number of years in order to get started in life. And, so they don't lose the ability to fund their retirement plans.

Don't shortchange your retirement savings plan in favor of college savings, unless you are sure that your children will land great jobs, and take care of you after you retire.

In most areas there is a Community College with reasonable costs that a child can attend for the first two years of a four-year plan. This can save thousands of dollars, and still allow a child to attend a regular university or college for the remaining two years.

Work-study programs are also available to make college more affordable.

Exhaust every other source of money for college, before you even think of reducing your retirement plan funding. This is clearly an area where emotions can cloud our judgment. No parent wants to say that they shortchanged their children so they could live better in retirement, even if it is the correct thing to do.

Sacrifice and Regret

Sacrifice is the word most often heard when parents talk about putting their children through a top-notch school. Regret is the word most often used when people discuss their lack of savings for retirement. No one wants to become a burden for their children in their later years.

How many children do you know that were unable to go to college due solely to lack of funds to pay for it? Ask your Good Financial Advisor to weigh the pluses and minuses before committing yourself to a specific plan, so you won't have to worry about your children taking care of you in retirement.

A retirement plan is a terrible thing to run out of,

especially if you are retired.

Chapter 10B – College Financial Assistance

"Watch out for little expenses. A small leak can sink a great ship"

Before raiding other sources seek financial assistance for college from a variety of areas. One of the best places to get help is your high school. They will direct you on how to apply for aid, and they usually know where the sources of grants and scholarships are, so you can get help from places that you do not have to pay back.

A second good place to look is at the college itself. They want your child, and will do what ever they can to enable him or her to attend their school. Financial assistance is a greatly overlooked area, so persistence here will pay off.

Loans, Grants and Aid

The government has provided help in the form of Hope and Lifetime Learning Credits, but you still can seek aid from other sources. Maximizing your financial aid is appropriate to do, since that is what it is there for.

There are PLUS loans, Stafford loans and other lending sources.

There are scholarships and grants, many of which go unused because people do not apply for them. Check out websites such as www.scholarships.com, www.petersons.com, and www.fastweb.com.

Do your homework and take advantage of the professionals who are there to help you. In general, do not pay for services that you can get at no charge, such as filling out your Free Application for Federal Student Aid (FAFSA) form. Check out the website www.fafsa.ed.gov where you can do this on line. Always apply for financial aid to determine your eligibility.

College Costs

Your child will get through college without incurring financial Armageddon because there are some ideas about college that are not as true as popularly believed.

First, the cost of college is not going up as fast as you might perceive due to the increased use of financial aid by the colleges themselves. Many students attend college at a public school where the cost is less than $15,000 a year. This is not trivial, but it is not $40,000 per year either. You have to question whether paying a lot for a private school is the best choice for your family, especially when you think of the value of the gift idea I mentioned in Chapter 10.

College Costs May Moderate

In my opinion, college costs cannot continue to outpace incomes or general inflation for the indefinite future. People are already questioning the extremely high cost of a private education, and changes will be forthcoming to make college more efficient and less expensive. One can foresee the day when much of our learning will be internet-based at very low cost. At the end of the day, learning is what college is supposed to be about, not sports and social activities.

Second, you may qualify for aid regardless of your income, especially if you have more than one child in college at the same time. Be sure to check to see if you qualify for assistance every year, if this is your situation.

Third, the more you save the less you will have to borrow, not the less aid you will receive. Save as much as possible in your name instead of your children's name, since assets in your name are counted at only 5.6% vs. 35% of funds in your children's name when calculating your expected family contribution. If you have funds in your child's name, consider spending them on your child's behalf, and saving an equal amount in your name in a 529 College Savings Plan or Coverdell Plan.

There is a substantial payoff for a college education in higher lifetime earnings, though not perhaps as much as some would have you believe. If you spend wisely for college, the rewards will be there for everyone. I have kept this chapter small because I think experts should handle college planning. It should not be done with generalized advice from a book.

Seek out the experts.

They know where the money is.

Chapter 11 – How To Get There From Here

"A journey of a thousand miles begins with a single step."

If you have read this book, you have my thanks and appreciation, but that is worth little in the overall scheme of things. You are likely not an expert in anything in the area of personal finance, and you should have many more questions than answers.

Continue to educate yourself in the basic areas I have covered in this book. The more knowledgeable you are, the better you will be able to communicate and work with the Good Financial Advisor. The better you can communicate, the more likely you are to reach your financial goals. And after all, that is what this book is all about. Reaching financial independence is not something that everyone will achieve. My hope is that you will be one of the chosen many.

The Next Step – Your Financial Plan

You have to take the next step by developing your own comprehensive financial plan, not just an investment strategy.

- Establish your goals, as difficult as they may be to define. They will be your roadmap to financial independence

- Develop a Spending and Savings Plan, no matter how hard you might think it is to accomplish. It will guide you on the correct path.

- Calculate your net worth, and see if it looks like you are on track to accomplish your goals, retirement or otherwise. Don't be afraid to find out where you are today. It is never too late to improve your situation.

- Get an opinion from someone you already trust as to how you are doing today. Get a second opinion if you are not sure of the first.

- If you are not on track, get help to get on track.

- When you get on track, monitor your financial plan carefully to be sure you remain on track.

Everyone Will Retire

Remember, everyone can and will retire, whether or not they have achieved financial independence. The only real questions are when, and in what kind of lifestyle. Some retirements will be voluntary, and some will be forced on people. Financial planning makes a difference, and the Good Financial Advisor might be just the catalyst you need to get a plan, and make a successful retirement and financial independence a reality.

Use the Good Financial Advisor

Remember my opening thought: The majority of the wealthy people in this country use a financial advisor, even though many of them are perfectly capable of handling their finances themselves. It is easy to find excuses, but excuses will not bring you financial independence. Do not forget the old saying: "I hear and I forget, I see and I remember, I do and I understand.

If I haven't given you enough reasons to use the Good Financial Advisor in the previous ten chapters of this book, here are a few more things you might do with the time saved by letting someone else do the heavy lifting.

- Teach a grandchild to fish. The look on my grandchild's face as he landed his first fish was priceless.

- Visit a museum and linger as long as you want. Stare at a painting until you see everything in it.

- Write a letter to an old friend. Talk about the good times that both of you may have forgotten.

- Call your brother or sister just to chat. Not to give them good news or bad news, just to talk about whatever crosses your mind.

- Tell your children you love them. Tell them how important they are in your life, no matter how old you are today.

- Sit and watch the stars for at least an hour. Buy a book on stargazing and thrill to the discovery that we are not the only planet in the universe.

- Drive 50 miles away to have lunch with a friend. It will give you time to talk about whatever you feel like for a few hours.

As I said in Chapter 2C, time is relentless. Do not let it pass without purpose. The time to act is now.

Get off your assets.

Find your Good Financial Advisor.

Get on the road to financial independence!

Chapter 12 - The Good Financial Advisor Credo

"......First, do no harm."

Hippocrates created the Hippocratic Oath as a guide for physicians of his day, and it has stood the test of time. Here is my idealistic take on a credo for the Good Financial Advisor.

The Good Financial Advisor Credo

I swear that I will fulfill the precepts of this credo, to the best of my ability and judgment.

I will always place the best interests of my client above everything else, holding the trust of my clients to be sacred and inviolable.

I will strive to keep my clients from financial harm, giving great care to the preservation of assets entrusted to my keep.

I will provide quality advice on a timely basis to assist my clients in the pursuit of their goals, and keep their goals at the forefront of all of my actions.

I will take such actions as needed to enable my clients to achieve their goals. Those actions shall be clear and understandable, and shall neither be excessive, nor less than required.

I will not attempt to perform tasks beyond my abilities or training, and will seek the assistance of others when my skills are not sufficient to meet the needs of my client.

I will charge fair, reasonable and competitive fees, and fully disclose all fees in a timely fashion.

I will conduct myself in a professional manner at all times. My relationship with my clients shall be appropriate and proper in every respect.

I will keep private all that transpires between myself and my clients, and will respect their emotions, concerns and feelings.

If I do not violate this credo, I hope to enjoy life and art, the respect of others, and a legacy of admiration and affection. May I always act to uphold the highest principles of the financial advisory profession, and experience the rewards of helping those who seek financial independence.

What does all of that mean in plain language? Simply that the Good Financial Advisor will try to act like this:

I will try to follow this credo.

I will place my clients' interests first.

I will try not to lose their money.

I will give good and timely advice related to their goals.

I will do only what is necessary for my clients. No more and no less.

If I cannot do it, I will find someone who can.

I will not overcharge and will disclose all of my fees.

I will behave myself in my client relationships.

I will always maintain confidentiality.

If I do a good job, I hope to live a good life.

Plain enough?

Chapter 13 – Acknowledgements

"You never stand so tall as when you stoop to help another."

You didn't think I wrote this book without help did you? We all need help at some time or another, and that is the main theme of this book. If you try to manage your finances alone, you run the risk of making the Big Mistake that can affect your financial future for years to come.

Unless you are truly qualified to do financial planning (not just picking an occasional stock or mutual fund), let someone help you. It will most likely be the best investment you ever make.

These are some of the people who helped me in writing this book:

My wife Joyce. For her nearly unlimited tolerance of my diversion of time from her to get this done, and her unwavering faith that I could finish it. She truly is one of a kind.

My children Jeff, Matt and Kathy. For giving me the inspiration to do this. Why else would I do this if not to make their future a little better?

My friend Ron. For showing me how to maintain a positive outlook on life in the face of overwhelming problems that no retirement plan could cure.

My friend Joan. For showing me how to maintain strength in the face of adversity. Few could walk in her shoes in the past few years.

My attorney Stan. For his constant support and direction over the years. He showed me how to give advice, even when the advice was tough to take.

My accountant Barry. For pointing out why I should get expert help with my taxes, and helping me greatly with them over the past 30 years.

My co-workers. For their support and guidance in pursuing this profession. They did not just help their clients, they taught me how to care for a clients' financial future

My colleague Wayne. For teaching me the human side of the financial services field. His care and concern for his clients is exceptional in many ways.

My Clients. Without whose ideas and input this book would have been impossible. They have put up with me as I tried to become the Good Financial Advisor and I owe them a debt that will be difficult to repay.

The great leaders in the financial services profession today. I am in their debt for the words of wisdom they have penned in the last two decades or so, and continue to learn from their experience and insight.

All of the others. They will remain nameless because I have forgotten some and cannot find others. Some have passed on. Their assistance will long be remembered, and their friendship will be treasured.

The essence of this book is simple,

It is difficult to do it alone.

Chapter 14 – Personal Thoughts

"The years teach much that the days cannot know."

I finished this book in my twelfth year in the financial services field as an independent financial advisor. I wanted people who were thinking of becoming clients of a financial advisor to know what it took to really benefit from the advisor's services. I also wanted people to know what it takes to become a financial advisor and run a successful practice. Understanding each other is the first step in trusting each other. For reasons I have not yet discovered, there seems to be a lack of understanding between advisors and clients in the financial services field.

We all know that being a client is difficult. It is hard to turn over to a stranger the management of assets that took 30 years of work to accumulate, and hope that they watch them as closely as you would. Advisors who understand this are far ahead of those who don't. Clients have earned the right to be eternally skeptical of their financial advisor.

How Do You Become A Financial Advisor?

Becoming a successful financial advisor is no easy task. The attrition rate for people who attempt to become advisors is as high as 90% after five years according to some studies. Dealing with rejection is a difficult task, and the stress of the profession can be overwhelming in difficult times. Burnout is a common occurrence.

Financial advisors have to start with a fair amount of education, both for their own benefit, and because their clients will expect someone who has a college background, similar to the other service professions, such as Accountants, Attorneys and Doctors.

Financial advisors need a high degree of maturity, and being older than 40 may be an advantage because of the typical age of clients with substantial assets. Youth can be a drawback in many cases, not unlike some other professions.

"Say Doctor, how many of these operations have you done?" asked the patient being wheeled into the operating room. "You are my first one" replied the young doctor with an eager smile.

Financial advisors have to study to become licensed in all of the areas they will practice. This takes about six months on average. Once licensed, they must continue to study each year to maintain their status.

Financial advisors usually have to utilize savings or incur debt to get established. Unless they work as a paid employee for a salary, their income on day one is minimal. If they are an employee, their income potential is not as high as that of an independent advisor.

Financial advisors work six and seven day weeks until they have acquired enough clients, with sufficient assets, to afford to take any significant amount of time off. This lasts for several years for most advisors. They struggle to maintain a family life and keep up relationships with their friends.

Financial advisors usually will work four or five nights a week until they are established, at which point they may cut back to one or two nights a week. They typically do not eat regular evening meals for several years.

As soon as they have a significant client base, they have to hire someone to be able to grow past that point and service those clients. Their income takes a dip for another year or so. They must continue to seek new clients to grow their practice to cover the added overhead.

They soon discover that they need an advanced designation to go further in their practice, so they spend a few more years getting a Certified Financial Planner (CFP®) or similar designation. Much of their free time is spent studying in this period.

Somewhere in the seventh or eight year, their steady recurring income actually becomes large enough to live on. They feel there is light at the end of the tunnel.

At about the tenth year, they regain modest control of their life.

In years 11 through 15 they begin to accumulate assets to replace what they were unable to save in the first ten years.

After 15 years they generally have a satisfying and financially rewarding life, accompanied by the constant pressure of knowing that people depend on them for their financial independence.

Good People Are Needed

As tough as this might sound, I do not want to discourage anyone from becoming a financial advisor. The profession needs many new people in the next decade to expand and replace retiring veterans. If you think you have the ability, and like working with people, please give it a try. The rewards are there for those who seek them.

When working with a financial advisor, try to keep this career path in perspective. The person you are working with may have had to give up a lot to get to the position where they can help you achieve your financial goals. I did, and even though it was worth it in many ways, the sacrifice was difficult at the time. I now spend my days trying to become the Good Financial Advisor for my clients.

Please encourage your Good Financial Advisor to do the best he or she can for you, and both of you will win in the long run. And when both of you win, it truly is a wonderful life. Now you know why I love this job.

<u>Thanks,</u> for making it possible.

Twelve Steps to Financial Independence

For those who have no time to read or cannot remember what they have read, I offer these twelve steps to financial independence. They are not comprehensive, but they are better than nothing. They are in no particular order, since each is important to your financial and overall health.

1. **Use a Good Financial Advisor**

2. **Develop a Financial Plan**

3. **Develop a Spending & Savings Plan**

4. **Invest Regularly**

5. **Invest Prudently**

6. **Protect Your Future**

7. **Keep Yourself Healthy**

8. **Enjoy Life Every Day**

9. **Educate Yourself**

10. **Behave Yourself**

11. **Plan Your Retirement**

12. **Avoid Excessive Risk**

About the Author

Dennis L. Morin is a Certified Financial Planner who runs his own financial services practice.

Dennis was born in 1945 in Hartford, CT, spent his early years on a farm in Vermont, and moved back to Manchester, CT in 1953, where he has lived for the past 55 years.

He attended the University of Connecticut (UConn) and graduated with a Bachelors of Science in Mechanical Engineering in 1968. After graduation he went to work for United Technologies as a development engineer.

He began investing in stocks in 1971, and within two years experienced the bear market of 1973-1974. Lack of diversification (his first Big Mistake) produced horrible results, which led him to drop out of investing in equities for many years (another Big Mistake). He obtained a Masters of Business Administration from UConn in 1977 and transferred to the sales department.

Dennis pursued his career in aircraft engine sales and financing for 13 more years. He left his 19-year career at United Technologies in 1987 to go into commercial real estate development. This move was just in time to see the real estate market enter a prolonged slump due to tax law changes. (Yet another Big Mistake).

He obtained his stockbroker's license in 1987, and returned to the financial services field in 1995. This was just in time for the big stock market run-up to 2000, followed by the second biggest market drop in 70 years. In spite of this, he managed to build a successful financial services practice that today consists of more than 200 clients.

Dennis gave seminars, taught adult education classes, and acquired the practices of two retiring colleagues in the course of building his business.

In 2006 he moved from a proprietary broker-dealer to an independent broker-dealer, where he continues to run his practice, in addition to writing and speaking about the financial services field.

He has been married to the love of his life, Joyce, for 31 years and they have two children, Matt (23) and Kathy (21). He has a son Jeff (37) from a previous marriage, who with his wife, Cathy, has a 8 year old son, Troy, and a 14 year old daughter, Megan.

His interests include boating, photography, hiking and an occasional motorcycle ride on his 1981 Honda 900.

Index

Additional Reading

These are books that I found helpful for the serious investor. They are not all easy reading, but they are informative. I do not necessarily agree with what I read in every one, but they will give you a broad view and a better understanding of the complicated world of finance as it pertains to you.

1) The Intelligent Investor: Benjamin Graham
2) Asset Allocation: Roger C. Gibson
3) Getting an Investing Game Plan: Vern C. Hayden
4) Get A Life – You Don't Need A Million To Retire Well: Ralph Warner
5) You're Fifty – Now What? Investing For The Second Half Of Your Life: Charles Schwab
6) A Random Walk Down Wall Street: Burton Malkiel
7) One Up On Wall Street: Peter Lynch
8) Beating the Street: Peter Lynch
9) Extraordinary Popular Delusions and the Madness of Crowds: Charles Mackay
10) 50 Ways To Spend Wisely: Ilycia Glink
11) Stocks for the Long Run: Jeremy J. Siegel
12) The Richest Man In Babylon: George S. Clason
13) Finance and Investment Handbook: Barron's
14) Simple Wealth, Inevitable Wealth: Nick Murray
15) Predicting The Markets of Tomorrow: James P. O'Shaughnessy
16) The Number: Lee Eisenberg
17) Against The Gods: Peter L. Bernstein
18) Basic Economics: Thomas Sowell

19) Your Complete Retirement Planning Roadmap: Ed Slott
20) The Seven Stages of Money Maturity: George Kinder
21) Your Money and Your Brain: Jason Zweig
22) Fooled By Randomness: Nassim Nicholas Taleb
23) The Black Swan: Nassim Nicholas Taleb
24) The Future for Investors: Jeremy J. Siegel
25) Economic facts and Fallacies: Thomas Sowell
26) The Only Three Questions That Count: Ken Fisher
27) What Works on Wall Street: James P. O'Shaughnessy

Appendix

Advisor Selection Questionnaire   Chapter 3B

Advisor Selection Questionnaire
Chapter 3B

1) Motivation

Q: What motivated you to become a financial advisor?

Good Answer: I like the work, and I enjoy working with and helping people.

Bad Answer: I heard it was a lucrative profession and I was out of work.

Select someone who is passionate about the profession. It is difficult enough to last when you are passionate, but those with little enthusiasm are likely to leave within five years.

2) Prior and Current Experience

Q: What was your prior job experience for the ten years before you became a financial advisor?

Good Answer: I worked 14 years as a teacher since college and changed careers.

Bad Answer: I have had so many jobs I don't know where to begin.

Relevant prior experience is a strong plus. Working with people is the best indicator of someone who is suited for the job.

Q: What is your experience as a financial advisor?

> Good Answer: I have been an advisor for more than ten years.
> Bad Answer: I have survived my second year so I think I can make it.

Five years experience is a minimum requirement unless they work under an experienced advisor. Do not let an advisor train on your accounts.

3) Education and Credentials

Q: What is your educational background?

> Good Answer: I have a Bachelor's degree in psychology.
> Bad Answer: You don't need college to do this job. You need common sense.

Insist on a college degree, with no exceptions. The training is very valuable, and especially so if it is in a related discipline.

Q: What licenses and credentials do you have, and how will they serve us?

> Good Answer: I have a Series 65 and Series 7 license, an insurance license, and can handle any type of transaction you might need in the future. I also have a Certified Financial Planner (CFP®) designation, which will allow me to more capably address your planning needs.
> Bad Answer: You don't have to worry about that. If I can't handle something because I don't have the right license, I'll find someone who can. Designations are just for show. I have experience from the school of hard knocks.

A Series 7 license is an absolute must. A Series 65 or 66 gets you a registered investment advisor. The CFP® is the gold standard of planning designations today. If you select someone who has all three of these, it will weed out most of the less competent advisors.

4) Practice Structure

Q: Describe your practice as to number and type of clients, and assets under management.

Good Answer: I have about 200 active client groups and have about $40,000,000 under management, primarily in mutual funds. Insurance and annuities are about 20% of my practice.

Bad Answer: That's confidential information. I would not want it to leak to my competitors.

An advisor with a normal sized practice is what you want. Avoid too large a practice (service may be lacking) or too small a practice (an unsuccessful advisor) if possible. It is not really confidential information.

Q: Why would you want me as a client?

Good answer: You fit my ideal client profile of a couple with clear goals and the desire to achieve financial independence. I lose about five clients per year due to death and transfers, and would like to maintain the size of my practice and grow it at 5% per year.

Bad Answer: You can always use fresh faces. Besides, I'm not very busy right now.

Avoid an advisor who is too anxious to get your assets.

5) Service

Q: What level and frequency of service will we receive?

Good answer: Based on your accounts I would recommend twice a year account reviews. One review will be in-depth and include a financial plan review.

Bad Answer: If things are going well there is no real need to meet. If things start to go bad, I will probably call you.

Once a year service is a must – Twice a year is preferable.

Q: What is your availability if we have a question or concern?

Good answer: Either myself or a colleague will always be available to talk to you during the business day. After hours and on weekends you may reach me or my designated backup in an emergency.

Bad Answer: I'm usually around, but nothing is so important that it can't wait a day or two or until Monday morning.

When you need money or help, someone must be available during normal business hours.

6) Fees

Q: What is your fee structure?

Good Answer: I run a hybrid practice. I can either charge commissions or fees as appropriate, and I structure my fees to keep your costs low, both initially and long-term.

Bad Answer: My fee structure is a competitive advantage so I keep it close to the vest. Don't worry about my fees, because I'll make you so much money you won't care how high they are.

Fees should be structured to best suit your account, and should be fully disclosed before you agree to them.

Q: Are you a Registered Investment Advisor?

Good Answer: Yes I am.

Bad Answer: No I am not. That's just a fancy title that means nothing.

> Insist on a registered investment advisor
> unless you simply want a stockbroker.

Q: How are you compensated?

Good Answer: As an independent advisor, I receive my compensation through my broker-dealer. It can be commissions or fees, depending on what fee structure we agree is best for your situation.

Bad Answer: I never reveal that type of information because it's too personal.

> Fees should always be fair, reasonable,
> and fully disclosed.

7) Competence

Q: What sets you apart from your competitors?

Good answer: I focus on what it takes to help you reach your goals.

Bad Answer: I have a secret way to make money. That's what really counts.

> Listen for an exaggerated claim on his ability to make
> money for you. Look for a focus on helping you reach
> your goals.

Q: Describe your investment philosophy in general and your risk management philosophy in particular?

Good Answer: I believe in investing to reach a specific goal, and it should always be done at the lowest level of risk consistent with that goal.

Bad Answer: No guts, no glory is my motto. If you take a chance you can hit it big someday.

> Be sure your risk tolerance matches
> the advisor's investment philosophy.

8) Financial Planning

Q: What area of financial planning is most important to our success?

Good Answer: Retirement planning is the key to meeting your most important goal once the children are through college.

Bad Answer: Just save as much as you can and we will hope for the best. All that fancy planning is meaningless until you pile up a ton of money.

> Insist on a focus on overall financial planning
> designed to meet your financial goals.

Q: Can you address all areas of traditional financial planning?

Good Answer: Yes, since I am a Certified Financial Planner.

Bad Answer: The only thing you need to worry about is how much money I will make for you in the years ahead.

> Accept no less than full service capability.
> You run a risk if you omit any area of financial planning.

9) Continuity

Q: Who will assume your role if you retire or are unable to do so?

     Good Answer: My business partner. You will know him well before long,

     Bad Answer: If I get hit by a truck, you are out of luck.

Continuity is important, but it is a judgment call.

10) References

Q: Can you provide two references from clients similar to us?

     Good Answer: I will have two of my clients contact you. You will have to promise to observe their request for confidentiality.

     Bad Answer: References don't mean anything in this business.

A refusal to provide any references is a cause for concern. Most references will be glowing.

Q: Have you had any problems in the past that we should know about?

     Good Answer: No. Check me out on the FINRA website.

     Bad Answer: All of the complaints against me were dropped. Those clients were just whiners anyway.

Avoid any advisor with valid complaints on his record.

11) Broker-dealer

Q: Do you work for an independent or proprietary broker-dealer?

Good answer: An independent broker-dealer, because I do not want any restrictions on the way I run my practice.

Bad Answer: A proprietary broker-dealer, but don't worry, I am as independent as they come.

This also is a judgment call. Good advisors work for proprietary broker-dealers and avoid using proprietary products. With an independent, there is no bias.

Q: Do you sell proprietary products?

Good Answer: I seldom do since I want to avoid even the appearance of bias.

Bad Answer: Of course, since my broker-dealer's funds are the best around.

If the product is the best available, it is no problem. If it is an inferior product you should look elsewhere.

12) Future Change

Q: If our relationship doesn't work out, will you help me to transfer to another advisor or firm?

Good Answer: Yes, even though I will be sorry to see you go.
Bad Answer: I really can't help you if I am not managing your money.

An advisor with character and confidence will reveal himself here. The right answer is yes.

It is Your Call

These twelve questions are not every question that you might ask of a prospective advisor, but they should help to sort out the Good Financial Advisors from the rest. If you have a particular concern by all means add that to the above list.

Keep in mind that you will have a limited time to interview a perspective advisor and you should ask only the important questions, not trivial ones such as "What is your opinion on our current policy on taxing capital gains." The answer is not relevant to your success.

If you get an answer on any of these questions that is not to your liking, be very careful in deciding on that advisor for a long-term relationship. (If all of the answers you get are precisely identical to the Good Answers I have listed above, ask for directions to the rest room and do not return. The advisor read this book!)

After you become a client, there are many more questions that I have indicated in this book that you should ask, but they do not go directly to the initial selection of an advisor. It is possible that you may change your mind after the initial selection, but those instances should be rare if the advisor satisfactorily answers the above questions.

Printed in the United States
211767BV00003B/2/P